Angles, Saxons, and Jutes

John Nowell Linton Myres (Society of Antiquaries)

ANGLES, SAXONS, and JUTES

Essays presented to J.N.L. Myres

EDITED BY
VERA I. EVISON

CLARENDON PRESS · OXFORD · 1981

Oxford University Press, Walton Street, Oxford OX2 6DP

London Glasgow New York Toronto
Delhi Bombay Calcutta Madras Karachi
Kuala Lumpur Singapore Hong Kong Tokyo
Nairobi Dar es Salaam Cape Town
Melbourne Wellington

and associate companies in
Beirut Berlin Ibadan Mexico City

Published in the United States
by Oxford University Press, New York

British Library Cataloguing in Publication Data

Angles, Saxons, and Jutes.
1. Europe—History—392–814
2. Saxons—Civilization
3. Jutes—Civilization
4. Angles—Civilization
I. Evison, Vera Ivy   II. Myres, John Nowell Linton
940.1'1   DD78.S3   80-41599
ISBN 0-19-813402-9

Printed in Great Britain by
Morrison & Gibb Ltd.,
London and Edinburgh

Preface

As Nowell Myres approaches his eightieth birthday, his colleagues and friends
feel it is an appropriate time to record their affection and their appreciation of
his pioneering studies of Angles, Saxons, and Jutes, and this is the inspiration
behind the assembling of the contents of this book. As he has always maintained,
the study of the Anglo-Saxons in England has to begin with the Angles, Saxons,
and Jutes on the Continent before, during, and after the migration of many of
them to England. All the contributions here are concerned with people of these
three tribes, either on the Continent or in England, from the beginning of the
migration to the time of the general acceptance of Christianity in the seventh
century which gradually put an end to furnished pagan burials in England, so
drastically diminishing a rich source of archaeological material. Some of the
articles are concerned with the fifth century, a period of knotty problems which
has always attracted the interest of scholars, and in which Nowell Myres's pottery
studies have been particularly fruitful.

The articles on continental archaeology are placed at the beginning, and a
source of information which has not so far been given the attention it deserves is
investigated in the first article, where parallels, which may have important
implications, are drawn by Hans Neumann between grave ritual in early Jutish
cemeteries in Jutland and later ritual observed in Kent. The Jutes are also
implicated in the chronological study by Egil Bakka of Scandinavian-type gold
bracteates in Kentish and continental grave finds. The contributions regarding the
continental side of the story include an article by Peter Schmid on some pottery
bowl types found in his excavation of the terp at Feddersen Wierde, a settlement
which came to an end just at the time when people using similar pottery landed in
England. A continental Saxon grave at Liebenau containing a belt suite unusual in
its ornamentation and its arrangement is described by Albert Genrich, and inlaid
metalwork of the fifth to seventh centuries which has been found in Lower
Saxony is discussed by Hans-Jürgen Hässler.

Amongst the articles on English subjects, the study by Catherine Hills of
combs with zoomorphic decoration, many of which were found in her

excavation of the prolific cremation cemetery with some inhumations at Spong Hill in Norfolk, provides a comprehensive view of one important group of artefacts of the fifth century. Information to be gained from distribution maps, and from some early inhumation graves at Mucking, Essex, on the two earliest phases of the Anglo-Saxon invasion enumerated by Myres, i.e. AD 360–410 and AD 410–50, is assembled by the editor. Leslie Alcock compares the contents of pagan cemeteries in the more southern parts of England with those in the Anglian graves of Bernicia in order to draw conclusions conerning the social system in this northern part of the country. Following on from a branch of Myres's pottery studies, Barbara Green, W.F. Milligan, and Stanley West have studied in exemplary detail the ornamented pottery emanating from the workshop of the Illington/Lackford potter in the sixth century, much of which found its way to the Illington cremation cemetery and the settlement at West Stow. A hanging bowl escutcheon inspired the thesis by David Brown regarding swastika patterns and the emergence of Anglo-Saxon enamel work as early as the sixth century. Finally, John Hurst examines the evidence for continuity of settlement at Wharram Percy in North Yorkshire, where extensive excavations have been going on under his direction for many years.

Although a historian by training, Nowell Myres was early attracted to dirt archaeology and undertook excavations on Roman sites, the reports of which figure amongst some of his earliest publications. The demands of teaching duties at Oxford, however, in time made it necessary for him, reluctantly, to give up this branch of archaeology, but his interest in the subject began to manifest itself in a different direction, in the study of Anglo-Saxon pottery. Although this area was more or less neglected by other contemporary workers in the field, it fortunately continued to fascinate him, and has always remained an important hobby. One article after another was published in learned journals, and he soon became the acknowledged authority on the subject. This continued to be the case, even during the deviation of a stint at the Ministry of Food during the war, and also between the years 1948 and 1965 when he served Oxford in another capacity as Bodley's Librarian.

This is the aspect of his life known to archaeologists, who value highly his basic contribution to the knowledge of this all-important and key subject in the Anglo-Saxon period, although, as he himself would point out, he was 'only a part-time archaeologist'! During all this time, the material for the definitive corpus of Anglo-Saxon pottery was being assembled, a difficult task to accomplish on a part-time basis, but this study was given a splendid fillip in more recent years when interest shown by various institutions enabled the work to progress at a more steady pace.

This bore fruit in 1969 with the publication of *Anglo-Saxon Pottery and the settlement of England* which summarized the essence of the results of his studies, and, eventually, in 1977, with the publication of the two volumes of the corpus of 3,470 Anglo-Saxon pots, with illustrations, catalogue, and commentary. Together with other major publications noted in the bibliography, they represent a formidable mine of information for the student of the period.

This part seen by archaeologists, however, is but one facet of the man, whose publications also reflect the other duties and interests which occupied him in his daily work first as an Oxford Fellow, and then as Bodley's Librarian. In this latter office the portrait collection, the painted frieze, and the reconstruction programme of the Old Library benefited from his attentions, and a fitting reminder in stone remains in the carved likeness of the then clean-shaven Bodley Librarian, nestling between a book and Anglo-Saxon pots, which was placed on the doorway of the Old Library as seen in the photograph, pl. I.

The list of learned bodies on which he has given his services is lengthy. Among them are the offices of President of the Council for British Archaeology, 1959–61, Member of the Ancient Monuments Board (England), 1959–76, and many others including Vice-President, Director, President, and Hon. Vice-President of the Society of Antiquaries of London, the Society awarding him its Gold Medal of 1976. Despite the gravity of these offices they were performed with a lack of pomposity, accompanied by a quiet charm and sense of humour.

These qualities have endeared him to those of his colleagues who have met regularly in various parts of north-west Germany, Holland, and Denmark under the auspices of the *Arbeitsgemeinschaft für Sachsenforschung,* some of whom have taken part in this present venture. The authors of the contributions to this book, however, are but a few of many colleagues who wish to be associated with this tribute.

As editor, I am very grateful for assistance which has been given by Grace M. Briggs and Valerie Cooper towards the correct presentation of the bibliography of Nowell Myres, and to Margaret Hardie for assistance in translating articles from German and in the general work of editing. Timely advice has been generously given by Hugh Thompson, General Secretary, and John Hopkins, Librarian of the Society of Antiquaries of London.

V.I.E.   1979

Contents

List of figures

Hans-Jürgen Hässler
Inlaid metalwork of the late migration period and the Merovingian period from Lower Saxony

Catherine M. Hills
Barred zoomorphic combs of the migration period

Vera I. Evison
Distribution maps and England in the first two phases

Barbara Green, W. F. Milligan, and Stanley E. West
The Illington/Lackford workshop

David Brown
Swastika Patterns

John G. Hurst
Wharram: Roman to Medieval

List of plates

(Plates fall at end of volume)

The published works of John Nowell Linton Myres

1926

1. 'Excavations on the Akeman Street, near Asthally, Oxon., Feb.–June, 1925' (with C.G. Stevens), *Antiq. J.* VI, 43–53.

1927

2. 'The campaign of Radcot Bridge in December 1387', *Engl. Hist. Rev.* XLII, 20–33.

1930

3. 'Saint Catharine's Hill, Winchester', (with C.F.C. Hawkes and C.G. Stevens), *Proc. Hampshire Fld. Club Archaeol. Soc.* XI.
4. (Anon.) 'The Castle Mill at Oxford', Letter to the Editor, *The Times*, 25 October, 8.

1931

5. (Anon.) 'Christ Church Hall, Oxford: a notable building. Links with Wolsey', *Sunday Times*, 1 February, 14.
6. 'A prehistoric settlement on Hinksey Hill, near Oxford', *J. Brit. Archaeol. Ass.* n.s. XXXVI, 360–90.

1932

7. 'Saxon Burial', Letter to the Editor, *Manchester Guardian*, 18 August, 16.
8. 'Three unrecognised castle mounds at Hamstead Marshall', *Trans. Newbury Dist. Fld. Club* VI (3), 114–26.
9. Report: 'International Congress of Prehistoric and Protohistoric Archaeology, Section V. The Transition from Prehistory to History', *Man* XXXII, 217–19.

REVIEWS:

10. *Roman Britain* by R.G. Collingwood, *J. Roman Stud.* XXII, 252–3.
11. *The transition from Roman Britain to Christian England, A.D. 368–664* by G. Sheldon, *J. Roman Stud.* XXII, 253–5.
12. *The Zimbabwe culture: ruins and reactions* by G. Caton-Thompson, *Antiq. J.* XII, 80–2.

1933

13. 'Butley Priory', Letter to the Editor, *Country Life*, LXXIII, 15 April, 379.

14. 'Butley Priory, Suffolk' (with W.D. Caröe and J.B. Ward Perkins), *Archaeol. J.* XC, 177–281.

REVIEW:

15. *Pre-feudal England: the Jutes* by J.E.A. Jolliffe, *Archaeol. J.* XC, 156–60.

1934

16. 'Excavations near Dorchester, Oxon.', *Antiq. J.* XIV, 55.
17. 'Notes on the history of Butley Priory, Suffolk', *Oxford Essays in Medieval History, Presented to H.E. Salter,* Chapter IX, 190–206.
18. 'Some thoughts on the topography of Saxon London', *Antiquity* VIII, 437–42.

1935

19. (Anon.), 'Excavation results at Aldborough: date of Roman town walls', *The Times,* 14 August, 10.
20. 'Roman Britain in 1934. Yorkshire: Aldborough (*Isurium Brigantium*)', *J. Roman Stud.* XXV, 205–6.
21. 'The medieval pottery at Bodiam Castle', *Sussex Archaeol. Collect.* LXXVI, 222–30.
22. 'Historical revision: LXXX—The Teutonic settlement of Northern England', *History* n.s. XX, 250–62.
23. 'Ancient Britain out of doors: Rome and after' (dialogue with Jacquetta Hawkes), *The Listener,* 24 April, 690–3.

REVIEW:

24. 'Britain in the Dark Ages. Review of *Map of Britain in the Dark Ages,* Ordnance Survey', *Antiquity* IX, 455–64.

1936

25. *Roman Britain and the English settlements. Oxford History of England* 1 (with R.G. Collingwood), First Edition, Oxford (J.N.L.M. 325–461 and 478–89).
26. 'A hoard of Roman coins from Ham Hill, Somerset' (with C.H.V. Sutherland), *Numis. Chron.* s.5. XVI, 30–42 (J.N.L.M. 30–3).
27. 'Roman Britain in 1935. Yorkshire: Aldborough (*Isurium Brigantium*)', *J. Roman Stud.* XXVI, 244.

REVIEWS:

28. *London and the Saxons* by R.E.M. Wheeler, *J. Roman Stud.* XXVI, 87–92.
29. *The birth of the Middle Ages, 395–814* by H. St. L.B. Moss, *Antiquity* X, 382–3.

1937

30. 'Saxon and Celt', *Times Trade & Engineering* (West of England Section), June, xlv.

31. *Roman Britain and the English settlements. Oxford History of England* 1 (with R.G. Collingwood), Second Edition, Oxford (J.N.L.M. 325–461 and 478–89).

32. 'The present state of the archaeological evidence for the Anglo-Saxon conquest', *History* n.s. XXI, 317–30.

33. 'Three styles of decoration on Anglo-Saxon pottery', *Antiq. J.* XVII, 424–37.

34. 'Some Anglo-Saxon potters', *Antiquity* XI, 389–99.

35. 'A prehistoric and Roman site on Mount Farm, Dorchester', *Oxoniensia* II, 12–40.

REVIEWS:

36. *The political ideas of St. Augustine's De Civitate Dei* by N.H. Baynes, *Class. Rev.* LI, 40–1.

37. *Early Anglo-Saxon art and archaeology* by E.T. Leeds, *Oxford Magazine* LV (19), 13 May, 616–18.

1938

38. 'The Saxon pottery from Theale', *Trans. Newbury Dist. Fld. Club* VIII, (1), 60–2.

39. 'Roman Britain: a survey of problems and needs', *Proc. Class. Ass.* XXXV, 34–7.

40. 'Hengist, Horsa, and Lord Raglan', *Man* XXXVIII, 96.

REVIEW:

41. *Verulamium: a Belgic and two Roman cities* by R.E.M. and T.V. Wheeler, *Antiquity* XII, 16–25.

1939

42. 'Roman Britain', *Hist. Ass. Pamphlet* No. 113, London, 1–30.

43. 'Roman Britain', in *The Year's Work in Classical Studies* 32, 57–76.

REVIEW:

44. *Saint Augustin et la fin de la culture antique* by H.-I. Marrou, *Class. Rev.* LIII, 22–3.

1940

REVIEWS:

45. *Nennius's History of the Britons* by A.W. Wade-Evans, *J. Theological Stud.* XLI, 196–8.

46. *The place-names of Hertfordshire* by J.E.B. Gover, A. Mawer, and F.M. Stenton, *Engl. Hist. Rev.* LV, 447–9.

47. *St. Ninian and the origins of the Christian Church in Scotland* by W.D. Simpson, *Archaeol. J.* XCVII, 181–2.

48. *Church and state in the later Roman Empire: the religious policy of Anastasius the First, 491–518* by P. Charanis, *Class. Rev.* LIV, 208–9.

1941

49. 'The Anglo-Saxon pottery of Norfolk', *Proc. Norfolk and Norwich Archaeol. Soc.* XXVII, 185–214.

REVIEW:

50. *An inventory of the historical monuments in the city of Oxford,* Royal Commission on Historical Monuments, England, *Antiq. J.* XXI, 77–80.

1942

51. 'Cremation and inhumation in the Anglo-Saxon cemeteries', *Antiquity* XVI, 330–41.

REVIEW:

52. *Archaeology and society* by G. Clark, *Engl. Hist. Rev.* LVII, 147–8.

1944

53. 'Wingham Villa and Romano-Saxon pottery in Kent', *Antiquity* XVIII, 52–5.

1945

REVIEW:

54. *The battle for Britain in the fifth century. An essay in Dark Age history* by T. Dayrell Reed, *Antiq. J.* XXV, 80–5.

1946

55. (Anon.), 'An Oxford quadringenary: the foundation and growth of Christ Church. Cathedral and Collegiate Body', *The Times,* 4 November, 5.

56. 'The coming of the Saxons', *New English Rev.* XIII (3), September (reprinted, revised, in 1951, as 'The *Adventus Saxonum*'), 271–82.

57. 'Anglian and Anglo-Danish Lincolnshire. 1: Lincoln in the fifth century A.D.', *Archaeol. J.* CIII, 85–8.

REVIEW:

58. *The three ages: an essay in archaeological method* by G. Daniel, *Engl. Hist. Rev.* LXI, 418–19.

1947

59. 'Anglo-Saxon urns from North Elmham, Norfolk: some corrected attributions', *Antiq. J.* XXVII, 47–50.

REVIEWS:

60. *England and the Continent in the eighth century* by W. Levison, *J. Theological Stud.* XLVIII, 99–104.

61. *A hoard of Roman Folles from Diocletian's reform (A.D. 296) to Constantine Caesar found at Fyfield, Berks.* by E.T. Leeds, *Oxoniensia* XI and XII, 185.

62. *The early history of Corpus Christi College, Oxford* by J.G. Milne, *Oxford Magazine* LXV (14), 13 March, 252–3.

1948

63. 'Anglo-Saxon England' in *Survey and policy of field research in the archaeology of Great Britain* (London: Council for British Archaeology), 75–8 and 112–20.

64. 'Some English parallels to the Anglo-Saxon pottery of Holland and Belgium in the Migration Period', *L'Antiquité Classique* XVII, 453–72.

65. 'Mr. L.W. Hanson', *Bodleian Library Record* II (27), 199–200.

66. Preface in *Italian Illuminated Manuscripts from 1400–1550. Catalogue of an Exhibition* (Oxford: Bodleian Library), 3–4.

REVIEW:

67. *Oxford replanned* by T. Sharp, *Oxoniensia* XIII, 89–93.

1949

68. Foreword in *Bibliotheca Radcliviana, 1749–1949. Catalogue of an Exhibition* (Oxford: Bodleian Library), 5–6.

1950

69. Foreword in H.M. Sinclair and A.H.T. Robb-Smith, *A short history of Anatomical Teaching in Oxford* (Oxford: Bodleian Library), 5.

70. 'The Bodleian coin cabinets', *Bodleian Library Record* III (29), 45–9.

71. 'The painted frieze in the picture gallery', *Bodleian Library Record* III (30), 82–91.

REVIEWS:

72. *Merowingerzeit: Original Altertümer des Römisch-Germanischen Zentralmuseums in Mainz Katalog 13* by G. Behrens, *Antiq. J.* XXX, 94–5.

73. *L'Eglise et les derniers Romains* by G. Bardy, *J. Theological Stud.* n.s.I, 114–15.

1951

74. 'The *Adventus Saxonum*', *Aspects of archaeology in Britain and beyond: Essays presented to O.G.S. Crawford*, ed. W.F. Grimes (London), 221–41.

75. Preface in *The Bodleian Library in the Seventeenth Century. Guide to an Exhibition* (Oxford: Bodleian Library), 5–6.

76. 'M.J.R(endall), 1862–1950' and Foreword, *The Register or Chronicle of Butley Priory, Suffolk 1510–1535*, ed. A.G. Dickens (Winchester), viii–xiii.

77. 'The Anglo-Saxon pottery from Elkington', *Archaeol. J.* CVIII, 60–4.

78. 'The Anglo-Saxon pottery of Lincolnshire', *Archaeol. J.* CVIII, 65–99.

REVIEW:

79. *Justin the First. An introduction to the epoch of Justinian the Great* by A.A. Vasiliev, *J. Theological Stud.* n.s. II, 206–8.

1952

80. Preface in *Latin Liturgical Manuscripts and Printed Books. Guide to an Exhibition* (Oxford: Bodleian Library), 7–8.
81. *Portraits of the sixteenth and early seventeenth centuries,* Bodleian Picture Book No. 6 (Oxford: Bodleian Library).
82. 'The Bodleian Library in post-war Oxford', *Oxford* XI (3), 64–71.
83. 'Thomas James and the painted frieze', *Bodleian Library Record* IV (1), 30–51.
84. 'A Restoration at Oxford', Letter to the Editor, *Country Life* CXII, 21 November, 1663.
85. 'Roman Britain', *The Making of English History,* ed. R.L. Schuyler and H. Ausubel (New York), 19–37, reprint of no. 42 above.

1953

86. Preface in *The History of the University of Oxford. Guide to an Exhibition* (Oxford: Bodleian Library), 3–4.

REVIEWS:

87. *The early cultures of north-west Europe (H.M. Chadwick memorial studies)* ed. C. Fox and B. Dickins, *Engl. Hist. Rev.* LXVIII, 264–6.
88. *New College and its buildings* by A.H. Smith, *Antiq. J.* XXXIII, 113–15.

1954

89. 'Modern History Lectures', Letter to the Editor, *Oxford Magazine* LXXII (16), 11 March, 266.
90. 'Two Saxon urns from Ickwell Bury, Beds., and the Saxon penetration of the eastern Midlands', *Antiq. J.* XXXIV, 201–8.
91. 'The Anglo-Saxon period', *The Oxford Region: a scientific and historical survey,* ed. A.F. Martin and R.W. Steel (Oxford), Chapter 10, 96–102.
92. 'Libraries', *The Oxford Region: a scientific and historical survey,* ed. A.F. Martin and R.W. Steel (Oxford), 191–5.

1955

93. 'Thomas James, *Concordantiae sanctorum patrum,* 1607', *Bodleian Library Record* V (4), 212–17.
94. Preface in *English Music. Guide to an Exhibition* (Oxford: Bodleian Library), 3.

REVIEWS:

95. *Language and history in early Britain* by K. Jackson, *Engl. Hist. Rev.* LXX, 630–3.
96. *The conquest of Wessex in the sixth century* by G. Copley, *Antiq. J.* XXXV, 242–3.
97. *Studies in early British history,* ed. N.K. Chadwick, *Engl. Hist. Rev.* LXX, 90–4.

1956

98. Preface in *Oxford College Libraries in 1556. Guide to an Exhibition* (Oxford: Bodleian Library), 3.
99. 'Further notes on the painted frieze and other discoveries in the Upper Reading Room and the Tower Room' (with E. Clive Rouse), *Bodleian Library Record* V (6), 290–308.
100. 'Bodleian reconstruction: an historic stage in the life of a great library', *The Times,* 3 January, 8.
101. 'Romano-Saxon pottery', *Dark-Age Britain: studies presented to E.T. Leeds,* ed. D.B. Harden (London), 16–39.
102. Comments on 'Decorated Anglo-Saxon pots' in 'A Saxon cemetery near the village of Harwell, Berkshire' by Joan R. Kirk and Kenneth Marshall, *Oxoniensia* XXI, 22–34 (J.N.L.M. 31–3).

REVIEW:

103. *An introduction to Anglo-Saxon England* by P.H. Blair, *Antiq. J.* XXXVI, 231–2.

1957

104. 'The reconstruction of the Bodleian Library', *American Oxonian* XLIV (April), 62–6.
105. 'A further note on the Saxon urns from Ickwell Bury, Beds.', *Antiq. J.* XXXVII, 224–5.

REVIEW:

106. *Formenkreise und Stammesgruppen in Schleswig-Holstein* by A. Genrich, *Antiq. J.* XXXVII, 83–4.

1958

107. 'Anglo-Saxon pottery', *Antiquity* XXXII, 274–6.
108. Introduction in *Notable Accessions, 1945–1957. Guide to an Exhibition* (Oxford: Bodleian Library), 5–9.
109. 'Oxford libraries in the seventeenth and eighteenth centuries', *The English Library before 1700,* ed. F. Wormald and C.E. Wright (London), Chapter XI, 236–55.

1959

110. 'The defences of *Isurium Brigantum* (Aldborough)' (with K.A. Steer and Mrs

A.M.H. Chitty), *Yorkshire Archaeol. J.* XL (Part 157), 1–77 (J.N.L.M. and Mrs A.M.H. Chitty, 12–39).

111. 'John Alan Barker and the palimpsest brass to Henry Dowe', *Ann. Rept., Friends of Christ Church Cathedral Oxford.*

112. '*Anglo-Saxon pottery of the Pagan Period*' in '*Anglo-Saxon Pottery: a symposium*' (held at Norwich, 1958), *Medieval Archaeol.* III, 1–78 (J.N.L.M. 7–13) (also published in *Council for British Archaeology Research Report,* No. 4).

REVIEW:

113. *Roman and native in north Britain,* ed. I.A. Richmond, *History* XLIV, 245–6.

1960

114. 'Pelagius and the end of Roman rule in Britain', *J. Roman Stud.* L, 21–36.

115. (Anon.), 'The Ewelme schoolmasters', *Bodleian Library Record* VI (4), 522–3.

116. 'Roman Britain', *Social life in early England,* ed. G. Barraclough (London), 1–28, reprint of no. 42 above.

117. '*Concordantiae sanctorum patrum*', *Bodleian Library Record* VI (5), 587–8.

REVIEWS:

118. *Das Alamannische Gräberfeld von Beggingen-Löbern* by W.U. Guyan, *Antiq. J.* XL, 85–6.

119. *Die Gräberfelder von Hemmoor, Quelkhorn, Gudendorf und Dühnen-Wehrberg* by K. Waller, *Antiq. J.* XL, 241–2.

120. *The northern seas* by A.R. Lewis, *History* XLV, 134–6.

1961

121. 'Archaeology and history: Britons and Saxons in the post-Roman centuries' (Presidential Address), *Council for British Archaeology Report No. 11 for the year ending 30th June, 1961,* 35–45.

122. 'The Bodleian Library: organisation, administration, functions', *Library World* LXII, 225–9.

1962
REVIEW:

123. *Litus Saxonicum* by D.A. White, *Engl. Hist. Rev.* LXXVII, 740–1.

1963

124. 'Presidential Address', *Library Association Record* 65 (8), 282–9.

125. 'The Bodleian', Letter to the Editor, *Oxford Magazine* n.s. 4 (7), 28 November, 107.

126. 'Repairs to Duke Humphrey's Library—made possible by the Oxford Historic Buildings Fund', *Illustrated London News,* 242, 18 May, 765–7.

127. 'The extra expense hidden under the floor' in 'Oxford Restored', *Supplement to the Oxford Mail*, 21 May, 6–7.

128. Discussion on 'The functions and planning of a National Library' in *National Libraries* (extracts from the Proceedings of the University and Research Section Conference, Bangor, 1963) (London: The Library Association).

REVIEWS:

129. *Westerwanna I by K. Zimmer-Linnfeld, H. Gummel, and K. Waller; Der Urnenfriedhof in Wehden by K. Waller; Fohrde und Hofenferchesar by A. von Müller, Antiq. J.* XLIII, 142–4.

130. *Humphrey Wanley: Saxonist and library keeper by C.E. Wright, Engl. Hist. Rev.* LXXVIII, 567–8.

131. *Anglo-Saxon coins. Historical studies presented to Sir Frank Stenton, ed. R.H. Dolley, Antiq. J.* XLIII, 153–4.

1964

132. 'The Wheatley Medal, 1962' (presented to Mr Michael Maclagan), 'The Library Association Medals', *Library Association Record* 66 (6), 261–3.

133. 'Wansdyke and the origin of Wessex', *Essays in British History presented to Sir Keith Feiling*, ed. H.R. Trevor-Roper (London), Chapter 1, 1–27.

134. Preface in *William Shakespeare, 1564–1964. A Catalogue of the Quatercentenary Exhibition* (Oxford: Bodleian Library), iii.

REVIEWS:

135. *Die Germanischen Funde der späten Kaiserzeit und frühen Mittelalters in Mittelfranken by H. Dannheimer, Medieval Archaeol.* VIII, 300–2.

136. *The rebellion of Boudicca by D.R. Dudley and G. Webster, Engl. Hist. Rev.* LXXIX, 809–10.

1965

137. *Culture and environment: essays in honour of Sir Cyril Fox*, ed. I.L.L. Foster and L. Alcock, *Engl. Hist. Rev.* LXXX, 571.

138. *Sutton Hoo: the excavation of a royal ship-burial by C. Green, Engl. Hist. Rev.* LXXX, 572–3.

1966

139. 'The Report of the Committee on University Libraries', *Oxford Magazine*, Michaelmas 8, 136–8.

140. 'Donald F. Hyde', *Oxford Magazine*, Hilary 5, 271–2.

141. 'The late Donald F. Hyde', *Bodleian Library Record* VII (6), 285–6.

REVIEWS:

142. *The Fifth-century Invasions south of the Thames* by V.I. Evison, *Engl. Hist. Rev.* LXXXI, 340–5.

143. *Gazeteer of early Anglo-Saxon burial sites* by A. Meaney, *Engl. Hist. Rev.* LXXXI, 138–9.

144. *Roman Cheshire* by F.H. Thompson, *Engl. Hist. Rev.* LXXI, 577.

1967

145. '*In memoriam* L.W. Hanson', *Bodleian Library Record* VII (6), 293–5.

146. 'Recent discoveries in the Bodleian Library', *Archaeologia* CI, 151–68.

REVIEW:

147. *The frontier people of Roman Britain* by P. Salway, *Engl. Hist. Rev.* LXXXII, 366–7.

1968

148. 'Notes for a speech that was not delivered in Congregation on 27th February 1968', *Oxford Magazine*, Hilary 7, 246.

149. 'The restoration of the Chapter House, Christ Church, 1968', *The Friends of Christ Church Cathedral*, 1967–8, 7–9.

150. 'Anglo-Saxon pottery from Mucking' in 'Crop-mark Sites at Mucking, Essex' by M.U. Jones, *Antiq. J.* XLVIII, 210–30 (J.N.L.M. 222–8).

151. 'The Anglo-Saxon cemetery' in 'The Early History of Abingdon, Berkshire and its Abbey' by M. Biddle, Mrs H.T. Lambrick and J.N.L. Myres, *Medieval Archaeol.* XII, 26–9 (J.N.L.M. 35–41).

152. 'Charlemagne on miniskirts', *Antiquity* XLII, 128.

153. Introduction in *Christianity in Britain, 300–700,* ed. M.W. Barley and R.P.C. Hanson (Leicester), 1–8.

REVIEW:

154. *The Iron Age in Northern Britain,* ed. A.L. Rivet, *Rural settlement in Roman Britain,* ed. C. Thomas, *The Civitas Capitals of Roman Britain,* ed. J.S. Wacher, *A north Somerset miscellany, Engl. Hist. Rev.* LXXXIII, 143–4.

1969

155. 'The Anglo-Saxon pottery' in 'The Iron Age and Anglo-Saxon site at Upton, Northants.', D.A. Jackson and D.W. Harding, *Antiq. J.* XLIX, 202–21 (J.N.L.M. 214–18).

156. 'Appendix: Comments on the pottery' in 'Saxon pottery from a hut at Mucking, Essex' by M.U. Jones. *Berichten van de Rijksdienst voor het Oudheidkundig Bodemonderzoek* 19, 145–56 (J.N.L.M. 150–3).

157. 'Appendix: Comments on the pottery' in 'Five Anglo-Saxon inhumation graves containing pots at Great Chesterford, Essex' by V.I. Evison, *Berichten van de Rijksdienst voor het Oudheidkundig Bodemonderzoek* 19, 157–73 (J.N.L.M. 169–71).

158. *Anglo-Saxon pottery and the settlement of England* (Oxford).

REVIEWS:

159. *The Church in early Irish society* by K. Hughes, *Engl. Hist. Rev.* LXXXIV, 109–11.

160. *Excavations at Shakenoak I* by A.C.C. Brodribb, A.R. Hands, and D.R. Walker, *Antiq. J.* XLIX, 422–3.

161. *The Sutton Hoo ship burial: a handbook* by R.L.S. Bruce-Mitford, *Antiq. J.* XLIX, 423.

1970

162. 'Introduction to the 1970 reprint' of E.T. Leeds, *The Archaeology of the Anglo-Saxon Settlements* (Oxford), nine pages not numbered.

163. 'Two Anglo-Saxon potters' stamps', *Antiq. J.* L, 350.

REVIEWS:

164. *Britannia: a history of Roman Britain* by S. Frere, *Engl. Hist. Rev.* LXXXV, 109–13.

165. *A history of Anglo-Latin literature 597–1066 vol i 597–740* by W.F. Bolton, *Engl. Hist. Rev.* LXXXV, 392–3.

1971

166. 'Sir L. Woodward: a gifted teacher', *The Times,* 20 March, 14.

167. 'May McKisack', *The Reign of Richard II: essays in honour of May McKisack,* ed. F.R.H. Du Boulay and C.M. Barron (London), xiii–xvi.

168. 'Anniversary Address' (delivered as President of the Society of Antiquaries of London on 23 April 1971—not as stated 23 April 1970), *Antiq. J.* LI, 167–76.

169. 'A Sermon preached in Christ Church Cathedral, Oxford, on the feast of St. Frideswide, 1970' in 'Christ Church Cathedral Oxford, 1970–71', *The Friends of Christ Church Cathedral,* 1970–1, 10–12.

REVIEWS:

170. *Bodenfunde der Völkerwanderungszeit aus dem Main-Tauber-Gebiet* by R. Koch; *Die Grabfunde der Merowingerzeit aus dem Donautal um Regensburg* by U. Koch, *Medieval Archaeol.* XV, 184–6.

171. *Bede's Ecclesiastical history of the English people,* ed. B. Colgrave and R.A.B. Mynors, *Engl. Hist. Rev.* LXXXVI, 344–6.

172. *The Will of Aethelgifu,* ed. Lord Rennell, *Engl. Hist. Rev.* LXXXVI, 603.

173. *Britannia: a journal of Romano-British and kindred studies Vol. i, Antiq. J.* LI, 349–50.

1972

174. 'Anniversary Address' (delivered as President of the Society of Antiquaries of London on 20 April 1972), *Antiq. J.* LII, 1–7.

175. 'The Angles, the Saxons, and the Jutes', Raleigh Lecture on History, 1970. *Proc. British Academy* LVI, 145–74.

REVIEWS:

176. *Die Bodenfunde des 3. bis 6. Jahrhunderts nach Chr. zwischen unterer Elbe und Oder* by H. Schach-Dörges, *Antiq. J.* LII, 220–1.

177. *Die Alamannen in Südbaden: Katalog der Grabfunde* by F. Garscha; *Die alamannischen Gräberfelder von Güttingen und Merdingen in Südbaden* by G. Fingerlin, *Medieval Archaeol.* XVI, 215–17.

178. *The history of All Souls College Library by Sir Edmund Craster,* ed. E.F. Jacob, *Antiq. J.* LII, 394–5.

1973

179. 'Anniversary Address' (delivered as President of the Society of Antiquaries of London on 3 May, 1973), *Antiq. J.* LIII, 1–8.

180. 'A Genius for friendship' in *David W. Davies: a bibliography* compiled by D.W. Keran (Orangerie Press, California State University, Fullerton), 28–9.

181. The Anglo-Saxon cemeteries of Caistor-by-Norwich/Markshall, Norfolk (with Barbara Green), *Reports of the Research Committee* XXX, *Society of Antiquaries of London.*

182. 'Ordnance Survey maps', *The Times,* 30 July, 13.

183. 'Ordnance Survey finance', Letter to the Editor, *The Times,* 8 November, 21.

184. 'The Anglo-Saxon cremation cemetery of Sancton, East Yorkshire' (with W. Southern), *Hull Museum Publications,* 218.

185. 'A fifth-century Anglo-Saxon pot from Canterbury', *Antiq. J.* LIII, 77–8.

186. In 'Two nineteenth-century Anglo-Saxon finds from Lincolnshire', by D. Parsons, *Antiq. J.* LIII, 78–81 (J.N.L.M. 80).

187. 'An Anglo-Saxon *Buckelurne* from the Mucking, Essex, cemetery', *Antiq. J.* LIII, 271–2.

REVIEWS:

188. *The coming of Christianity to Anglo-Saxon England* by H. Mayr-Harting, *J. Theological Stud.* n.s. XXIV, 271–3.

189. *England before the conquest: studies in primary sources presented to Dorothy Whitelock,* ed. P. Clemoes and K. Hughes, *Antiq. J.* LIII, 126–8.

1974

190. 'The Anglo-Saxon pottery' in 'The Roman fortress at Longthorpe—the Anglo-Saxon cemetery' by S.S. Frere and J.K. St. Joseph, *Britannia V* (J.N.L.M. 113–21).

191. 'Anniversary Address' (delivered as President of the Society of Antiquaries of London on 25 April, 1974), *Antiq. J.* LIV, 1–7.
192. 'The Burial Urn' in 'A late fourth-century cremation from Billericay, Essex' (with S.G.P. Weller and B. Westley), *Antiq. J.* LIV, 282–5 (J.N.L.M. 284–5).
193. 'The Broadwater helmet and the alienation of church treasures', Letter to the Editor (with others), *The Times,* 21 May, 17.
194. 'Sale of church treasures', Letter to the Editor, *The Times,* 29 May, 15.

REVIEWS:

195. *Issendorf; ein Urnenfriedhof der späten Kaiserzeit und der Völkerwanderungszeit I* by W. Janssen, *Medieval Archaeol.* XVIII, 224–5.
196. *Anglo-Saxon England I,* ed. P. Clemoes, *Antiq. J.* LIV, 120–1.
197. *Reihengräberfelder von Heidelberg-Kircheim* by G. Clauss, *Antiq. J.* LIV, 338.
198. *Three Lives of English saints,* ed. M. Winterbottom, *J. Theological Stud.* n.s. XXV, 197–8.
199. *The agrarian history of England and Wales Vol. Iii A.D. 43–1042,* ed. H.P.R. Finberg, *Engl. Hist. Rev.* LXXXIX, 845–9.

1975

200. 'Anniversary Address' (delivered as President of the Society of Antiquaries of London on 23 April, 1975), *Antiq. J.* LV, 1–10.
201. 'The Anglo-Saxon vase from Mitcham Grave 205' in 'Mitcham Grave 205 and the Chronology of applied brooches with floriate cross decoration' by M.G. Welch, *Antiq. J.* LV, 86–95 (J.N.L.M. 93–5).
202. 'Public Records', Letter to the Editor (with others), *The Times,* 1 February, 15.
203. 'A Home for the Turners', Letter to the Editor, *The Times,* 25 March, 17.

REVIEWS:

204. *The age of Arthur: a history of the British Isles from 350–650* by J. Morris, *Engl. Hist, Rev.* XC, 113–16.
205. *Early Christian Ireland: introduction to the sources* by K. Hughes, *Engl. Hist. Rev.* XC, 156–7.
206. *Catalogue of the Anglo-Saxon ornamental metalwork 700–1100 in the Ashmolean Museum* by D. Hinton, *Engl. Hist. Rev.* XC, 874–5.
207. *La cimetière de Lavoye: nécropole merovingienne* by R. Joffroy, *Antiq. J.* LV, 432–3.

1976
REVIEW:

208. *The northern barbarians 100 B.C.–A.D. 300* by M. Todd, *Antiq. J.* LVI, 100–1.

1977

209. *A corpus of Anglo-Saxon pottery of the pagan period*, 2 Vols. (Gulbenkian Archaeological Series. Cambridge).

210. 'Zoomorphic Bosses on Anglo-Saxon pottery' from *Studien zur Sachsenforschung* (Hildesheim), ed. H.-J. Hässler, 251–93.

REVIEWS:

211. *Die Merowinger und England* by Annette Lohaus, *Engl. Hist. Rev.* XCII, 180–1.

212. *The Sutton Hoo ship-burial vol. i* by R. Bruce-Mitford, *Engl. Hist. Rev.* XCII, 847–51.

1978

213. 'The Origin of the Jersey parishes—some suggestions', *Bulletin of the Société Jersiaise* 22, 163–75.

214. 'Amulets or small change?', *Antiq. J.* LVIII, 352.

REVIEWS:

215. *The Anglo-Saxon cemetery at Spong Hill, North Elmham I. Catalogue of cremations 20–64 and 1000–1690* by C. Hills, *Antiquity* LII, 166.

216. *The Roman forts of the Saxon shore* by S. Johnson, *Engl. Hist. Rev.* XCIII, 897.

1980

REVIEW:

The Sutton Hoo ship-burial vol. ii: Arms, armour and regalia by R. Bruce-Mitford, *Engl. Hist. Rev.* XCV (1980), 607–11.

In the press   **? 1980**

Myres Memorial Lecture, given at New College, 29 May 1979, 'Commander J.L. Myres R.N.V.R. the Blackbeard of the Aegean'.

? 1981

'The stone vaults of the churches of Jersey: their historical significance', *Bulletin of the Société Jersiaise*.

REVIEWS:

The South Saxons, ed. P. Brandon, *Antiq. J.*
A corpus of wheel-thrown pottery in Anglo-Saxon graves by V.I. Evison, *Antiq. J.*
Later Roman Britain by S. Johnson, *Antiq. J.*
From Roman Britain to Norman England by P.H. Sawyer, *Engl. Hist. Rev.*

I

Jutish burials in the Roman Iron Age

HANS NEUMANN

In a remarkable lecture, 'The Angles, the Saxons and the Jutes', held in the British Academy in 1970,[1] J.N.L. Myres spoke on the continental background of those three peoples mentioned by Bede.[2] The Saxons are said to come from 'that region, which is now called that of the Old Saxons' and the Angles are said to come from 'that country, which is called Angulus'. Further, Bede relates that the Angles lived between the provinces of the Saxons and the Jutes, which means that the Jutes must have had their settlements in the area which is today called north Slesvig and south Jutland, although it does not expressly exclude their presence further north.

From an archaeological point of view, the supposition of their presence in north Slesvig and south Jutland could be correct, because it agrees with the maps of settlements already drawn by continental archaeologists. According to the archaeological finds, Schleswig-Holstein is divided into three areas:[3] one with Angeln as a centre, but also including Sundeved and Als to the north and perhaps the southern part of Funen (fig. 1,D); south of this area one or several areas in Holstein (not marked on fig. 1); and to the north an area in north Slesvig and south Jutland which German archaeologists call the Ober Jersdaler Kreis (fig. 1,C).

North of these regions, Danish archaeologists distinguish two others: one in east and central Jutland, especially concentrated around Århus and Randers (fig. 1,B); and one in north Jutland, including Himmerland, Vendsyssel, and Thy (fig. 1,A).[4]

The three areas in the south (fig. 1,C,D, and Holstein) correspond to Bede's positioning of the three 'very powerful Germanic tribes'. Still, Bede's statement that the Jutes settled in Kent, on the Isle of Wight, and in the parts of Wessex situated opposite the Isle of Wight is well known to have caused much debate. For several decades it was almost generally accepted that whoever these Jutes in Kent might be, they could not possibly have come from Jutland.

Bede's clear and detailed statement makes such a rejection appear unwise. In fact reaction has started and Myres's lecture emphasizes the fact that the oldest post-invasion pottery in Kent might very well have a Jutish background. Thus

Bede might be correct in his statement. The problem arose not only because of the strong Romano–Frankish influence which could be noticed in the Kentish material, but also because the material available for comparison with the finds from south Jutland made comparison difficult. This is particularly the case with the pottery, the design and ornament of which is simple, and which cannot at all compare with what Anglian and Saxon areas in England and on the Continent could offer.

Comparisons between Kentish and Jutish pottery, however, have been made, and with positive results.[5] Clay vessels from the earliest cemeteries in Kent, especially low spherical jars decorated with simple linear patterns but without boss ornament, may be compared with very similar clay vessels from cemeteries in Jutland, especially in south-west Jutland.[6] However five or six of these cemeteries are situated north of the area of settlement in Jutland which adjoins the northern boundary of the Angles, and are thus from a region with a different sort of pottery. These clay vessels can hardly be typical for these northern regions as well, but the lack of sufficiently comprehensive publications makes it impossible to be more exact. However, this instance provides an opportunity to emphasize the point that in comparing archaeological regions in order to assign them to various tribes, the basis of comparison must be the major characteristics of the areas, that is, their typical objects. The more simple a clay vessel is in form and ornament, the easier it will be to find similar objects elsewhere.

The value of comparing such simple ornamented clay vessels as those discussed here is correspondingly low, and therefore for further illustration of the Jutish problem, we would appreciate documentation from fields other than that of pottery and small finds. Such documentation might be available as regards funeral customs. In south Jutland and north Slesvig an important change took place in the first centuries of this era in that a new custom, inhumation, was accepted in addition to cremation, which had been universal here for a millennium.

The equipment of these first inhumation graves and their construction suggest that this new custom starts off among the leading and most prosperous classes. Furthermore it is important that this new custom is known only in the Jutish region, the northern of these three areas of settlement, whereas the southern areas, Angeln, Sundeved, and Holstein, kept the cremation habit for some centuries. English archaeologists will notice that this difference in burial customs[7] recurs in England. Inhumation is particularly common in Kent. Therefore it might be worth a closer study of this burial custom to determine whether its details also are similar.

It is fortunate that excavations during the last few decades have provided us with detailed knowledge of how Iron Age inhumation actually took place. In the following account typical examples of this will be given. The starting-point chosen is a photograph from an excavation at Hørløk, a cemetery with inhumation graves from the second century AD, 15 km west of Haderslev. This simple photograph (pl. II) clearly shows how the grave appeared in different stages during the excavation. On level A, immediately under the plough level, the outline of the grave was visible because of the different colour of its fill. The digging was continued by emptying this grave, still keeping a flat level. When level B was reached, another rectangular figure appeared. This was the coffin itself. In some places a thin layer of decayed wood had survived, so that the coffin could be emptied in its exact form, while the rest of the filling in the grave was left intact.

This phenomenon is known from a great number of excavations. It is evident that if the coffin remains as a mark only, this technique is the only way in which to show the coffin in the grave and this is the reason for its adoption. However, the following will demonstrate that this photograph shows not only an excavation situation but also a prepared and intentional situation during the burial itself.

Another excavation photograph from a different grave in the same cemetery shows the same situation (pl. III). The big oak coffin has been emptied in the grave except for a block of earth in the middle of the coffin, on top of which is a pot which apparently had never been inside the coffin, but was placed on top of it after the funeral.

Just as important is the fact that a big pot is placed next to the coffin. This pot was not placed in the grave at the same time as the coffin, because it stands, not on the floor of the grave, but on the earth at the middle of the side of the coffin. The little ceremony, as it can be called, of placing this pot beside the coffin, must have been carried out after the coffin had been put in the empty grave and the grave filled up with earth to half the height of the oak coffin. This custom is characteristic of the Roman graves in this area. It is a custom also known on Funen,[8] while graves in central Jutland (pottery graves, fig. 1,B) and north Jutland (fig. 1,A) do not seem to have it.

We may now call attention to another grave, where details of the funeral ceremonies can be studied still more clearly. At Højvang near Skodborg two graves of a special construction were found. In 1953 the find was published in *Kuml*,[9] but in this connection we shall concentrate on what these graves have to say about the funeral rites.

In one of these graves, that of the woman, the grave itself was 260 × 160 cm in area, with the walls quite steep at the top (fig. 2 and pl. IV). While this grave was being emptied during the excavation, it was strange to notice that on three of the walls, directly on the undisturbed subsoil, a brown layer, only a millimetre thick, could be seen. Unfortunately this layer was not analysed, but it must have been due to some kind of wall-covering of wood or cloth which was used during the funeral. At a depth of 115 cm there were a great many stones, especially along one of the sides and the two ends of the coffin. At the northern side was a regular stone-paving made of small stones. At the eastern end were big stones, and at the western end a single stone set on its edge. These stones therefore surrounded a rectangular shape in the grave, which represented the position of the coffin, and it was situated somewhat south of the middle of the grave.

At this level the coffin appeared as a wooden plank standing on its edge up to and below the paving along the north side of the grave. The coffin itself was not a plank coffin but the bottom half of a trunk coffin, the sides of which had been heightened by the addition of planks to make the grave more suitable for its purpose and more impressive.

The coffin was placed on a layer of blue clay, known to have wood-preserving properties, and on the section (fig. 2) it can be seen that the grave-diggers saved themselves work by making the wall on the north side of the grave slope inwards under the paving, while the south side was made vertical down to the floor.

In this grave careful preparations for an impressive funeral were made, for it is evident that the situation which is here described, and which can be seen in the photograph (pl. IV), is the one that existed at the funeral itself, that is, when the body was placed in the coffin already *in situ* in the grave.

The grave-diggers dug the grave in the shape we can see. Then they placed the empty coffin on a layer of blue clay, added upright boards to the sides of the coffin, put earth into the grave up to this level, and put paving down beside the grave, mainly to the north, where there was most room. The coffin was, of course, empty during these preparations. There would be no purpose in all this if the entombing was not to take place in the grave arranged as it is shown here, and in view of the entombing it is understandable that they wanted to cover the sides of the grave with wood or leaves or even cloth.

The same situation prevailed in the other graves, where pots stand next to the coffin. While these other graves are not paved, they are similar in having a level on which people could walk during the funeral and other ceremonies in connection with the funeral.

The man's grave was only 8–9 m away but was built in quite a different way.[10] A burial chamber had been built of vertical planks. Its bottom had been about 45 cm above the dug-out floor of the grave, and on the same level some stones were placed like a small paved area at the end of the grave. During the funeral, this chamber was presumably open at one end. The funeral took place on this paving. In spite of the difference in the construction of the chambers there may have been considerable similarity in the procedure of the funeral.

At the beginning of the first century AD the new custom of inhumation came to north Slesvig from the east, from Funen, for there were close points of contact between these two areas during the first part of the Roman Iron Age. In this connection it is important to notice that this influence only holds good for the northern settlements (the above-mentioned Ober Jersdaler Kreis), which include the northern part of north Slesvig and south Jutland. In this area where, according to Bede, the Jutes lived, these rather deep and narrow inhumation graves of the first part of the Roman period have been recognized, and through additional graves of this kind and by means of the pottery we can define the northern border of this settlement as a line between Horsens and the south end of Ringkøbing Fjord. The southern border of the area has been known from recent excavations at the fortification line, the Olgerdige,[11] approximately on a line between Tønder and Åbenrå. This settlement (fig. 1,C), covers an area of about 8,400 km², which is double the size of the county of Kent, and Bede may well have been right in counting the Jutes among the 'very powerful Germanic tribes'.

There are two reasons for attempting to give English readers these observations. It is an opinion widely held that archaeology, which from its beginning is a science of objects, often tends not to attach sufficient importance to the fact that other sources exist besides small finds. It is well known that useful results have been obtained by arranging archaeological objects in geographic and chronological systems. Still, careful excavations can tap new sources, which, as in similar reports from later periods, give certain, though incomplete, information on the course of events. And where a funeral is concerned the sources must be of considerable importance, because the natural veneration involved causes strict adherence to custom and ritual.

The article by A.C. Hogarth about structural features of graves in Kent is interesting in this connection.[12] The cemetery of St Peter's dates from the seventh century AD, and various influences seem to have resulted in different constructions of graves. Some graves with postholes seem to have had a wooden building over the grave, and may have their parallels in Germany. But other graves show ledges on two, three, or four sides, and this feature seems to be directly comparable to the filled-up and sometimes paved sides of the Jutish graves. The difference could be due to the difference of the soil. In the hard chalk of Kent the digging was kept to a minimum and even a wooden coffin was often omitted. Thus, from the level of the Jutish pavement, only the coffin-like grave was made, so that the funeral could take place.

Several of the graves at St Peter's are surrounded by circular ditches, some of them penannular. At the Jutish cemetery of Endrupskov one of the graves shows the same kind of penannular ditch and inside this, two burnt patches with charcoal and burnt stones. It is the only example known in Denmark and it might be significant that this parallel to Kentish graves also occurs in the area from which, according to Bede, the Jutes came.

Further investigations, especially in unpublished excavation records of graves in Kent, may increase the number of parallels, and may contribute to the solution of the problems regarding the Jutes in Kent.

Acknowledgments

I would like to express my grateful thanks to Dr J.N.L. Myres for kind information and encouragement, to Mrs M.U. Jones and Mr W.T. Jones, the excavators of Mucking, for information about Kentish excavations, to Mrs Barbara Bluestone for great help with the manuscript and above all to Mr Dafydd Kidd, Assistant Keeper at the Department of Medieval and Later Antiquities, British Museum, for much valuable advice.

Bibliography

ALBRECTSEN, E., *Fynske Jernaldergrave*, II (København, 1956); III (København, 1968).

BEDE, *Historia ecclesiastica gentis anglorum*, ed. C. Plummer, *Venerabilis Bedae Opera Historica*, (Oxford, 1896).

BRØNDSTED, J., *Danmarks Oldtid*, III (København, 1960).

HOGARTH, A. C., 'Structural Features in Anglo-Saxon graves', *Archaeol. J.* 130, (1973), 104–19.

JANKUHN, H., *Die römische Kaiserzeit und die Völkerwanderungszeit (Geschichte Schleswig-Holsteins Volquart Pauls, 2)*, (Neumünster, 1964).

NEUMANN, H., 'Et løveglas fra Rinlandet', *Kuml*, (1953), 137–54.

Notes

1. Myres, 1971 (No. 175).
2. Bede, *Hist. Eccles.* I, 15.
3. Jankuhn, 1964, Abb. 3.
4. Brøndsted, 1960, 139ff., 165ff.
5. Myres, 1969 (No. 158), 95–9, Map 7 and fig. 40.
6. Ibid., Map 7.
7. Myres, 1937 (No. 25), 362.
8. Albrectsen, 1956, 74; 1968, 73.
9. Neumann, 1953, 137.
10. Ibid., 140, fig. 3.
11. Publication of the Olgerdige excavation is under preparation and will appear in *Jysk Arkaeologisk Selskabs Skrifter*.
12. Hogarth, 1973, 104–19.

Fig 1. Archaeological find regions in the Early Roman Iron Age, as characterized by various types of pottery and graves
A. North Jutland with large stone-built graves, for pottery see Brøndsted 1960, 166 ff.
B. East and central Jutland with broad, flat, so-called pottery graves, Brøndsted 1960, 144 ff. and 167   C. South Jutland and north Slesvig with narrow, deep graves, Brøndsted 1960, 150 ff. and 168   D. Angeln with other regions, where the custom of cremation is preserved

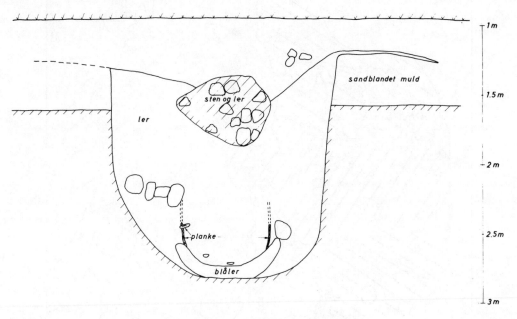

grav 2 , tværsnit

sandblandet muld

sten og ler

ler

planke

blåler

1 m

1.5 m

2 m

2.5 m

3 m

Fɪɢ 2. Højvang 1952, cross-section of grave 2. Ler = clay, Blåler = blue clay

2

Scandinavian-type gold bracteates in Kentish and continental grave finds

EGIL BAKKA

The finds of Scandinavian-type gold bracteates, mainly D bracteates, in western and central Europe, provide an important field of study for throwing light on cultural contacts between the North and the rest of Europe in the first half of the sixth century. They serve to illustrate the character of the contact, to define more closely the areas and lines of contact, and they also give one of the best chronological links between Scandinavia and the rest of Europe, by making it possible to synchronize a stage in the Scandinavian relative chronology with a certain stage in the far better dated continental system.

Most of the relevant finds come from Kent, where a number of rich grave groups contain typical Kentish objects associated with continental objects as well as with Scandinavian-type gold bracteates. There are, furthermore, important finds in France and central Europe, and finds along the North Sea coast, in Frisia and north-west Germany, mark the line from the western centre in Kent to Jutland, which has produced the most relevant comparative material in Scandinavia for the west European finds.

An important difference in find contexts should be emphasized at the outset: in Jutland, north Germany, and Frisia the finds are hoards, votive offerings, or stray finds, but farther to the west and south they come from graves. This must be a warning that numbers should not be used indiscriminately, and, moreover, that hoards and votive offerings are not associations that carry equal weight to grave finds in drawing chronological conclusions.

The finds have repeatedly attracted the interest of earlier research, and some of the main points need only be briefly summarized. The gold bracteate finds are definitely later than the historically recorded Jutish conquest of Kent, which has been studied from the archaeological point of view on the basis of pottery and cruciform brooches of an earlier date.[1] The bracteate finds serve rather to illustrate continued contacts with the old homeland, and at a time when the Jutes of Kent had established even more important contacts with the Franks of the Rhineland

and northern Gaul. For the time in between the Jutish invasions and the D bracteate period there is also the introduction of the square-headed brooch and Salin's Style I in England from Scandinavia, and again with Denmark and Kent as the focal points at either end of the line of contact.[2] The movement of skilled craftsmen in the service of members of the leading social levels may be the explanation here, and a similar explanation may be the more likely one for the further spread of square-headed brooches and Style I to the Continent, where Kentish influence or mediation has to be considered just as seriously as a more direct spread of Scandinavian fashion along more easterly lines of contact to central Europe.

For the spread of Scandinavian-type gold bracteates of the next stage, trade has been considered the most convincing answer,[3] still with Kent and Jutland as the focal points geographically. The central European material, however, has been taken to indicate more direct and easterly lines of contact than the detour via Kent. The character of contact is, however, not sufficiently clear.

To me an explanation in terms of trade alone is not fully satisfactory, and a high proportion of imitative bracteates certainly indicate something more than trade alone. It also seems that versions of late Scandinavian Style I animal ornament caught the interest of south German people, the Alamanni of south Germany and no less the Lombards of western Hungary, at a time before the Lombard migration to Italy in 568 and probably in or towards the end of the D bracteate period. At some time after the Lombard migration to Italy strong return impulses from Italy and central Europe introduced Style II in the animal ornament and other new fashions into England and the North, in evidence of lively and far-reaching international contacts among members of the leading social classes, where exchange of gifts, diplomatic contacts, intermarriages, and the movement of skilled craftsmen in the service of the aristocracy may be more convincing reasons than trade, or a slow, general diffusion.

We are here dealing with a long and unbroken sequence of international contact, to be studied in precious objects and in changing fashions of art styles, personal ornaments, arms, drinking vessels, and horse-gear of the aristocracy, in short, on their visible symbols of prestige. It is a fascinating, varied, and complicated story, far from clear on many points, and the finds with Scandinavian-type bracteates occupy a central position in it, representing, however, neither the beginning nor the end.

A total of 287 D bracteates from 156 different stamps were on record in 1977, as part of the more than 800 Scandinavian-type gold bracteates known.[4] Fifty-two D bracteates from thirty-three dies come from outside Scandinavia, being twenty-three from nineteen dies in England (all from Kent), twenty-three from nine dies in Germany, and six from three dies in Frisia. Two bracteates from Normandy and two from Rheinhessen should probably be added to these numbers.[5] On the whole, then, between one-fifth and one-sixth of the total of D bracteates, and about one-fifth of the dies are known from finds outside Scandinavia.

The more closely comparable material in Scandinavia to the non-Scandinavian finds is, however, more restricted in number and distribution. The bracteates in question, of Mackeprang's Jutish group I and his north Jutish–west Swedish group I,[6] make up a total of some fifty dies, of which about half come from outside Scandinavia, and the nineteen examples from Kent at the same time form a remarkably high proportion of the total and undoubtedly the most dense concentration within the distribution area, which extends from Normandy and south Germany to middle Sweden and south-western Norway.

All D bracteates found outside Scandinavia can ultimately be derived from three Scandinavian prototypes (fig. 1), while the many other Scandinavian D groups are of no importance here. The three in question are, however, also closely related to each other, two of them evidently being varieties derived from a prototype. It would all have started with one particular design (here variety 1), which was closely copied and imitated, more than once debased, and slightly changed. The beginning of the other two varieties should be seen as successful and deliberate improvements and perfections of the already existing basic pattern.

General *Jutish type*: the basic pattern is a ribbon-shaped animal with its head turned backwards over an S-shaped body, with loop-shaped shoulder and thigh, and legs bent first in an angle and then making a curve, the foreleg crossing the neck and the hindleg crossing the body. *Variety 1* (fig. 1) has a head with U-shaped eye frame, originally with a notched outer contour, and a transverse moulding (lower eyelid) in front of it, the jaws formed like a beak with rounded base and hollow inside. I consider this head diagnostic for the variety. In front of the beak the primary design has a small C-scroll. The foreleg crosses over both neck and body. This variety corresponds to Mackeprang's first division of his Jutish group I.[7] *Variety 2* (fig. 1) has a more open U-shaped eye frame and the lower eyelid placed inside it, loop-shaped jaws, the long lower jaw crossing over the body. The artistically best design (like M 16:24) should be considered as the result of a deliberate act of improvement and perfection, not merely chance imitation of some secondary and probably late bracteates of variety 1 (like M 16:19–20), where the (more inconspicuous) loop-shaped jaws are there already, but the eye frame and lower eyelid are still those of variety 1, as well as the crossing of the foreleg over the body, another detail which was usually changed with variety 2. This variety corresponds to Mackeprang's third division of his Jutish group 1. *Variety 3* (fig. 1) has a U-shaped eye frame with the eyelid placed inside it, and a curved beak with an angular hook downwards at its squared-off base. In the original design a small and simplified animal figure is found between the shoulder and the hind leg. This variety corresponds to Mackeprang's north Jutish–west Swedish group 1. I consider the animal heads as the primary diagnostic detail of the varieties, and the secondary figures of the C-scroll and the additional small animal as further diagnostic features for varieties 1 and 3 respectively. Varieties 2 and 3 can best be explained as derived from variety 1, and independently of each other.

The distribution of the three varieties may be seen on the distribution map, fig. 1. In Scandinavia varieties 1 and 2 have very much the same distribution, i.e. in Jutland, with scattered finds of variety 1 farther to the east, on Fyn and in Scania. Variety 3 covers the same area and goes in addition somewhat farther to the north and east, with a number of finds in western Sweden and outlying examples in south-western Norway, east and south Sweden.

The gold bracteates from outside Scandinavia (pl. V) are partly of good Scandinavian standard and in all respects indistinguishable from bracteates of the same standard found in Scandinavia, but partly, however, they are imitations of inferior quality, some of them degenerate. Nevertheless, poor and degenerate imitations are also well known in Scandinavian finds, and there is also every reason to believe that good standard copies could also have been produced outside Scandinavia, based on imported Scandinavian originals, for instance in Kent. Of variety 1 there are eight good standard bracteates of five dies in five finds in Kent and Normandy (pl. V,1–6), with two dies represented in Finglesham grave D3. The bracteates from Sarre grave 90, Kent (pl. V,2) and Hérouvillette grave 39, Normandy (pl. V,1), are made with the same die. Furthermore, three of the bracteates from Sarre grave 4, from the same die (pl. 1,7) are degenerate imitations of variety 1. There is nothing like them elsewhere, and I think L. Webster[8] is probably right in suggesting that they were made in Kent. For the identification of the model as belonging to variety 1, the C-scroll must be decisive.

One more imitation, from Bad Kreuznach, Rheinhessen (pl. V,8), can be derived from variety 1. It is a very small bracteate, with the lower part of the animal missing and otherwise garbled, which shows that it is not just a section of an ordinary stamp. Its animal head, however, can be identified as belonging to variety 1, with the beak and the transverse moulding in front of the eye frame, which also has the serrated outer contour.

Variety 2 bracteates are on the whole known in smaller numbers. In west European grave finds there are four of them, two of a good standard, from Bifrons grave 64 (pl. V,14) and Sarre grave 4 (pl. V,10), Kent, and two not so good, from the same Sarre grave 4 (pl. V,9) and Hérouvillette grave 11 (pl. V,11), Normandy. Varieties 1 and 2 are also known in Frisian and north German finds from terps, hoards, and bog finds, where they are mainly of good quality.

Variety 3, on the other hand, is known outside Scandinavia in stylistically inferior or debased imitations only. They make up two distinctly different groups, one Kentish and one continental, differing in design and distribution, having only the original Scandinavian prototype in common. The Kentish group comprises three bracteates, one from Bifrons grave 29 (pl. V,13) and another, made with the same die, from Bifrons grave 64 (pl. V,14). The third one, from Lyminge grave 16 (pl. V,15), is a still more simplified imitation of those from Bifrons. Animal head and foreleg on these bracteates are reduced beyond recognition, and important for the identification of the prototype is the additional small animal between shoulder and foreleg on the Bifrons bracteates. A Kentish production is very likely for these bracteates, as has also been suggested by Webster,[8] although they are the only indication known so far of a model bracteate of variety 3 finding its way to Kent.

The continental imitative group of variety 3 bracteates comes from Germany, Obermöllern grave 20 (pl. V,19) in Thuringia, Schretzheim grave 33 (pl. V,18) in Baden-Württemberg (five bracteates of the same die), and a recent find from Wörrstadt (pl. V,17) in Rheinhessen. These bracteates, from three different dies, differ stylistically from the Scandinavian examples and resemble each other and it seems to be generally agreed that they are of German production, copying one particular Scandinavian model. The small extra figure between shoulder and hind leg is the decisive detail for identifying the model as belonging to variety 3. It has been suggested that the Scandinavian inspiration of these bracteates reached the Danube and Rhine valleys by means of Thuringian mediation, along with other Thuringian influences in those areas, an explanation which is very likely.

Lastly, the three smaller gold bracteates from Várpalota, grave 21, western Hungary[9] are likely to be derived from a variety 3 model, and possibly from the German group of Obermöllern/Schretzheim/Wörrstadt, as might be argued from the circular eye frame and the beak. With them, in the same grave, was found a fourth gold bracteate, a unique B bracteate, also most likely of Scandinavian derivation, if not of Scandinavian production.

No long discussion will be undertaken here of the few A, B, and C bracteates found in graves outside Scandinavia, in England and Germany, where associated finds contribute little to their dating (Market Overton, Longbridge, Meckenheim),[10] or where the style of the artistically inferior designs allows no dating in the Scandinavian development (Aschersleben, Obermöllern 6).[11] The B bracteates of two finds, however, may contribute something more specific: Bifrons grave 29, Kent, has in addition to the three D bracteates, a B bracteate with its closest parallels in three finds from Fyn, Denmark, and can stylistically be attributed to Mackeprang's bracteate period 2. It is much worn, and was probably old at the time of burial.

Freilaubersheim grave 68, Rheinhessen, which has two B bracteates (pl. V,20) with a close parallel in northern Jutland, can stylistically be dated to bracteate period 3, and is contemporary with the D bracteates.

Chronology

The Scandinavian-type bracteates in datable grave groups form fundamentally important links between the chronological systems of Scandinavia, Kent, and parts of the continent. Datings should primarily be given in terms of relative chronologies, and absolute-chronological terms should be taken in a relative-chronological sense, a point which has been clearly understood by some of our continental colleagues for a long time already, and which has been argued theoretically most recently by myself for Scandinavia[12] and for the continent by H. Ament.[13] For Scandinavia I have proposed a system of four stages for the migration period (Fvt. I–IV), with the beginning of stage III defined by the beginning of the square-headed brooch with undivided foot, and the beginning of stage IV defined by the beginning of D bracteates. These criteria were deliberately chosen as they can also be related to west and central European chronologies.

Much of the more relevant literature for studying the chronological relationships appeared after my first discussion of them in 1958. I touched upon them again in 1973, but a more comprehensive presentation of the main evidence in the light of the present state of research would, I think, be useful. Firstly, however, it should be noted that in Kentish relative chronology I find it convenient for the present purposes to use two defined landmarks: 1, the beginning of the square-headed brooch and Salin's Style 1 in Kent (Bakka 1958), and 2, the beginning of the Kentish keystone-garnet disc brooch. This type of object has recently been systematically studied by R. Avent (1975), and the Kentish garnet-inlaid disc brooches may conveniently serve as the backbone of Kentish archaeological chronology for a hundred years or more, from an early date in the sixth century onwards (Avent seems to base his absolute chronology on the state of research of 1958). The square-headed brooch represents a somewhat earlier intrusion in a Germanic or Jutish cultural pattern already established in Kent, and its beginning there cannot, therefore, designate anything like a 'first period', but rather a second one, following an earlier one, which in the Kentish cemeteries has left such things as early, handmade pots, cruciform brooches, buckles with late Roman and early Frankish affinities, and ornaments in the quoit-brooch style.[14] How and where the beginning of the square-headed brooch should be placed in relation to these elements, is not very clear, due to a general shortage of good, informative grave groups, and due to the fact that the early square-headed brooches have come down to us either with no associations or as much worn and fairly old objects at the time of burial, like the Finglesham D3 and Bifrons 41 brooches, so one can only say that they belong to a time prior to that of their associations. For the present purpose I shall in the following use the term 'Kentish stage II' for a period starting with the square-headed brooch, and 'Kentish stage III' for that which starts with the Kentish keystone-garnet disc brooch.

The basis for dating our bracteate finds in absolute-chronological terms must necessarily be Frankish chronology, which is based on large numbers of finds from the Rhineland and adjoining areas first of all, and has also proved its validity and adaptability for most of the *Reihengräber* civilization of western and central Europe. Coin-datings and datings based on historical events (the Gothic migration to Italy AD 489, the Lombard occupation of western Hungary, AD 530 and of Italy, AD 568) and the graves of historically known persons (Childeric, Arnegunde), are here possible. The *Stand der Forschung* in Frankish chronology has recently been summarized by K. Böhner,[15] who has also pointed out the importance of Frankish chronology for Anglo-Saxon and Scandinavian chronology:

Une grande partie des fouilles anglo-saxonnes peut également être datée grâce aux découvertes du pays franc (par exemple: E. Bakka. *Universitetet i Bergen, Årbok 1958, Hist. ant. rekke 3*, 1–83). La fixation chronologique des découvertes franques sera également d'une grande importance pour la datation des fouilles scandinaves.[16]

In the following I am going to use the chronological system of K. Böhner, first worked out for the antiquities of the Trier region,[17] and now generally used and referred to for large parts of the Continent, with such adjustments, elaborations, and refinements as have been made possible by later discoveries and results of research, as discussed by Böhner and H. Ament, while I shall refer also to the analyses of completely excavated cemeteries and their internal, independent, relative chronologies.[18]

The more important refinement of the system for our purposes is a division of Böhner's *Stufe* III (about AD 525–600 into an earlier and later part, with a division about 560, as was first suggested by B. Schmidt[19] for the Thuringian finds of central Germany (*Gruppe* IIIa and IIIb), and later also established more generally and corresponding to Ament's periods AM II and AM III.[20] For the present purposes I shall use a subdivision of Böhner's *Stufe* III into 'early' and 'late', of '*Stufe* IIIa' and '*Stufe* IIIb', corresponding to Ament's AM II and AM III.

Table 1

Grave group	Gold bracteates	Bow brooches	Other brooches	Other ornaments	Buckles and strap fittings	Other objects
Finglesham D3	3 D var. 1	1 square-h. 2 radiate-h. w. straight-sided foot	2 bird br.	glass and amber beads	1 buckle 2 belt rivets	glass beaker weaving batten bronze tube knife, 2 keys
Bifrons 29	2 D var. 1 1 D var. 3 1 B	2 radiate-h. w. straight foot	2 keystone disc	gold braid 2 silver rings bronze bracelet	1 buckle	Roman bronze coin knife 3 keys wooden pail pottery vessel bronze and iron rings
Bifrons 63	1 D var. 2	1 square-h.		beads		
Bifrons 64	1 D var. 3	2 square-h.	1 keystone disc	gold braid beads		crystal ball knife
Sarre 4	3 D var. 1 2 D var. 2 1 D indeterm.	2 square-h.	2 keystone disc	gold braid silver ring bronze pin glass and amber beads	1 buckle 2 belt rivets	glass beaker silver spoon crystal ball 2 Rom. bronze coins 2 knives, comb
Lyminge 16	1 D var. 3	1 radiate-h. w. lozenge foot	1 button br.	bronze bracelet silver toe ring glass and amber beads	1 buckle	knife
Buckland Dover 20	1 D var. 1	2 square-h.	1 cloisonné disc	2 bracelets silver pin beads	1 buckle 2 belt rivets	glass beaker bronze bowl weaving batten knife, keys
Hérouvillette 11	1 D var. 2		cloisonné mount reused as brooch	2 finger rings 6 amber beads	1 buckle 3 belt rivets	earthenware jug knife
Hérouvillette 39	1 D var. 2		2 S-brooches	finger ring 7 glass and amber beads	2 buckles	3 bronze rings bronze hook iron shears glass and pottery fragments

Table 1 cont.

Grave group	Gold bracteates	Bow brooches	Other brooches	Other ornaments	Buckles and strap fittings	Other objects
Wörrstadt	1 D var. 3	2 w. oval foot	2 cloisonné rosettes	glass beads	1 buckle	silver coin (Valentinian III, 425–45) glass beaker glass whorl clay whorl, comb knives coin (lost)
Bad Kreuznach	1 D var. 1	2 radiate-h. w. straight-sided foot		beads (lost) finger ring (lost)		
Freilaubers-heim 68	2 B	2 w. oval foot	1 bird brooch 1 S-brooch	4 ear-rings bracelet finger ring glass and amber beads	1 buckle	wooden pail 2 pottery vessels spinning whorl
Schretzheim 33	5 D var. 3	2 bow brooches (unidentified)	2 cloisonné brooches (unidentified)	glass and amber beads	2 buckles	crystal whorl bone comb knife
Obermöllern 20	1 D var. 3	2 volute-headed w. oval foot	2 cloisonné disc brooches	3 gold pendants beads	3 buckles 2 strapends	clay pot glass whorl loom weights 2 knives shears

In Table 1 I have listed 14 grave finds with Scandinavian-type B and D gold bracteates, the dating of which will be discussed in the following. The large majority of these finds can be dated in *Stufe* IIIa (about AD 525–560), none of them tending to be really late within that span of time. Indications for datings earlier than *Stufe* IIIa, i.e. in the later part of *Stufe* II, are also present, and the beginning of the D bracteates would, in my opinion, be likely to fall in the first quarter of the sixth century.

I propose to start with the associations of the imitative and therefore later bracteates. Imitative bracteates of variety 3 can be dated in the grave groups Bifrons 64, Lyminge 16, Bifrons 29, Obermöllern 20, Schretzheim 33, and Wörrstadt.

Imitative bracteates of variety 1 can be dated in Sarre grave 4 and Bad Kreuznach, imitative bracteates of variety 2 likewise in Sarre 4 and Hérouvillette grave 11.

The Kentish finds *Bifrons 29, Bifrons 64,* and *Sarre 4* have gold bracteates in association with keystone-garnet disc brooches, and can accordingly be dated straight away in my Kentish stage III. Bifrons 64 and Sarre 4 also contain square-headed brooches, which continued in use in this stage, the end of which may conveniently be placed where the square-headed brooch went out of use in Kent. From Avent 1975 it appears that keystone-garnet disc brooches and square-headed brooches are found associated in ten finds, two of them being very firm associations, with the keystone-garnet disc fixed to the bow of square-headed brooches from Dover and Howletts. The ten finds are the following (for further references, see Avent, 1975, part II):

Table 2

Find	Keystone-garnet disc brooch Avent 1975			Square-headed brooch
	Corpus No. and fig.	Class	Diameter cm	
Finglesham E2	8	1.1	2.4	1 large, 2 small. Chadwick 1958, 19, fig. 11a–c, pl. IV A–B
Mersham	17	1.2	2.6	1 small. Bakka 1958, fig. 52
Bifrons 64	22	2.1	2.8	2 small. Fig. 2:9
Dover	27	2.1	2.85	Brooch with disc on bow. Avent 1975, pl. 4 no. 27
Howletts	29	2.1	2.8	Brooch with disc on bow. Avent 1975, pl. 5 no. 29
Lyminge 44	31–2	2.1	2.8	2 large. Warhurst 1955, pl. XII. Leeds 1957, pl. 5A
Chessel Down	37	2.2	3.0	3 large. Kendrick 1938, pl. XXX
Howletts A	41	2.2	3.0	? 1 small (association uncertain)
Sarre 4	42–3	2.2	3.1	1 large, 1 small. Fig. 2: 11, 14
Howletts 18	57	2.5	2.8	? 2 headplates of brooches (association uncertain)

The small sizes of the keystone-garnet disc brooches, with a diameter variation 2.4–3.1 cm indicate an early date, being consistently smaller than any brooch with Style II ornament (diameter 4.2–5.1 cm) or associated with Style II ornamented objects (diameter from 3.9–4.3 cm upwards.[21]

The square-headed brooches in association with keystone-garnet disc brooches are all typologically fairly evolved. With the exception of the Bifrons 64 brooches, they have pronouncedly late features in the Kentish development; garnet inlay, square or lobe-shaped foot terminal, extra border enclosing the foot-plate or parts of it, short and low bow (so also the Bifrons 64 brooches), just to mention some of the typologically secondary features. The Bifrons 64 brooches (fig. 2,9) would typologically be the earliest of the lot, and minor versions of the Gilton and Richborough brooches,[22] but as such later than the Buckland, Dover brooches (fig. 2,6), which have the higher and longer, convex bow.

The associated types of Kentish garnet disc brooches and square-headed brooches can be dated in relation to Frankish chronology in a number of finds, all indicating *Stufe* IIIa, with contact to late *Stufe* II in some cases, and no clear indications for contact with *Stufe* IIIb. Both types together are found in the

Mersham grave,[23] associated with two small Frankish brooches, one square and one circular, of the first half of the sixth century.[24] The grave also contained an ornamented buckle with thickened base of the tongue, which has a close parallel in a rich and well-datable grave of *Stufe* IIIa, Pry grave 18, Belgium.[25] Similar buckles were in use in the Namur area as early as the fifth century.[26]

The bracteate grave *Bifrons 29*, with a pair of Class 2.1 brooches (pl. VI:2), also contained a pair of Frankish radiate-headed brooches with straight-sided foot of Kühn's type of Bonn,[27] or Böhner's type Trier A 2[28] of *Stufe* IIIa and stylistically related to late *Stufe* II brooches, and a square buckle with shield on tongue,[29] also of *Stufe* IIIa.

Small Kentish square-headed brooches of the types of my Kentish stage III are found with Frankish brooches in the following graves: Chatham Lines grave 2[30] with a pair of small three-knob brooches of *Stufe* II, Chatham Lines grave 18 with a brooch of type Hahnheim[31] of *Stufe* IIIa (cf. Lyminge grave 14 in the following), Bifrons 42[32] with two small cloisonné disc brooches of *Stufe* IIIa (its pair of square-headed brooches are very similar to the small brooch of the bracteate grave Sarre 4, fig. 2,14), Bifrons 41[33] with a Frankish bird brooch and buckle with shield on tongue, also indicating *Stufe* IIIa.[34] Lastly it may be mentioned that the cloisonné style of the bow of the Lyminge 44 square-headed brooches,[35] with the notched cell partitions, is a characteristic and widespread feature which has been discussed by Werner and dated in the first half of the sixth century,[36] late *Stufe* II and *Stufe* IIIa.

On the whole, then, my Kentish stage III, starting with the beginning of the keystone-garnet disc brooches and ending with the end of Kentish square-headed brooches, can be firmly dated as contemporary with the Frankish *Stufe* IIIa, probably starting no later than the beginning of IIIa (about AD 525), and probably not outliving it.

The imitative variety 3 bracteate (pl. V,15) in *Lyminge grave 16*[37] can be dated by a Frankish brooch with semicircular head-plate and lozenge-shaped foot (pl. VI,3) of type Hahnheim, named after the coin-dated find of Hahnheim grave 57, *terminus post quem* AD 552 (Werner 1935, Taf. 4 A). The type has been discussed by Kühn, Werner, and most recently by M. Martin.[38] It has a clearly Frankish distribution, with an eastern and western variety, the Lyminge brooch belonging to the eastern variety of the Rhineland. There is nothing to indicate that it continued in use after *Stufe* IIIa, and the coin-dated Hahnheim find is likely to be a late association for the type. In Basel-Bernerring grave 42 it belongs to the first generation of Frankish settlers, arriving a short time before the middle of the sixth century and buried with an old woman, whose other ornaments can be dated to the first half of the century. The associations of type Hahnheim with small brooches are discussed by Martin, and they are most common in the second quarter of the sixth century, more rare in the third quarter.

Obermöllern grave 20 is a richly furnished grave with three more gold pendants (pl. VI,9) in addition to the gold bracteate (pl. V,19), and as the more closely datable objects there are a pair of Thuringian bow brooches with a pair of bird-headed volutes for the head-plate, and oval foot with chip-carved diagonal angular twist and animal head terminal (pl. VI,11), and a pair of small, circular, cloisonné disc brooches (pl. VI,10), dated by Schmidt in his *Gruppe* IIIa.[39] The one known close parallel for the Thuringian bow brooches of the find comes from Schretzheim grave 197, and is dated by U. Koch in her *Stufe* 1 of the Schretzheim cemetery (AD 525/35–45/50).[40]

The *Wörrstadt* grave[41] (bracteate pl. V,17) contained as its more closely datable objects a pair of small bow brooches with square head-plate and oval foot ornamented with chip-carved diagonal angular twist (pl. VI,6), a pair of quite small rosette cloisonné brooches (pl. VI,5), a glass beaker, bronze buckle, bone comb, etc., and is dated by Clauss in the decennia just before the middle of the sixth century.

The bow brooches belong to a rather widespread type,[42] with the majority of finds in south Germany. Brooches from Niederösterreich (Poysdorf grave 6) and western Hungary would according to Werner[43] belong to the Lombard north Danubian phase (AD 489–526/7) and the following Pannonian phase AD 526/27–68. A pair from Cividale St Giovanni grave 12 would have been brought to Italy in the Lombard migration of AD 568. A closely related pair from Schretzheim grave 31 is dated by Koch in her *Stufe* 1 (AD 525/35–45/50) of that cemetery, with the primary typological dating in full agreement with the location of the grave in the primary and central part of the cemetery.[44]

Freilaubersheim grave 68,[45] a child's grave with two late B bracteates (pl. V,20), has a pair of bow brooches (pl. VI,14) very similar to those of the Wörrstadt grave and Schretzheim grave 31, as well as a bird brooch (pl. VI,13), and an S-shaped brooch (pl. VI,12). The dating can only be the same as for the Wörrstadt grave.[46]

Schretzheim grave 33 contained five D bracteates of the same die (pl. V,18), imitative of variety 3, and closely related to the bracteates from Obermöllern grave 20 and Wörrstadt. Of the rich equipment of this grave[47] a pair of bow brooches and a pair of cloisonné disc brooches can no longer be identified, and an S-shaped brooch (pl. VI,7) and glass beads remain as the more closely datable items of the grave group. The location of the grave in the cemetery is close to the dividing line between *Stufe* 1 and 2,[48] beads of both stages are present in it, and

Koch refers the grave to the beginning of her *Stufe* 2 (AD 545/50–65/70). The S-brooch could, according to Koch, have been an old piece at the time of burial. It belongs to the widespread Anhausen/Nordendorf type, discussed by Werner[49] and most recently by Koch. Its presence in west Hungary[50] dates it in the Lombard Pannonian phase (AD 530–68). The type is more common in south-west Germany and northern France, and appears in associations with bow brooches of the first half of the sixth century.[51]

The imitative D bracteates of variety 3 of the finds so far discussed seem all to be securely dated in *Stufe* IIIa (AD 525–60). What then about the good standard variety 1 and 2 bracteates and their imitations?

Bad Kreuznach has a small imitative D bracteate of variety 1 (pl. V,8). Its association with a pair of bow brooches has been checked and confirmed by Clauss, who has also discussed the find.[52] The brooches have semicircular headplates with five bird-headed knobs and straight-sided foot (pl. VI,8). They belong to a rather distinctive type, distributed in the Rhineland and northern France.[53] A brooch very similar to the Bad Kreuznach brooches has been found in a datable association in Rittersdorf grave 15, dated by Böhner in *Stufe* III.[54] Its bird brooch (Trier C 14b) and glass beaker (*Sturzbecher* Trier A) of *Stufe* II/III date the grave more closely in *Stufe* IIIa. The bird-headed knobs of the bow brooches is also an element which otherwise started in *Stufe* II.

Hérouvillette grave 11[55] has a D bracteate (pl. V,11) imitative of variety 2, associated with a rectangular cloisonné brooch (fig. 2,1), which seems to be a reused (scabbard?) mount of *Stufe* II, and could be an old piece at the time of burial.

The good standard 'originals' of D bracteates can be dated in five grave groups, in Kent and Normandy. Two of these finds, Bifrons grave 29 and Sarre grave 4, also contained imitative D bracteates and have been dealt with already.

Bifrons grave 63 contained a D bracteate (pl. V,12), variety 2, of good standard, associated with a large Kentish silver square-headed brooch (fig. 2,4) of a typologically and stylistically fairly early character,[56] which I would attribute to my Kentish stage II. The brooch is much worn, and was evidently older than the gold bracteate at the time of burial.

Hérouvillette grave 39[57] contained a D bracteate (pl. V,9) of variety 1, struck from the same die as the bracteate in Sarre grave 90.[58] It is associated with a pair of S-shaped brooches (fig. 2,2–3) of type Cléry, variety A,[59] with garnet eyes, straight, parallel, short jaws, ear at the back of the head, and chip-carved chevrons and strokes filling the body. These brooches are found in northern France and in the Rhineland, with a few finds in south Germany. They are stylistically closely related to animal-shaped brooches of type Herpes—the two types have conveniently been listed and mapped together by Werner.[60] In Westhofen grave 48, Rheinhessen, a brooch very similar to those from Hérouvillette, was found with a pair of bow brooches and a pair of strap-ends,[61] to be dated in *Stufe* IIIa. The pair of bow brooches with square headplate and oval foot, with meander and angular twist in chip-carving, can by size and style be grouped with what is characteristic for *Stufe* I in the Schretzheim cemetery and for the Lombard Pannonian phase (AD 530–68). The animal brooches of type Herpes, stylistically closely related to variety A of type Cléry, are also dated by Werner in the first half of the sixth century,[62] cf. also Oberwerschen grave 2, dated by Schmidt to his *Gruppe* IIIa[63] and Schretzheim grave 472, dated by Koch to her *Stufe* I.[64]

Buckland Dover grave 20 is an important new find, unpublished, and I am indebted to Vera I. Evison for her kind permission to utilize it here. Its D bracteate (pl. V,6) of variety I is associated with a pair of small Kentish square-headed brooches (fig. 2,6), a small circular cloisonné brooch (fig. 2,5), a buckle with shield on tongue (fig. 2,7) and two disc-headed strap-rivets (fig. 2,8), a glass claw-beaker and a bronze bowl with beaded rim as the more important datable items. Claw-beaker and bronze bowl are datable in *Stufe* II and IIIa in continental chronology, so also the small cloisonné brooch, the rim of which is unusual, however. Buckles with shield-on-tongue came into use in the later part of *Stufe* II and were common in *Stufe* III, to be further discussed on p. 27. The small square-headed brooches (fig. 2,6) would in my opinion be early in the particular Kentish development, of my Kentish stage II, with the high, convex bow and the narrow shape of the footplate, typologically earlier than the related Bifrons 64 brooches (fig. 2,9), and contemporary with the Canterbury Martyr's Field brooch.[65] In comparison with the larger square-headed brooches, which they evidently imitate, they should probably be placed at the same stage as the Richborough and Gilton brooches.[66] The more closely defined date of these brooches depends on Finglesham grave D3 and Basel-Kleinhüningen grave 74, to be discussed in the following, but with Buckland Dover grave 20 as an important additional link in the chronological argument.

Finglesham grave D3[67] is in various respects a key find in the cultural and chronological triangle Scandinavia, Kent, and the Continent. There are the three good standard D bracteates (pl. V,3–4) of variety I, one of the earliest Kentish square-headed brooches (fig. 3,1), with all of its preconditions in south Scandinavia, marking the beginning of my relative-chronological Kentish stage II, a pair of probably Kentish-made bird brooches (fig. 3,2), made after a Frankish model, and a pair of Frankish bow brooches with semicircular headplate with five knobs, and straight-sided foot-plate (fig. 3,3), Frankish imports from the Rhineland, and a Frankish-type buckle with shield-on-tongue (fig. 3,5) with shoe-shaped rivets (fig. 3,4). Furthermore there is a Frankish glass claw-beaker.

In addition to the associations, the degree of wear of the brooches should also be considered in a chronological discussion. The square-headed brooch is extremely badly worn, and must have been an old piece at the time of burial. The Frankish bow brooches are less worn, but, judging from a photograph, the niello triangles of the middle of the bow are clearly smaller than elsewhere, indicating undoubted wear on this exposed surface. So these brooches were not new at the time of burial, and could also be considered as older than the bracteates, bird brooches, and buckle at the time of burial. These things have not been taken into consideration by Kühn in his last treatment of the find,[68] and he rather seems to reverse the relative age of the bow brooches. Rather questionable also is his use of Mackeprang's absolute chronology of the gold bracteates, and his misleading quotations of S. Chadwick 1958. I am altogether unable to accept as valid Kühn's general view of the origin and date of the square-headed brooches in his works of 1940 and 1974, the first of which has, however, influenced others in their chronological discussions.

For the dating of the Finglesham D3 square-headed brooch, Basel-Kleinhüningen grave 74 is of primary importance. In anticipation of U. Giesler's publication of the Basel-Kleinhüningen cemetery, I am indebted to her for permission to use her drawings, and refer to the treatment of the find by Moosbrugger-Leu 1971, Bakka, 1973, and Haseloff 1974.[69] Haseloff and I are in perfect agreement that the Basel-Kleinhüningen 74 square-headed brooches are among the immediate successors to the Finglesham, Engers, and Bifrons 41 brooches,[70] which I still consider as Kentish products. A minor difference of opinion between Haseloff and myself in this matter does not influence the chronological questions.

Important for the dating is a pair of miniature bow brooches (fig. 3,14–15) with semicircular headplate and lozenge-shaped foot, with three knobs, animal head terminal and spiral ornament,[71] of the second half of the fifth century, a buckle with kidney-shaped plate[72] (fig. 3,17) a clear *Stufe* II type, a silver bracelet with thickened, ornamented ends (fig. 3,16), twisted gold wire earrings, a silver hairpin (?), and other objects. Moosbrugger-Leu refers the find variously to the time 'about 500' (p. 214), and the square-headed brooches and the grave with them '*ins zweite Viertel des 6. Jh.s*' (p. 185), with reference to Kühn 1940, 170, and a note: 'Zu diesem Grab wäre zu bemerken, dass es in seinem Inventar eine grosse Spannweite aufweist d.h. relativ frühes und mittleres Material in sich vereint.' A similar late dating at other places (pp. 211, 122) is also evidently influenced by Kühn's dating of the square-headed brooches. If this dating is considered for what it is worth, however, the problem of a great difference in age of the objects disappears. The ornamented bracelets with thickened ends were in use in the second half of the fifth century.[73] Moosbrugger-Leu's dating of about AD 500 seems to be the most reasonable for the grave, and the square-headed brooches being much worn, they are likely to have been made some time before AD 500, giving the slightly older brooch of Finglesham D3 a date roughly in the middle of the second half of the fifth century, or, believe it or not, about a century and a half earlier than Kühn's 1974 attempt at a dating.

The brooches with semicircular head-plate and straight-sided foot of Finglesham D3 have been referred by H. Kühn[74] to his type no. 11 '*Gleichbreiter Fuss mit Laternenknöpfen*', '*Typ von Lavoye*', variety '*500–550 mit Ranken*'. Two finds are coin-dated, Lavoye grave 307 bis, *terminus post quem* AD 491, and Chaouilley grave 19, *terminus post quem* AD 527.[75] The ornamentation of bow and foot-plate is different from that on the Finglesham D3 brooches, which have exact parallels in two finds, Westhofen grave 49[76] and Basel-Kleinhüningen grave 94.[77] Westhofen 49 contained, among other things, a square brooch with garnet corners[78] and an unusual S-shaped brooch.[79] The square brooch is related to one from Mersham, Kent,[80] referred to above, pp. 20–1, and can be dated in the first half of the sixth century.

The rich grave of Basel-Kleinhüningen 94 is a clear and undoubted association of *Stufe* II. In the mouth of the dead person was a coin of Valentinian III (AD 425–55).[81] In addition to the bow brooches (fig. 3,9) there are a pair of bird brooches (fig. 3,10), a pair of ear-rings (?) with lunate pendants (fig. 3,6–7), a pair of strap-ends (fig. 3,11), a silver hair-pin with bird-head terminal (fig. 3,8), a silver neck-ring,[82] glass and amber beads, an iron buckle, iron knife, a glass bottle, and a clay pot (fig. 3,12). Moosbrugger-Leu dates the grave to the end of the fifth century.[83] Böhner dates the Finglesham D3 and Basel-Kleinhüningen brooches as '*zweifellos in die Zeit um 500*', and refers in particular to the clay pot of Basel-Kleinhüningen 94 as no longer possible after AD 525.[84] The pot would correspond to the type Trier B 6, of *Stufe* II.[85] Some of the objects would fit equally well in the late fifth and early sixth century, ie the bird brooches,[86] the hair-pin,[87] and the glass bottle, while the lunate pendants with garnet settings[88] would be more likely to be of fifth than sixth-century date. Lunate pendants start in the fourth century. From the middle of the fifth century there is a good parallel with garnet setting in Arcy Ste Restitue grave 127,[89] coin-dated with more than 20 silver coins, some of them imitative, *terminus post quem* AD 429, and somewhat later is a garnet-set lunate pendant in a rich grave from Gava, Hungary, of the time before the Ostrogothic migration to Italy, AD 489.[90]

The bird brooches of Finglesham D3 (fig. 3,2), with garnet eye and tail, and a Style I animal inside the body, contribute little to an exact dating, and depend on the rest of the find for their own dating. Their precondition, however, is most likely to be a fairly early type of bird brooch from the Rhineland and northern Gaul.[91] The latest datable items of the grave group seems to be the silvered buckle with shield-on-tongue (fig. 3,5) and the two shoe-shaped, tinned-bronze strap-rivets (fig. 3,4). Buckles with shield-on-tongue are common in the sixth century, first of all in *Stufe* III, starting towards the end of *Stufe* II. I refer to Böhner's discussion 1958 and 1968.[92] In *Stufe* II can be dated some finds with weapons, the more outstanding of them being the princely graves of Planig, with *Goldgriffspatha,* the boy's grave of Cologne Cathedral, and Krefeld-Gellep grave 1782, the latter coin-dated with a solidus of Anastasius (491–518), in mint condition, in the mouth of the dead man.[93] These three graves would be completely contemporary, and are in a way the latest representatives of the Flonheim-Gültlingen group of graves, representing the high nobility whose rich equipment was dominated by the fashions found in the grave of Childeric (d. 481) and predominating during the reign of Clovis. Of the buckles with kidney-shaped, inlaid plates of the period, only one, from Rittersdorf grave 45,[94] has the shield-on-tongue, an additional indication that this feature only appeared towards the end of *Stufe* II. In addition to the early finds with buckles with shield-on-tongue, mentioned by Böhner 1958,[92] reference may be made to Krefeld-Gellep graves 964, 1307, 2134, and 2162, in the latter there is also a shoe-shaped rivet, as in the grave at Planig.[95] There is, on the whole, strong evidence for Böhner's conclusion that the buckle with shield-on-tongue first appeared towards the end of *Stufe* II, which in my opinion would be the date of the burial of the Finglesham D3 grave. I consider the same date as the most likely one for Buckland Dover grave 20, likewise because of its buckle.

In conclusion, then the D bracteates of Jutish type, variety 1, are likely to have started in the later part of *Stufe* II (or a short time before AD 525), and went on into the earlier part of *Stufe* IIIa. The derivative varieties 2 and 3 may have started early in *Stufe* IIIa, but the material is conclusive only so far that they existed in the Kentish stage III and *Stufe* IIIa, with no find necessarily later than the middle of the sixth century, and Schretzheim grave 33 probably the latest burial, with imitative D bracteates of variety 3.

The period of Scandinavian-type D bracteates in west and central Europe appears to have been a short one, perhaps something like that of a generation.

Non-Scandinavian imitations constitute a fairly large proportion of the total, so that it seems that the supply of good standard Scandinavian originals was insufficient to meet the demands of fashion. Typologically and stylistically they do not, strictly speaking, seem to have initiated any further development outside Scandinavia. It is a relevant question, however, how far the idea of a circular golden pendant with animal ornament as an amulet contributed to the creation of non-Scandinavian types, sometimes ornamented with designs in Style II, sometimes with ribbon interlace. They have been found in particular in Kent,[96] but also on the Continent,[97] and no direct connection with Scandinavia can be demonstrated by them.

Bibliography

ÅBERG, N., *The Anglo-Saxons in England* (Uppsala, 1926).

AMENT, H., 1974 see NEUFFER-MÜLLER, C. and AMENT H., 1974.

AMENT, H., 'Zur archäologischen Periodisierung der Merowingerzeit', *Germania*, 55 (1977): 1/2, 133–40.

ANNIBALDI, G. and WERNER, J., 'Ostgotische Grabfunde aus Acquasanta, Prov. Ascoli Piceno (Marche)', *Germania*, 41 (1963), 356–73.

AVENT, R., *Anglo-Saxon garnet inlaid disc and composite brooches*, British Archaeological Reports, 2 vols. (Oxford, 1975).

BAKKA, E., *On the beginning of Salin's Style I in England*, Univ. i Bergen. Årbok (1958), Hist. ant. rekke, No. 3.

BAKKA, E., 'Goldbrakteaten in norwegischen Grabfunden. Datierungsfragen', *Frühmittelalterliche Studien*, 7 (1973), 53–87.

BAKKA, E., 'Norwegische Kontakte mit Westeuropa in der frühen Merowingerzeit', *Union internationale d. sciences préhist. et protohist. Congrès IX, Colloque XXX: Les relations entre l'empire romain tardif, l'empire franc et ses voisins* (Nice, 1976), 24–41.

BÖHNER, K., *Die fränkischen Altertümer des Trierer Landes* (Germ. Denkmäler d. Völkerwanderungszeit, Ser. B, Bd. 1), (Berlin, 1958).

BÖHNER, K., 'Zur Zeitstellung der beiden fränkischen Gräber im Kölner Dom', *Kölner Jahrbuch für Vor- und Frühgeschichte*, 9 (1967/1968), 124–35.

BÖHNER, K., 'La chronologie des antiquités funéraires d'époque mérovingienne en Austrasie', *Problèmes de chronologie relative et absolue concernant les cimetières mérovingiens d'entre Loire et Rhin*, eds. M. Fleury and P. Périn (Paris, 1978), 7–12.

CHADWICK, S., 'Note on an early Anglo-Saxon square-headed brooch from Canterbury', *Antiq. J.*, XXXVIII (1958), 52–7.

CHADWICK, S., 'The Anglo-Saxon cemetery at Finglesham, Kent: a reconsideration', *Medieval Archaeol.* 2 (1958), 1–71.

CLAUSS, G., 'Ein neuer Grabfund mit nordischen Goldbrakteaten aus Wörrstadt. Kr. Alzey-Worms', *Arch. Korrespondenzblatt*, 8 (1978): 2, 133–40.

DASNOY, A., 'Quelques tombes du cimetière de Pry (IVᵉ–VIᵉ siècles) (Belgique, Province de Namur)', *Problèmes de chronologie relative et absolue concernant les cimetières mérovingiens d'entre Loire et Rhin*, eds. M. Fleury and P. Périn (Paris, 1978), 69–79.

DECAENS, J., 'Un nouveau cimetière du haut moyen âge en Normandie, Hérouvillette (Calvados)', *Archéologie Médiévale*, 1 (1971), 1–124.

DECAENS, J., 'Problèmes de datation au cimetière d'Hérouvillette (France Calvados)',

Problèmes de chronologie relative et absolue concernant les cimetières mérovingiens d'entre Loire et Rhin, eds. M. Fleury and P. Périn (Paris, 1978), 143–4.

DOPPELFELD, O., and PIRLING, R., *Fränkische Fürsten im Rheinland* (Düsseldorf, 1966).

EVISON, V.I., *The fifth-century invasions south of the Thames* (London, 1965).

FLEURY, E., *Antiquités et monuments du département de l'Aisne* (Paris, 1878).

HASELOFF, G., 'Salin's Style I', *Medieval Archaeol.,* 18 (1974), 1–15.

HAWKES, S.C. and DUNNING, G.C., 'Soldiers and settlers in Britain, fourth to fifth century', *Medieval Archaeol.,* 5 (1961), 1–70.

HAWKES, S.C. and DUNNING, G.C., 'Krieger und Siedler in Britannien während des 4. und 5. Jahrhunderts', *43.–44. Bericht d. Römisch-Germ. Kommission,* 1962–3 (1964).

JESSUP, R.F., 'An Anglo-Saxon cemetery at Westbere, Kent', *Antiq. J.* XXVI (1946), 11–21.

JESSUP, R.F., *Anglo-Saxon jewellery* (London, 1950).

KOCH, U., *Die Grabfunde der Merowingerzeit aus dem Donautal um Regensburg, Germ. Denkmäler d. Völkerwanderungszeit,* Ser. A, Bd. X (Berlin, 1968).

KOCH, U., *Das Reihengräberfeld bei Schretzheim, Germ. Denkmäler d. Völkerwanderungszeit,* Ser. A, Bd. XIII (Berlin, 1977).

KÜHN, H., *Die germanischen Bügelfibeln der Völkerwanderungszeit in der Rheinprovinz* (Bonn, 1940, reprinted Graz, 1965).

KÜHN, H., *Die germanischen Bügelfibeln der Völkerwanderungszeit in Süddeutschland* (Graz, 1974).

KÜHN, H., 'Das Problem der S-Fibeln der Völkerwanderungszeit', *Jahrbuch für prähistorische und ethnographische Kunst,* 24 (1974–7), 124–35, Taf. 60–2.

LEEDS, E.T., *Early Anglo-Saxon art and archaeology* (Oxford, 1936).

LEEDS, E.T., 'Denmark and early England', *Antiq. J.* XXVI (1946), 22–37.

LEEDS, E.T., *A corpus of early Anglo-Saxon square-headed brooches* (Oxford, 1949).

LEEDS, E.T., 'Notes on Jutish art in Kent between 450 and 575', ed. S. Chadwick, *Medieval Archaeol.,* 1 (1957), 5–26.

MACKEPRANG, M., *De nordiske guldbrakteater* (Århus, 1952).

MARTIN, M., *Das fränkische Gräberfeld von Basel-Bernerring* (Basel, 1976).

MOOSBRUGGER-LEU, R., *Die Schweiz zur Merowingerzeit, Handbuch der Schweiz zur Römer- und Merowingerzeit* (Bern, 1971).

MOREAU, F., *Album Caranda aux époques préhistorique, gauloise, romaine et franque. Premier volume. Planches* (Saint-Quentin, 1873–87). Text *Album Caranda (Suite). Les fouilles d'Arcy-Ste. Restitue 1878* (Saint-Quentin, 1879).

MÜLLER, H.F., *Das alamannische Gräberfeld von Hemmingen (Kr. Ludwigsburg), Forsch. und Berichte zur Vor- und Frühgeschichte in Baden-Württemberg,* 7 (Stuttgart, 1976).

MUNKSGAARD, E., 'Nye fund af guldbrakteater', *Nationalmuseets Arbejdsmark,* 1963–5 (1965), 19–24.

NEUFFER-MÜLLER, C. and AMENT, H., *Das fränkische Gräberfeld von Rübenach, Germ. Denkmäler d. Völkerwanderungszeit,* Ser. B, Bd. VII (Berlin, 1973).

PADBERG, L., von, 'Brakteaten: Tabelle', *Johannes Hoops: Reallexikon der germ. Altertumskunde*, Bd. 3 (Strassburg, 1977), 347–51.

PIRLING, R., 'Ein fränkisches Fürstengrab aus Krefeld-Gellep', *Germania*, 42 (1964), 188–216.

PIRLING, R., 1966 see DOPPELFELD, O. and PIRLING, R. 1966.

PIRLING, R., *Das römisch-fränkische Gräberfeld von Krefeld-Gellep, Germ. Denkmäler d. Völkerwanderungszeit*, Ser. B, Bd. II (Berlin, 1966).

PIRLING, R., *Das römisch-fränkische Gräberfeld von Krefeld-Gellep, 1960–1963, Germ. Denkmäler d. Völkerwanderungszeit*, Ser. B, Bd. VIII (Berlin, 1974).

REICHSTEIN, J., *Die kreuzförmige Fibel, Offa-Bücher*, Bd. 34 (Neumünster, 1975).

ROEREN, R., 'Ein münzdatierter Grabfund der frühen Merowingerzeit aus Heilbronn-Böckingen', *Fundberichte aus Schwaben*, N.F. 16 (1962), 119–31.

ROTH, H., 'Der Pressblechmodel aus Liebenau, Kr.Nienburg (Weser), Niedersachsen, Körpergrab VIII/100', *Studien zur Sachsenforschung*, ed. Hans-Jürgen Hässler (Hildesheim, 1977), 343–56.

SCHMIDT, B., *Die späte Völkerwanderungszeit in Mitteldeutschland, Veröffentlichungen d. Landesmus. f. Vorgesch. in Halle*, 18 (Halle, 1961).

SZONDREY, A.V., 'Der gotische Grabfind von Miszla', *Archaeologiai Ertesito* (1928).

THIRY, G., *Die Vogelfibeln der germanischen Völkerwanderungszeit, Rheinische Forschungen zur Vorgeschichte*, Bd. III (Bonn, 1939).

VIERCK, H., 'Der C-Brakteat von Longbridge in der ostenglischen Gruppe', *Karl Hauck: Goldbrakteaten aus Sievern, Anhang VIII*, 331–9, *Münstersche Mittelalterschriften*, 1 (München, 1970).

VOGT, E., 'Das alamannische Gräberfeld am alten Gotterbarmweg in Basel', *Anzeiger f. schweizerische Altertumskunde*, N.F., Bd. 32: 3 (1930), 145–64.

WARHURST, A., 'The Jutish cemetery at Lyminge', *Archaeol. Cantiana*, LXIX (1955), 1–40.

WEBSTER, L., 'Brakteaten. 1. Archäologisches, § 2, England', *Johannes Hoops: Reallexikon d. germ. Alertumskunde*, Bd. 3 (Strassburg, 1977), 341–2.

WERNER, J., *Münzdatierte austrasische Grabfunde, Germ. Denkmäler d. Völkerwanderungszeit*, Bd. III (Berlin, 1935).

WERNER, J., 'Eine nordfranzösische Tierfibel von Basel (Bernerring)', *Ur-Schweiz*, XX (1949), 60–8.

WERNER, J., *Beiträge zur Archäologie des Attila-Reiches, Bayerische Akad. d. Wissensch., Phil. hist. Kl. Abhandl.*, N.F. 38A, B (München, 1956).

WERNER, J., 'Eine ostgotische Prunkschnalle von Köln-Severinstor', *Kölner Jahrbuch f. Vor- und Frühgesch.* 3 (1958), 55–60.

WERNER, J., *Katalog der Sammlung Diergardt*, Bd. 1: *Die Fibeln* (Berlin, 1961).

WERNER, J., *Die Langobarden in Pannonien, Bayerische Akad. d. Wissensch. Phil. Hist. Kl. Abhandlungen*, N.F. H.55, A–B (München, 1962).

WERNER, J., 1963, see ANNIBALDI, G. and WERNER, J. 1963.

Notes

1. Myres, 1969 (No. 158); Reichstein, 1975; Myres, 1977 (No. 209).
2. Bakka, 1958.
3. And not the migration of Jutes from Jutland to Kent, see Webster, 1977, with references.
4. Padberg, 1977, 349.
5. Decaens, 1971; Clauss, 1978.
6. Mackeprang, 1952, 56–9, Catalogue 106–94. Additional finds: Vamdrup and Grathe hede, Jutland, Munksgaard, 1965, 20 f. figs. 2–4. Lyminge, Kent, grave 16; Warhurst, 1955, 15, pl. VII (a) 1. Buckland, Dover, Kent, grave 20, unpublished. Hérouvillette, Normandy, graves 11 and 39, Decaens, 1971, 18, 40, 74, 124 fig. 28. Decaens, 1978; Wörrstadt, Rheinhessen (Rheinland-Pfalz), Clauss, 1978, 133 ff., Taf. 21–3, 24. 1 a–b; Bad Kreuznach, Rheinhessen, Clauss, 1978, 133 ff., Taf. 23,3–5, 24.2 a–b.
7. Mackeprang, 1952, 56 f.
8. Webster, 1977, 342, Taf. 20 a.
9. Werner, 1962, Taf. 7,7–9.
10. Mackeprang, 1952, 175. Vierck, 1970, 331–9, fig. 49. Clauss, 1978, 139 no. 4, pl. 24,7–8.
11. Mackeprang, 1952, 184.
12. Bakka, 1973.
13. Ament, 1977.
14. Myres, 1969 (No. 158); Reichstein, 1975; Hawkes and Dunning, 1961, 1964; Evison, 1965.
15. Böhner, 1978, 7–12.
16. Ibid., 12.
17. Böhner, 1958.
18. Böhner, 1978; Ament, 1977. Cemetery chronologies utilized for the present purposes are for instance those of Schretzheim, Koch, 1977, Rübenach, Neuffer-Müller and Ament, 1973, Basel-Bernerring, Martin, 1976, Hemmingen, Müller, 1976.
19. Schmidt, 1961.
20. Ament, 1977.
21. Avent, 1975, Corpus nos. 126, 127, 128, 129, 81, 114, 135.
22. Bakka, 1958, figs. 44–5.
23. Ibid. fig. 52.
24. Square brooch: Böhner, 1958, 97, Trier C 13, Taf. 13,12; Werner, 1961, 37 no. 173–4,

list of finds 5 p. 58, distribution map Taf. 53; Moosbrugger-Leu, 1971, 192. Circular brooch: Werner, 1961, 38, no. 177.

25. Dasnoy, 1978, 75, fig. 5.
26. Ibid. 78.
27. Kühn, 1940, 125–7; Kühn, 1974, 677–82.
28. Böhner, 1958, 84, Taf. 10.2.
29. Bakka, 1958, fig. 53.
30. Åberg, 1926, fig. 152; Jessup, 1950, pl. VI.
31. Åberg, 1926, fig. 162, Tab. II: 105 and Tab. III: 31. Small square-headed brooch illustrated Kühn 1940, 156, Abb. 48.
32. Bakka, 1958, fig. 53.
33. Ibid. figs. 51 and 53.
34. Thiry's (1939, 54–7) late dating of the bird brooch type with strongly broken contour (Thiry, 1939, Abb. 475–7) is based on a typological assumption more than on associated finds, the one important association being Bifrons 41. I know of no indication that bird brooches outlived *Stufe* IIIa.
35. Warhurst, 1955, pl. XII. Leeds, 1957, pl. IV A.
36. Werner, 1958.
37. Warhurst, 1955, 15, pls. VII (a), VIII,5, figs. 9,3 and 10,5–7; Bakka, 1958, fig. 53.
38. Kühn, 1940, 151–61; Kühn, 1974, 799–811; Werner, 1961, 56, list of finds 2, distribution map Taf. 51; Martin, 1976, 77–81, with references and distribution map Abb. 24.
39. Schmidt, 1961, Taf. 76.
40. Koch, 1977, 49 f. Taf. 191.6–7.
41. Clauss, 1978, 133 ff., Taf. 21–4.
42. Kühn, 1940, 283–93; Kühn, 1974, 996–1006. Typ von Goethes Fibel.
43. Werner, 1962, 65 f.
44. Koch, 1977, 51, Taf. 190.5–6, 17, Abb. 2.
45. Kühn, 1974, 196 f. no. 76, Taf. 28 and 166; Clauss, 1978, Taf. 24.3–4.
46. Clauss, 1978, 136.
47. Koch, 1977, vol. 2, 17 f., Taf. 13.9–17.
48. Ibid. Abb. 1 and 2.
49. Werner, 1962, 44, 76, list of finds no. 6 p. 170 ff., distribution map Taf. 70.2. Koch, 1977, 65.
50. Werner, 1962, Taf. 3,5 36,33–4. Werner's dating of Várpalota grave 34, on the basis of the location in the cemetery, as buried after the Avar settlement, is uncertain. Martin 1976, 194–9, has discussed the layout and character of the Várpalota cemetery and interpreted it differently by a comparison with the Basel-Bernerring cemetery. Várpalota 34 agrees well in location and character with an original, Germanic plan, and the Avar graves nearby are more likely to be later intrusions.
51. I am not convinced that the western Merovingian brooches of the type should be

derived from, and be secondary to the Lombard Pannonian ones, and would not let such an assumption influence the dating of the western finds.

52. Clauss, 1978, 133 f., 136, with references, Taf. 23,3–5 and 24,2a–b.

53. Kühn, 1940, 236–9; Kühn, 1974, 956–60; Böhner, 1958, 84, type A 4.

54. Ibid. 50 f., 84 f., 94 f., 228, Taf. 4,3, 10,3–4, 12, 16, 13, 14. Kühn, 1974, 956 Abb. 113.

55. Decaens, 1971, 18, 73, 122 fig. 26, 124 fig. 28; Decaens, 1978, pl. XX 1.

56. Åberg, 1926, 76, fig. 122. Leeds, 1949, Corpus no. 2. Bakka, 1958, fig. 53.

57. Decaens, 1971, 39–42, 107 fig. 11, 124 fig. 28. Decaens, 1978, 143 f., pl. XX 2.

58. Leeds, 1946, pl. VIII.

59. Werner, 1949, 67 note 6 and fig. 44, 12–14; Werner, 1961, 63, list of finds 11, distribution map 11 Taf. 56.

60. Werner, 1961, as in note 59.

61. Kühn, 1974, 41 f., no. 403, Taf. 130 and 213. The S-brooch also Kühn, 1977, Taf. 61, 11.

62. Werner, 1949, 67.

63. Schmidt, 1961, Taf. 77.

64. Koch, 1977, 64, Taf. 194,2.

65. Chadwick, 1958 (*Antiq. J.*); Chadwick, 1958 (*Medieval Archaeol.*) pl. V A.

66. Bakka, 1958, 50, fig. 44–5.

67. Chadwick, 1958 (*Medieval Archaeol.*), 11–18, figs. 6a,j, 7e, 9a–f, pls. II–III, IV C. pp. 40–57; Bakka, 1958, 66–8, fig. 50; Bakka, 1973, 75–7, fig. 2. p. 83 (printing error line 27 '575' for '475', and line 28 '6. Jahrh.' for '5. Jahrh.').

68. Kühn, 1974, 1160.

69. Moosbrugger-Leu, 1971, 122, 182–5, 211; Bakka, 1973, 78; Haseloff, 1974, 11–14.

70. Bakka, 1958, 49–53; Haseloff, 1974, 11–13.

71. Moosbrugger-Leu, 1971, Taf. 47,6.

72. Ibid. 122 with note 7, Taf. 22,11. Here illustrated as fig. 3:17 after an unpublished drawing for U. Giesler, by courtesy.

73. Examples: Heilbronn-Böckingen, Forchenweg grave 2, Roeren 1962, 121 Abb. 2, 11, p. 126 f.; Laa an der Taya, Austria, Werner, 1956, Taf. 9,6–7; Domolospusza, Hungary, Werner, 1963, Taf. 45,4–5; Miszla, Hungary, Szendrey, 1928, pl. VII,7–8; Basel-Gotterbarmweg 12, Vogt 1930, Taf. VII,3; Basel-Kleinhüningen 126, Moosbrugger-Leu 1971, Taf. 53,4 and 56. For a discussion of the bracelets with thickened ends, ornamented and plain, worn as pairs or single, by men or women, see Koch 1968, 47–50.

74. Kühn, 1940, 140 ff.; Kühn, 1974, 694 ff.

75. Werner, 1935, Taf. 1C–D.

76. Kühn, 1974, 442 no. 404, Taf. 130 and 213.

77. Kühn, 1940, 144 f., Abb. 41 and Taf. 76; Moosbrugger-Leu, 1971, Taf. 47,11, 46,25, 52,2, 50,5, 68,3, 66,24.

78. Böhner, 1958, 98, Abb. 4a1; Werner, 1961, 58, list of finds 5, *Sonderform* Bingen, distribution map 5, Taf. 53.

79. Kühn, 1977, Taf. 61,12.

80. Bakka, 1958, fig. 52.

81. Moosbrugger-Leu, 1971, 61.

82. Kühn, 1940, 145 Abb. 41,19 and Moosbrugger-Leu, 1971, Taf. 52,2 is not the same ring.

83. Ibid. 185, 189, 248.

84. In Chadwick 1958 (*Medieval Archaeol.*), 41, note 119.

85. Böhner, 1958, 45.

86. Thiry, 1939, Taf. 24,10.

87. Koch, 1968, 43, list of finds 7, distribution map 7, Taf. 94.

88. Kühn, 1940, 145, Abb. 41,16 and 18.

89. Moreau, 1879, pl. L.; Fleury, 1878, 245, fig. 317j.

90. Werner, 1963, Taf. 44,6.

91. Thiry, 1939, Taf. 18,412–19. In addition Krefeld-Gellep grave 643, Pirling, 1966, 178 and Abb. 20,5, dated in *Stufe* II.

92. Böhner, 1958, 182; Böhner, 1968, 132.

93. Pirling, 1964; Doppelfeld/Pirling, 1966, 54, 50–6; Pirling, 1974, Taf. 44–52.

94. Böhner, 1958, Taf. 36,7.

95. Pirling, 1966, Taf. 77; Pirling, 1974, 158. The buckle with shield on tongue appears in *Stufe* II also in the Rübenach cemetery in Koblenz, Neuffer-Müller/Ament, 1973, 100, 144–50.

96. Åberg, 1926, figs. 246–52; Jessup, 1946, pl. II; Leeds, 1936, pls. XVIII, XXIXa, XXXI; Jessup, 1950, pl. XXIX,9 and 11.

97. Schmidt, 1961, Taf. 45,a–e; Roth, 1977, 343–51, Abb. 1–5.

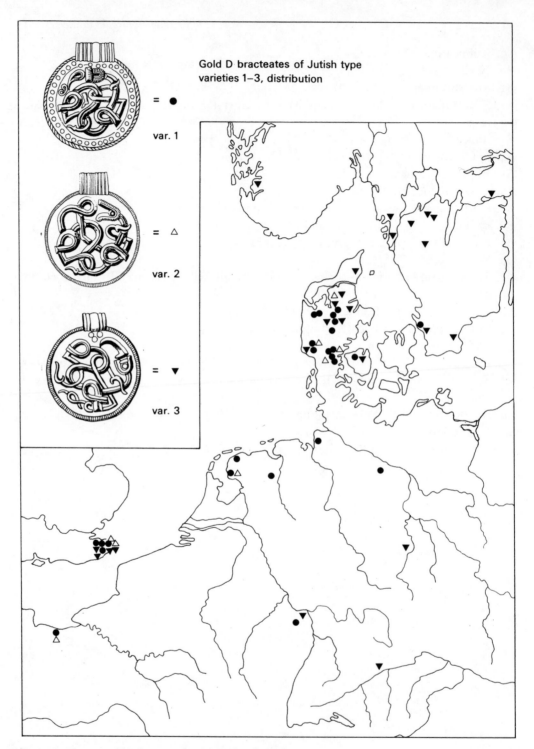

Gold D bracteates of Jutish type
varieties 1–3, distribution

= ● var. 1

= △ var. 2

= ▼ var. 3

FIG. 1. Jutish type gold D bracteates and their distribution

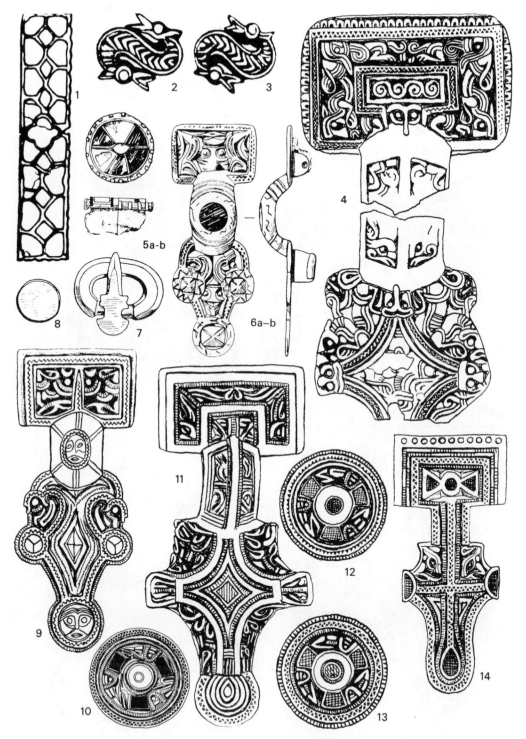

Fig. 2. Objects associated with D bracteates in grave finds. 1. Hérouvillette 11. 2, 3 Hérouvillette 39. 4 Bifrons 63. 5–8 Buckland Dover 20. 9, 10 Bifrons 64. 11–14 Sarre 4.   Scale *c.* 1/1

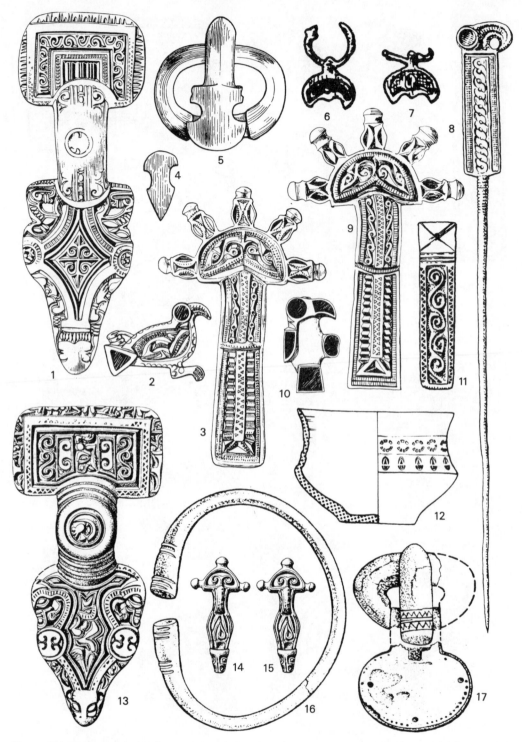

Fig. 3. Objects associated with D bracteates in grave finds. 1–5 Finglesham D3. 6–12 Basel-Kleinhüningen 94. 13–17 Basel-Kleinhüningen 74.   12 scale 1/2, the rest 1/1

3

Some bowls from the excavations of the terp at Feddersen Wierde near Bremerhaven*

PETER SCHMID

In quite early works analysis of pottery, chiefly from the cemeteries of the second and third centuries AD in the southern coastal region of the North Sea, made it possible to distinguish a spread of pottery shapes which later was designated as the *Nordseeküstennahe Gruppe* (North Sea coastal area group).[1] Particularly characteristic of this group are above all the carinated bowls and carinated pedestal bowls, homogeneous characteristics of which can be seen not only in the shape but especially in the ornamentation. In the region of the Elbe and Weser estuaries the credit goes mainly to K. Waller for having made the rich collection of forms accessible by means of numerous rescue excavations and in publications of the material. Thus Waller has already indicated that the 'ornamental designs of the widespread carinated bowls with horizontal lines, hatched triangles, rows of dots, pendant triangles and angled shoulder are numbered among the characteristic features which differentiate the pots of the Cuxhaven Group from the common West Germanic group'.[2]

This regional demarcation of a spread of pottery shapes based on criteria of typology and ornamentation could also be confirmed later in the arrangement of the existing pottery of the Roman period from the southern North Sea coastal area.[3] Above all, analysis of the large amount of pottery from the marsh and sand settlements showed that the homogeneous distribution area of pottery forms on the coast in the west of the Netherlands and north-west Germany stretched beyond the Elbe to the north into the region of Eiderstedt.[4] On the other hand, analysis of the settlement pottery also allows it to be recognized that the style characteristics of this group west of the Weser no longer appear to be as numerous as in the main distribution area between the Eider and the Weser. This fact made it possible to speak of the appearance of stylistic and cultural movements across the Weser towards the west.[5] More recent analyses of material have brought forward an increasing amount of evidence that the group of finds of the later Roman period west of the Weser show many correspondences in form and decoration of

* Translated from German by Miss Margaret Hardie and V.I.E.

the pots to the finds of the Rhenish-Westphalian region.[6] According to the evaluation of grave and settlement finds, therefore, the north-west German coastal area west of the Weser can be designated as a transition zone during the later Roman period between a Rhine-Weser Germanic group of finds and a group of finds in the North Sea coastal area. Having regard to these facts, the pottery of the late Roman period appearing in this transition zone was recently featured as 'A group in the north of N.W. Germany'.[7]

If we now turn to the Elbe estuary area as the central region of distribution of typical style elements of the 'North Sea coastal area' find group, then this includes, together with other pot forms, a large number of carinated bowls and carinated pedestal bowls.[8] They appear in the coastal region between the Elbe and the Weser in small cemeteries, but also in the earliest finds level of the large cemeteries which continued in use into the Migration period, and which are characterized by abundant finds of Saxon pottery in both cremations and inhumations. As is well known, this change in form and style in the pottery has given rise to manifold discussions, since the beginning of the analysis of the finds, about the origin of the Saxons and their 'expansion south of the Elbe'.[9] In current research, there is also a complex of questions of whether we can interpret Saxon find material as the result of immigration, conquest, upper-class assimilation, or even identification with the Chauci who were settled in the Elbe–Weser region, a crux problem of interdisciplinary research in the north-west German coastal area.[10]

Settlement research in the area of the southern North Sea coast has a special significance in the solving of these questions. Thus numerous settlement excavations in the Netherlands and in north-west Germany have shown that the great village sites in the marsh and sand areas were continuously occupied from the first to the fifth centuries AD. The excavation results from the terp at Feddersen Wierde and the sand settlements of Wijster and Flögeln furnished typical examples of this.[11] Inter-regional comparisons of settlement pottery from various settlement areas also led to important discoveries. They showed that during the Roman period until the fifth century AD economic contacts between the separate coastal regions were becoming stronger. As a result there was a mutual increase of foreign style influences in the find material, especially in the pottery. Thus processes of stylistic fusion in the designing of the groups of pottery shapes became noticeable, which can be recognized particularly in the finds of the third to fourth century AD. This is mainly the pottery which comes from the later levels of the continuously occupied village sites of the coastal area, while tendencies in design of the Chaucian and Saxon pottery which often persist in regions also appear in contemporary cemeteries.

With the extensive excavation of the settlement terp at Feddersen Wierde, a large amount of pottery became available which made it possible to answer the question of the demarcation of the distribution areas of forms and their variations.[12] The stratigraphical order of the settlement levels was of value for the analysis of the find material, and we are indebted to it for detailed information concerning the relative chronological sequence of the individual pottery groups from the first century BC to the fifth century AD. Thus after the typologically latest pottery and Saxon grave pottery of comparable form groups were mapped, it was established that their distribution began in level 7 of the settlement. In this phase they are found in all household industries and working areas of the village.[13] This pottery characterizes also level 8 of the settlement and with it the final phase of occupation which can be dated to the period from the fourth until the middle of the fifth century on the basis of the metal finds discovered.[14]

To the typical pot forms of the two latest settlement levels of the village terp at Feddersen Wierde belong different variants of narrow- and wide-mouthed pots with offset neck, and some have rich shoulder ornamentations.[15] As in the cemeteries and also other settlement sites of the Elbe–Weser region, these pot forms lead into tall, narrow-mouthed, almost biconical shapes provided with geometrical ornament.[16] Except for these forms which are comparable to the grave pottery, a large part of the settlement pottery naturally consists of plain ware for daily use, which consists mostly of wide-mouthed globular cooking-pots with upright, sometimes rather incurved rim, or globular bowls with short, flared lip.[17]

For the pottery from the two latest settlement levels of Feddersen Wierde, except for the various cooking-pot shapes, several groups of bowl-shaped pots are characteristic. The first group is of bowls with steep-sided walls, mostly round bellied, with high cylindrical neck and flared rim (S.1), (fig. 4). The ornamentation of the shoulder area consists mostly of combinations of lines and grooves, dimples and rosette patterns, also notched borders and broad, undulating, parallel diagonal grooves. These pots, which are comparable to the so-called bowl-shaped pots (*Schalenurnen*), display many features parallel to the Germanic Elbe distribution area of forms, the influence of which is also clearly visible on the grave pottery of the Lower Elbe region.[18] Different variants of this group of bowls are also widespread in other coastal areas of the North Sea, thus north of the Elbe up to the North Frisian islands, west of the Weser in marsh and sand settlements as far as the north-east Netherlands.[19]

The second group of bowl-shaped vessels which appear in settlement levels 7 and 8 of Feddersen Wierde consists of biconical shapes with a low and sharp shoulder angle and hollow neck with flaring rim (S.2), (fig. 5). These shapes, called by A. Genrich 'shoulder vessels mostly with richly ornamented upright neck',[20] are often ornamented at the neck with encircling horizontal grooves, and on the shoulder with dimples, bosses, and stamp patterns. Broad, undulating diagonal grooves covering the shoulder, which give the effect of a plastic surface design on the pots, again represent a popular decoration. In some cases the so-called 'faceted' ornament is achieved on the shoulder angle by means of deep indentations in a row, which again finds many parallels in the area of the middle Elbe. This bowl group is very strongly represented in Schleswig-Holstein, as may be seen from numerous comparable finds in Angeln, East Holstein, and the North Frisian islands. Close parallels are known from England as well.[21] The bowl group is widespread in the cemeteries of the Elbe–Weser coastal region. Thus accessory vessels from inhumation graves are often to be classified in this group.[22] The associated finds available there make possible a date in the second half of the fourth and into the fifth century.

The third bowl group appearing in settlement levels 7 and 8 of Feddersen Wierde comprises the so-called *Trichterpokale* (carinated bowls with hollow neck), or bowls of the Dingen type (T.4), (fig. 3). The lower part of the pots of this group is incurved like a *situla,* and has only a small base. In some variants it develops into a pedestal. The typologically older forms still display a narrow shoulder over the sharply bent carination, which completely disappears in the later bowls. Moreover, the vertical, and strongly flaring S-shaped hollow neck is characteristic of this younger type of carinated bowl which also generally characterizes the change in style to Saxon pottery. The grave finds belonging to this group of shapes are often dated by plain bow brooches with parallel-sided, facetted foot, which were very widespread in the area between the Elbe and the Rhine during the fourth century.[23] The occurrence together of globular pot shapes with S-shaped flaring rim and carinated bowls with hollow neck is known from stratified settlements and closed grave finds of the Elbe–Weser area. Both groups of forms also show the same decoration, which often consists of the combinations of grooves, dimples, and stamps typical of the older Saxon pottery.

On the question of the origin and chronological arrangement of this group of pots, the possibility of imitation of Roman vessels has already been pointed out in earlier literature.[24] Further, the close relationship in form of the carinated bowls with hollow neck to similar vessels of the Rhine–Weser Germanic find group is often put forward. These are likewise bowls with S-shaped flaring, vertical rim profiles and mostly with offset rim, which are characteristic of the group of forms I/II, and II presented by R. von Uslar.[25] This pottery, distributed in the Rhineland, Westphalia and Hessen, shows a continuous development from the earlier to the later Roman period. There also the change of style in the pottery in most of the vessel shapes, partly in the plain and coarse domestic ware, is characterized by an S-shaped rim formation.[26] Among wheel-thrown ware of the fourth century AD the proportion of small bowl-shaped vessels, often with a foot, is also very large. These were also produced during the later Roman period in other Germanic areas, and have a wide distribution.[27]

In the 'Rhine–Weser Germanic find group' therefore, from the end of the older Roman period until the fourth century, a richly varied development of bowl-shaped vessels is to be observed. This often makes it difficult to establish a chronological connection between the comparable shapes in the coastal region and the vessels of the 'Rhine–Weser Germanic find group'. This difficulty occurs particularly in the coastal area west of the Weser but also in the northern Netherlands, where carinated bowls with hollow neck (*Trichterpokale*) of the earlier and later shape are likewise distributed in the sand and marsh settlements, and they are known in England, too.[28] Thus, for example, among the bowl group IC presented by W.A. van Es there are numerous vessels with globular lower part, short shoulder, and sometimes an applied pedestal, which with this form indicate connections with the Rhenish–Westphalian material of von Uslar's forms I/IIa, and II. Apart from these variants, however, numerous carinated bowls with hollow neck of the coastal shape are also extant in the Netherlands, which W.A. van Es has arranged in type-group ID. This group ID from the Netherlands, comparable with north and north-west German forms, also agrees chronologically with the adjoining coastal material to the east, as is shown by stratified settlement finds and some closed grave finds which belong to the fourth century AD.[29]

With the three groups of bowl-shaped vessels mentioned above, we find ourselves in a period level which, on the basis of metal finds in Feddersen Wierde, is classified in the fourth and the first half of the fifth century. To this period belong, therefore, the settlement levels 7 and 8, i.e. in the middle of the fifth century a disruption of settlement is to be recorded in the Feddersen Wierde terp. The function of the settlement is also clearly visible in the structural remains. Thus in level 8 fairly large farm units no longer appear but instead smaller houses are dispersed over the whole terp. Thus the radial arrangement of the farm units, which was characteristic of the earlier periods of the terp buildings, was also broken up.[30] The areas of craft activity in this latest phase were extended over the entire terp, but were obviously organized as before by a farmstead of special importance for the development of craft activity which still existed. Yet the recognizable change in the way of life and industry in the village, with the growth in craft and a falling-off in agriculture, brings only a temporary protection of the basis of existence. The influx of the sea in the final phase of the settlement caused such a great reduction of the agricultural acreage that the terp village had to be abandoned in the middle of the fifth century AD after a continuous settlement of almost 500 years.

If we turn to the earlier settlement level 7, then the above-mentioned three bowl groups are widespread there, together with other pottery types (fig. 7). In this settlement phase the radial structure of the village is maintained, and with it the position of the farm units around an open space, as in the earlier settlement stages. The peasant farmsteads, however, have become smaller, that is, a change in the form of the economy is also visible in this level. The rise in the water table and the resultant salt damage to open farmland affected agriculture to a considerable degree. Thus at this stage the smaller workshops increased in number, as well as the small houses used for handicrafts. The farmstead of the headman represents an economic centre in this stage also, and was built in the same place as before. The workshop area of metalworking which already existed is extended in this phase to the north and south-west, and lies partly outside the excavation area. In the region of the former working areas smaller aisled hall buildings used for handicraft are erected. All in all, therefore, the continuous development of most of the industry and also of the farmstead of the headman is maintained in this period, as a comparison of the ground plans of settlement levels 6 and 7 shows (figs. 6 and 7). Only in the method of the economy are changes in pattern visible. They lead to an increase in handicraft activities and with this to the erection of further craftsmen's houses in the peripheral area of the settlement already built over with workshops.

In addition, if the distribution of the groups of pots discussed here is considered, i.e. carinated bowls with hollow neck (T.4), the steep-sided bowls (S.1), and the biconical bowls (S2), then concentrations of finds are illustrated both in the area of the rural farmsteads and also in the settlement area used for handicrafts (fig. 7). The bowl vessels are especially widespread in the centre of the settlement, i.e. in the area of a group of farmsteads which includes houses 17, 27, 40, 47, and 52. They also appear, however, and in greater quantity, in the adjoining northern farm area. The area of the headman's farmstead with its nearby buildings used for craftwork, is likewise covered with a dense spread of find spots (houses 12, 13, 37, 53, and 54). A further concentration of finds of the three bowl groups occurs then in the east peripheral region of the settlement where, in this stage of settlement as already mentioned, several craftsmen's houses are erected in the area where metalworking previously took place (houses 48, 49,

50, 51, and 56). This expansion of craft, carried out dependent on the farmstead of the headman, is continuously maintained until level 8 of the settlement, in which, however, traces of the breaking-up of the settlement are visible in other places. According to these facts, therefore, the three groups of bowl-shaped pots dealt with belong to the characteristic forms which are widespread in level 7 of the settlement, and are also in use until the abandonment of the village in the middle of the fifth century, as their occurrence in the latest level 8 shows.

According to the evidence of the distribution map the carinated bowls with hollow neck, the steep-sided bowls, and biconical bowls appear in the farmsteads of level 7 of the settlement which developed continuously from the earlier farmsteads of level 6. It is therefore necessary to investigate which types of bowl-shaped vessels are characteristic of level 6. Here it must again be emphasized that the individual groups of bowl-shaped vessels in level 7 are not concentrated separately in definite areas of the village layout, but are associated with each other within the various house and farm sites. The same is valid for the village area to the east which was extended after level 6 of the settlement and built over with craftsmen's houses. These facts show above all that new pot types with style characteristics of early Saxon pottery appear with the bowl groups S1 and S2. Here, however, in Feddersen Wierde, there is obviously a transmission of style elements of a new find group which cannot be considered as a sign of the invasion of a new group of settlers. The evidence of continuity of settlement and constancy of dwelling sites, as well as the general occurrence of old and new style elements in the pottery of level 7, indicate the continued existence of the early group of settlers until the abandonment of the terp in the fifth century.

This question must, however, subsequently be tackled again with the analysis of the existing bowl vessels from level 6 of the settlement. In this settlement phase at Feddersen Wierde, as also in other settlements and among the grave finds of the Elbe–Weser region, the various forms of the carinated bowls with or without a pedestal base are a particularly characteristic group of pots. As it is mostly rim and wall sherds that are dealt with in the case of settlement pottery, it can only rarely be determined whether a pot fragment belongs to the series of carinated bowls or pedestal bowls. From settlement level 6, however, numerous sherds of pedestals occur, which shows that carinated bowls with a foot are also widespread among the find material. As however there is no difference in the typological development of both variants, they can also be treated as a homogeneous group of forms.[31]

As mentioned at the beginning, the decorative design on these bowls with horizontal lines, hatched triangles, rows of dotting, 'swags' and shoulder angles is extraordinarily rich in variety (figs. 1 and 2). The carinated bowls with this ornamentation belong to the characteristic type forms of the 'North Sea coast area'. They are prevalent from the southern part of Schleswig-Holstein through north-west Germany into the north Netherlands. The relations in forms between the bowl vessels of the 'North Sea coast area' and the 'Rhine–Weser Germanic find group' has already been pointed out in connection with the carinated bowl with hollow neck. These parallels have often led to the Rhenish–Westphalian finds being taken into consideration for the dating of the coastal pottery. In the carinated bowls with hollow neck however, and also in the carinated bowls in the coastal area, numerous individual shapes and characteristics of decoration are present which differentiate them from the 'Rhine–Weser Germanic find group'. More attention must be paid to these difficulties in chronological comparisons. Despite this, however, in Feddersen Wierde as in other find spots of north-west Germany and the Netherlands, forms appear here and there among the carinated bowls which are completely comparable with individual pot types of the 'Rhine–Weser Germanic find group'. They correspond to pot groups I, I/II, and II of von Uslar.[32]

Apart from these individual occurrences, however, the carinated bowls of Feddersen Wierde have particularly characteristic forms (figs. 1 and 2). The style characteristics of the carinated bowls widespread in level 6 of the settlement are typical of the typologically later forms of this group.[33] These are bowls with long conical lower part and usually very narrow shoulder, which is frequently offset from the lower part by a sharp angle. The rim formation of the carinated bowls widespread in level 6 is different. There are sharply everted rims with triangular section (T.1), (fig. 1). Further, sharply everted rims ending in a point, flat outside and rounded inside, also occur (T.2), (fig. 2 Nos. 1–5). The third variant is characterized by a nearly vertical, long drawn-out rim running to a point (T.3), (fig. 2, Nos. 6–10). Carinated bowls with these rim shapes can be distinguished stratigraphically and chronologically from earlier forms in other settlements and in cemeteries of the North Sea coast area. They were collected, e.g. in the finds of the settlement at Wijster, into pottery group IB.[34] On the basis of stratified settlement and closed grave groups, these later forms of carinated bowls are classified in a period which stretches from the end of the second to the end of the third century. Moreover for the variants with long drawn-out rim and frequently very short shoulder (T.3), (fig. 2, Nos. 6–10), which are typologically at the end of the carinated bowl development, there are stratified data from settlements and some grave finds which indicate that these forms are already in transition to the carinated bowls with hollow neck. These pots were already featured as a typical group of forms of level 7 of the settlement of Feddersen Wierde. In addition it is to be noted that in the typologically latest carinated bowls there is often only a very short shoulder offset. The style change to the biconical form of pot repeatedly caused this pot shape to be separated typologically from the carinated bowls and carinated bowls with hollow neck as carinated bowls with short shoulder (*Trichternapf*).

On the basis of the stratigraphical data, the three variants of carinated bowls mentioned from Feddersen Wierde are classified in a find level from which there are also some metal finds. These are e.g. two-part bow brooches with long pin-catch, disc brooches, and other forms, which make a date in the third century AD possible. If we now turn to the distribution of the carinated bowls in level 6 of the settlement, the distribution map shows that a thick network of finds covers all the farmsteads (fig. 6). Particularly well represented is the variant T.1 which, however, is not found separately but always in connection with the other variants T.2 and T.3. A collection of carinated bowls is found in the north part of the settlement (houses 22, 26, 33, 31, 41). The same is valid for the south-west area of the settlement, where the concentration of carinated bowls gives chronological evidence of the extension of the settlement and the erection of new houses (e.g. house 42). Particularly striking is the dense distribution of carinated bowls in the area of the farmstead of the headman of the village, which was erected on the same spot as before (house 12), while a second adjoining house to the east, probably serving as accommodation for craftsmen or ships' crews, was newly included in the farmyard of the headman (house 43). The workshop area was also increased in comparison with the previous stage of the settlement. On the other hand agricultural production declined as the predominance of smaller household industries becomes evident. Regarding the question of continuity, it can be established that the group of carinated bowls is especially densely distributed in the area of the farmstead of the headman, which until the abandonment of the settlement in the fifth century maintained its importance for the organization of craft and trade (houses 12, 13, 37, 43).

Finally, if we again compare the house remains of levels 6 and 7 of the settlement, the continuity of the dwelling sites, and with that the entire structure of the settlement and the economy, is clearly recognizable in all areas of the village (figs. 6 and 7). In level 6 of the settlement a new economic orientation is marked by an increase of craft activities just as in level 7 of the settlement. If we consider the pottery as well, in level 7 of the settlement a change in style of the pottery can be established, as the analysis of the various groups of bowl-shaped vessels has shown. But the distribution map of the bowl groups within the settlement does not change in either phase. The concentration of the various bowl groups in the area of the farmstead of the headman and of the adjoining working area is an especially striking example of this. While, therefore, new characteristics of style appear in the pottery finds, on the basis of the house remains no break in the development of the settlement can be recognized which suggests a new immigration of another group of people. That the style change in the pottery is also not concerned with a sudden process is already obvious in the decoration of the pottery of level 6 of the settlement. Thus, beside the typical geometrical ornamentation on the carinated bowls of Feddersen Wierde, here and there rosette patterns appear, and in one instance the swastika motif (fig. 1, Nos. 2, 3; fig. 2, No. 8). These decorative elements are, as everyone knows, very popular in conjunction with stamp patterns on the later Saxon pottery. The process of stylistic change is already indicated, therefore, in the pottery of the third century, and then leads in the fourth century to a new design in form and ornament in many forms of vessels, for which some bowl types have been presented as examples. The excavation finds of Feddersen Wierde have shown, however, that this process of change in a group of finds takes place in an area in which the settlement develops continuously without any traceable foreign influence from the first until the fifth century AD. This settlement period in the coastal region only came to an end in the middle of the fifth century with the discontinuance of cemeteries and dwelling sites.

Bibliography

BANTELMANN, A., *Tofting, eine vorgeschichtliche Warft an der Eidermündung, Offa Bücher* 12 (1955).

BÖHME, H.W., *Germanische Grabfunde des 4.–5. Jahrhunderts zwischen unterer Elbe und Loire* (München, 1974).

VAN ES, W.A., *Wijster, A Native Village beyond the Imperial Frontier, A.D. 150-425, Palaeohistoria* 11 (Groningen, 1967).

GENRICH, A., 'Neue Gesichtspunkte zum Ursprung der Sachsen', *Archiv für Landes- und Volkskunde von Niedersachsen*, 16 (1943), 83.

GENRICH, A., 'Über Schmuckgegenstände der Völkerwanderungszeit im nordöstlichen Niedersachsen', *Neues Archiv für Niedersachsen*, 23 (1951), 221–81.

GENRICH, A., *Formenkreise und Stammesgruppen in Schleswig-Holstein nach geschlossenen Funden des 3. bis 6. Jahrhunderts* (Neumünster, 1954).

GENRICH, A., 'Der Ursprung der Sachsen', *Die Kunde* N.F. 21 (1970), 66–112.

HAARNAGEL, W., *Die Grabung Feddersen Wierde, Methode, Hausbau, Siedlungs- und Wirtschaftsformen sowie Sozialstruktur* (Wiesbaden, 1979).

MILDENBERGER, G., *Römerzeitliche Siedlungen in Nordhessen* (Marburg, 1972).

PLETTKE, A., *Ursprung und Ausbreitung der Angeln und Sachsen, Die Urnenfriedhöfe in Niedersachsen*, 3 (Hildesheim/Leipzig, 1921).

PLETTKE, F., *Der Urnenfriedhof von Dingen, Kr. Wesermünde* (Hildesheim, 1940).

SCHMID, P., 'Die Keramik des 1. bis 3. Jahrhunderts n. Chr. im Küstengebiet der südlichen Nordsee', *Probleme der Küstenforschung im südlichen Nordseegebiet*, 8 (Hildesheim, 1965), 9–72.

SCHMID, P., 'Bemerkungen zur Datierung der jüngsten Siedlungsphase auf der Dorfwurt Feddersen Wierde, Kreis Wesermünde', *Neue Ausgrabungen und Forschungen in Niedersachsen*, 4 (Hildesheim, 1969), (a), 158–69.

SCHMID, P., 'Die Siedlungskeramik von Mucking (Essex) und Feddersen Wierde (Kr. Wesermünde)—Ein Formenvergleich', *Berichten van de Rijksdienst voor het Oudheidkundig Bodemonderzoek*, 19 (1969), (b), 135–44.

SCHMID, P. and ZIMMERMANN, W.H., 'Flögeln—zur Struktur einer Siedlung des 1. bis 5. Jhs. n. Chr. im Küstengebiet der südlichen Nordsee', *Probleme der Küstenforschung im südlichen Nordseegebiet*, 11 (Hildesheim, 1976), 1–78.

SCHMID, P., 'Zur chronologischen Auswertung von Siedlungsfunden des 4.–5. Jahrhunderts n. Chr. im Küstengebiet zwischen Elbe und Weser', *Archäologische Beiträge zur Chronologie der Völkerwanderungszeit, Antiquitas*, Reihe 3, Band 20 (1977), 29–41.

TISCHLER, F., 'Der Stand der Sachsenforschung, archäologisch gesehen', *Bericht der Römisch-Germanischen Kommission 1954* (1956), 21–215.

VON USLAR, R., *Westgermanische Bodenfunde des 1. bis 3. Jahrhunderts n. Chr. aus Mittel- und Westdeutschland* (Berlin, 1938).

VON USLAR, R., 'Spätkaiserzeitliche Funde in Westfalen', *Bodenaltertümer Westfalens* 12 (1970), 107–10.

VON USLAR, R., 'Zu einer Fundkarte der jüngeren Kaiserzeit in der westlichen Germania libera', *Prähistorische Zeitschrift* 52 (1977), 121–47.

WALLER, K., *Der Galgenberg bei Cuxhaven* (Leipzig, 1938).

WALLER, K., 'Der Duhner Wehrberg', *Hammaburg* 10 (1955), 162–71.

Notes

1. von Uslar, 1977.
2. Waller, 1955, 162 f.
3. Schmid, 1965.
4. Schmid, 1965, Taf. 12.
   van Es, 1967, 183 ff.
5. Tischler, 1956.
6. von Uslar, 1938; von Uslar, 1970, 107 ff.; Mildenberger, 1972.
7. von Uslar, 1977, 134 f.
8. Tischler, 1956; Schmid, 1965; Genrich, 1970.
9. Plettke, 1921.
10. von Uslar, 1977, 135 f.
11. Haarnagel, 1979; van Es, 1967; Schmid and Zimmermann, 1976.
12. Schmid, 1969 a, b; Schmid, 1977.
13. Schmid, 1977, Abb. 2.
14. Schmid, 1969 a, Abb. 4.
15. Schmid, 1977, Abb. 1 Nr. 2, 3, 9.
16. Schmid, 1977, Abb. 1 Nr. 4, 5.
17. Schmid, 1977, Abb. 1 Nr. 10, 11.
18. Genrich, 1951, 251 ff.
19. van Es, 1967, 315 ff.
20. Genrich, 1943, 92.
21. Genrich, 1943, 92; Genrich, 1954, 27; Bantelmann, 1955, Taf. 23, Nr. 2, 10, 17; Myres, 1977 (No. 209), fig. 95.
22. Waller, 1938, Taf. 36–51.
23. Böhme, 1974.
24. Plettke, 1940, S. 34 f.; Tischler, 1956, 57.
25. von Uslar, 1938.
26. von Uslar, 1970, 107 ff.; Mildenberger, 1972, 80 f.
27. von Uslar, 1977, 129 ff.
28. van Es, 1967, 195 ff.; Myres, 1975 (No. 201), 93 ff.; Myres, 1977 (No. 209), fig. 201.
29. van Es, 1967, 298 ff.
30. Haarnagel, 1979, 202 ff.
31. Schmid, 1965, 19 ff.
32. von Uslar, 1938.
33. Schmid, 1965, 20 ff.; van Es, 1967, 187 ff.
34. van Es, 1967, 293 ff.

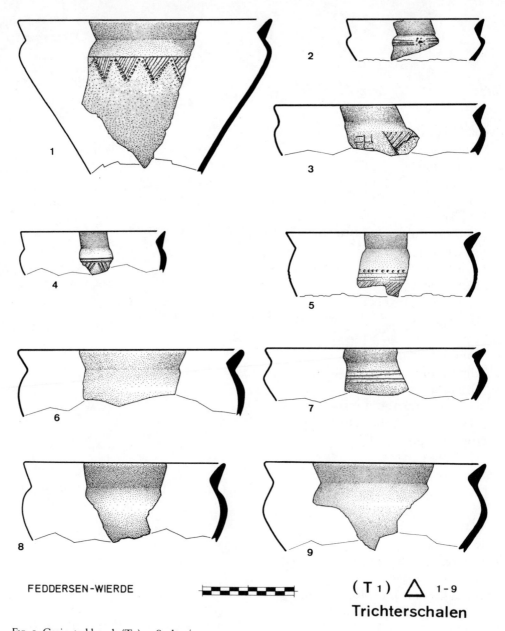

FEDDERSEN-WIERDE

(T_1) △ 1-9
Trichterschalen

FIG. 1. Carinated bowls (T1). Scale 1/4

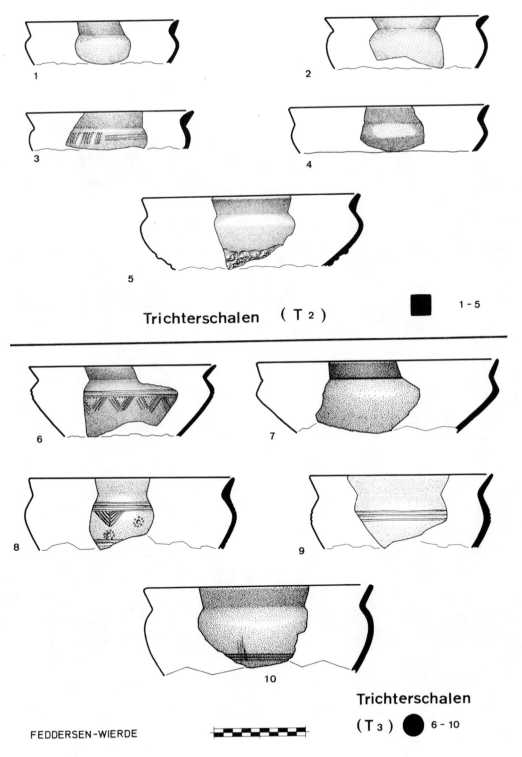

Trichterschalen (T 2)

1 - 5

Trichterschalen (T 3) 6 - 10

FEDDERSEN-WIERDE

Fɪɢ. 2. Carinated bowls (T2 and T3).   Scale 1/4

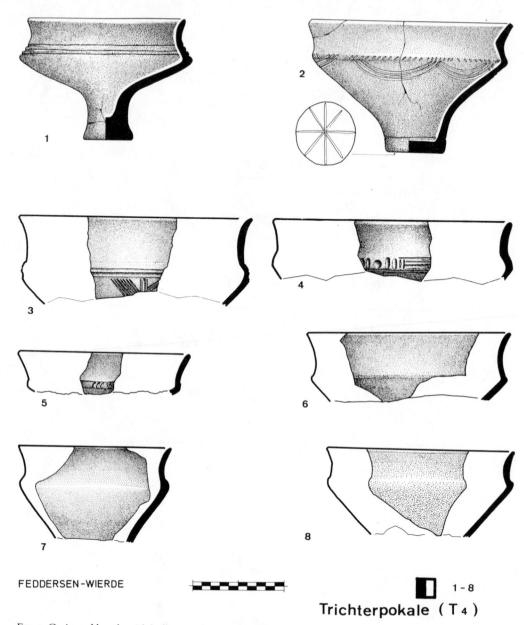

FEDDERSEN-WIERDE

Trichterpokale (T 4)

1 - 8

FIG. 3. Carinated bowls with hollow neck (T4).   Scale 1/4

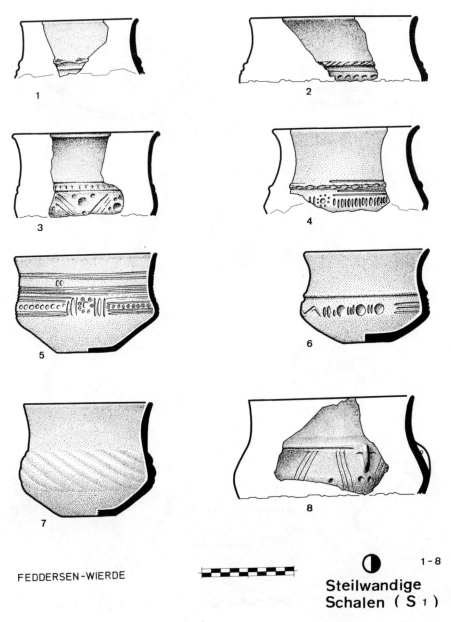

1 - 8

**Steilwandige
Schalen (S 1)**

FIG. 4. Steep-sided bowls (S1).   Scale 1/4

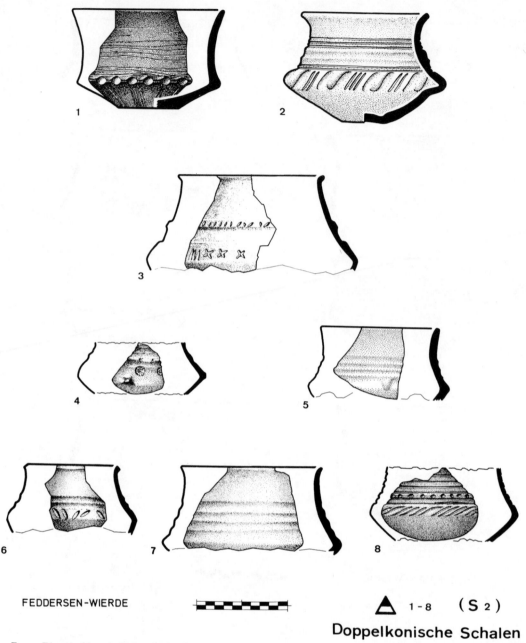

FEDDERSEN-WIERDE

1-8 (S 2)

Doppelkonische Schalen

FIG. 5. Biconical bowls (S2). Scale 1/4

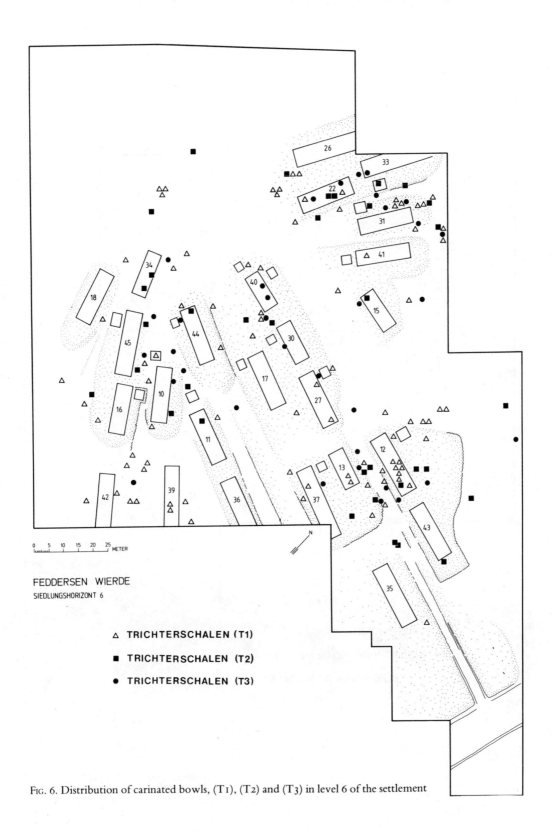

FIG. 6. Distribution of carinated bowls, (T1), (T2) and (T3) in level 6 of the settlement

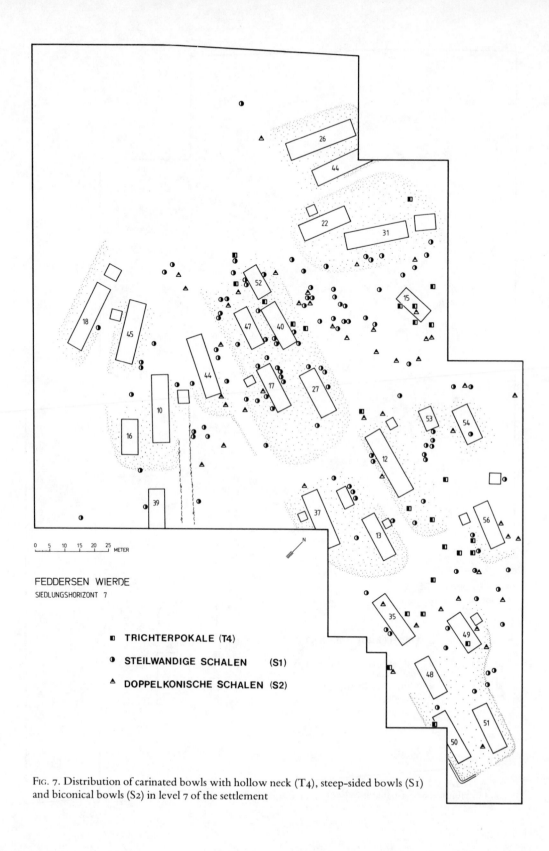

FEDDERSEN WIERDE
SIEDLUNGSHORIZONT 7

- ▯ **TRICHTERPOKALE (T4)**
- ◑ **STEILWANDIGE SCHALEN (S1)**
- ▲ **DOPPELKONISCHE SCHALEN (S2)**

Fig. 7. Distribution of carinated bowls with hollow neck (T4), steep-sided bowls (S1) and biconical bowls (S2) in level 7 of the settlement

4

A remarkable inhumation grave from Liebenau, Nienburg, Germany*

ALBERT GENRICH

In his articles about Anglo-Saxon pottery in England, J.N.L. Myres has occasionally pointed out products which illustrate the work of an individual craftsman or a single workshop.[1] F. Roeder[2] has already observed that similar statements can also be made for some metal objects ornamented with chip-carving. The author was able to supply some further examples.[3] The subject being offered in this volume in honour of J.N.L. Myres is the contents of an inhumation grave in Liebenau, which contained two belt buckles noteworthy in this respect, and which were arranged in an extremely unusual fashion on the belt.

The cemetery from which these grave goods came is briefly described here for the English reader, for whom the German literature is perhaps not easily accessible.[4] It lies left of the Weser between the villages of Liebenau and Steyerberg (fig. 1), on a small tributary of the river "Warme" Aue, within a sand dune area which has only quite recently been used for forestry and has never been ploughed. Thus finds and traces near the surface were preserved which, in similarly placed cemeteries of the region of the middle Weser like Stolzenau, Schinna, Dörverden, and Mahndorf,[5] had been destroyed by agricultural or industrial use of the land. Because of this it was possible to gain valuable information, particularly about the cremation burials at Liebenau. Extensive areas blackened by charcoal with a diameter of 2–3 m, which, in addition, were strewn with cremated bones and in which an astonishing quantity of grave goods was preserved, could be recognized as the remains of funeral pyres. Noteworthy discoveries about burial customs can be established. During the burning of the dead on the funeral pyre whole series of pots were broken. Sherds of these fell into the fire and therefore show a secondary burning, while other sherds of the same pots fell beside the funeral pyre. Some of the grave goods, the sherds of the broken pots and the burnt bones were selected and buried in cremation pits (*Brandgruben*), cremation heaps (*Brandschüttungen*), or urns within the funeral pyre or in the

* Translated from German by Miss Margaret Hardie and V.I.E.

vicinity of it. After that the cremation area was covered over with a layer of earth to form a flat mound. Postholes were found occasionally, but not always, within the funeral pyre areas. Some of these were undoubtedly recognizable as the stakes used in the construction of the funeral pyre, while on the other hand, others were arranged in circles, in triangles, or as the ground plan of miniature houses. In this way they served as the external mark of the funeral pyre mounds, which are shown by these means as the actual grave monuments. These were also very rarely marked by a stone. Correspondence between the finds from the funeral pyres and the actual burials could be found in most cases by means of laborious comparison. It may be important for our present article that such complete sequences of everyday pottery are dated by grave accessories and, moreover, from periods when, on the Continent, urns contain not one example of datable accessories.

This unusual grave custom has been practised on the spot since the later Bronze Age. The few finds from this and the following periods, however, do not allow continuity of settlement to be established. It could just be that the older finds were destroyed by later burials. On the other hand, the barrenness of the earth may have encouraged burials at this place at all periods. For what farmer deprives himself of a fruitful acre to set up a cemetery there if barren land is available in the vicinity! Thus the continuity of the burial site need not correspond absolutely to a continuity of the accompanying settlement. In any event the cemetery was in use from the beginning of the fourth century AD until the middle of the ninth century, which is long after the conversion of the Saxons to Christianity.

In the second half of the fourth century inhumations as well are laid down in the cemetery. They are aligned from south to north. Some of them keep exactly to the south–north direction, while others are angled from south-east to north-west. From this time until the end of the pagan period Liebenau is a mixed cemetery. It is revealing for the importance of the various forms of burial that almost all materially valuable objects, such as silver and gold, the remains of bronze and glass vessels, and particularly rich belt sets are mostly found in cremation burials from which, however, the heavy weapons of the inhumation graves are lacking. It therefore seems that religious differences rather than social differences are to be recognized in the different burial rites.

The chronological end of the cemetery is formed by a concentrated group of west–east inhumations in the eastern part which, on account of their alignment and also their small number of accessories which are late in date, can be considered as Christian. One of them contained the fragment of a denarius of Louis the Pious from the *Christiana-Religio* type. In the west–east burials as well two general alignments have been observed. Some are aligned exactly from west to east, others turned to a south-west/north-east direction. They are, therefore, aligned exactly at right angles to the predominant directions of the south–north burials.

Some of these Christian graves which belong to the end of the eighth and the ninth century are overlaid by cremation burials. It can be assumed that this reversion to pagan burial customs is connected with the Stellinga uprising of AD 841/842.

The inhumation grave of which the grave goods are presented here, lies in the north part of the cemetery (fig. 2). It was discovered in a trial trench (II 25) and received the working number of 119. In the forthcoming publication it will be entered in square 0.8 of the plan and receive the designation A 1. It was aligned from south-east to north-west (designated as south and north in the following) (fig. 3a). In the south-east corner of the grave near the head of the body was a pottery vessel (fig. 4a). The body itself lay on its left side, almost on the stomach, squeezed right up to the west side of the grave. There was no coffin extant. The position of the body can be explained by the assumption that it was lowered into the grave with ropes, and that these were pulled away from under the corpse at the east side of the grave.

The head of the body looked to the west. The right arm, the first to emerge, was slightly bent, the hand was on the edge of the grave, the left arm, lower down, was under the body. It also was bent so that the two hands lay close together. Two rings were on the ring finger of the clenched left hand. The lower ring was of twisted silver wire (fig. 4b), the other, of bronze, had the form of a modern wedding ring (fig. 4c). A leather strap was uncovered at the waist position of the body. On the front of this small bronze bars were riveted at regular intervals. As a result of the metal salts from these, a broad leather trace had been preserved over the belt which developed further away from the bronze bars into a dark humous discolouration (pl. VII,c). This was probably part of a covering or clothing. The belt was removed by the chief conservator W. Reuter in a block, and was examined and conserved in the museum. There it was established that two belt buckles, 21 cm apart with the tongues pointing inwards, were attached to it. Of the total of seventeen bronze bars, two were furnished with pendant bronze rings which served as a device on which to hang a purse, and were attached on the left side of the body beside the left buckle. In the immediate vicinity of this was found a small iron belt buckle and an iron strap-end, obviously the fastening of the purse. Two flint chips, which might have served as striking flints, can be regarded as contents of the purse. The waist measurement of 77 cm, and the lack of any weapons in an otherwise relatively rich burial, suggests the grave of a woman (figs. 4d and 5).

The pot is a wide-mouthed bowl with slightly everted rim. The base is convex and not offset from the body. The colour is light brown with large dark brown smoke patches (fig. 4a).

The twisted silver wire finger-ring (fig. 4b) belongs to Form 16 of Germanic finger-rings according to C. Beckmann, which she describes [6] as 'rings with bezels in the shape of discs formed by wires spiralling round each other'. They are found mainly in the east Germanic region, and come chiefly from burials there, while rings of this form in the Rhineland, according to Henkel, were known exclusively from settlements. There are also some rings of this type from Anglo-Saxon graves.[7] Beckmann's deduction that this ring form is predominantly east Germanic is therefore not convincing. The distribution map merely shows that it was indeed present in the western distribution area, but was not included in burials until the exception of our example from Liebenau. Apart from the main area of finds in the east Germanic region, concentrated in East Prussia west of the River Passarge, a few pieces are found in free Germania, in Norway and Denmark, three in Bohemia, and two in Dowesee in Lower Saxony. In addition there is our piece from Liebenau.[8]

The dating is difficult. According to Henkel, rings of this form already occurred in Bohemia in the La Tène period.[9] In the Rhine provinces they appear mainly in the middle and later Roman period. Yet the form is also known from a Frankish grave worn together with a plain silver circlet on one finger as in Liebenau. The closed finds from free Germania collected by Beckmann refer to the periods C and D (after Tischler and Eggers). The long life of this form of jewellery is astonishing. Perhaps a magical significance is attached to the complicated entwined spirals so that, for this reason, it was immune to the influence of fashion.

The second finger-ring of bronze (fig. 4c) has the form of a wedding ring. It is flat inside and slightly convex outside, and therefore belongs to Beckmann's Form 2 with plano-convex cross-section. Such rings occur, according to Beckmann,[10] in periods B to D, but appear also in quite different periods and are therefore not useful for dating purposes.

Particularly remarkable is the belt set (fig. 5), not only on account of the manner in which it was worn but also on account of the ornamentation of the buckles (fig. 3b, c) and the manufacturing technique deduced from this. Late Roman buckles with biting animal heads at the base of the tongue are obviously their model.

Their loops are shaped as animals in Salin's Style I. On the right of the tongue base the head of a bird with a strongly curved beak is recognizable. Then follows a thigh joint shaped as a human mask. A segmented ribbon in relief forms the animal's body, which is defined on the outside border of the buckle by a contour line, and on the inner border by two lines. The inner line, which emanates from the mask forming the thigh on the right, apparently bends round upwards in one buckle and ends in a three-toed foot at the position of the tongue base. It therefore represents the front leg bent under the body. The hind thigh is also formed by means of a mask. On one buckle a line comes out from the left eye which continues to the outer border the very rudimentary hind leg bent on to the back of the large animal. Moreover on this buckle a dimple on the chin of the mask forms the eye of a bird's head, the lower beak of which is represented by the hind leg of the large animal. In a similar manner the dimple on the chin of the front thigh mask can also be interpreted as the eye of a bird's head. The tongues of the buckles are cast in different shapes. One is ornamented with five notches, the other with four hollows on top of the axis of the tongue.

The metal plates are of sheet bronze. The rectangular plate is ornamented on the upper surface with double lines scored parallel to the edges. A continuation of the plate is turned back as a flap which is fastened to the back of the plate by a rivet. The middle of the flap is cut out to accommodate the tongue, and the edges are smoothed by a file.

At first glance the two buckles appear to come from the same mould, but that is not so. It is true the basic shapes and many of the details are identical on both pieces. Other details deviate from one another. Thus the middle point within the beak of the great animal on one buckle is a hollow, on the other it is pierced. The eye of the bird's head cannot be recognized in the latter. The animal's foot is offset on one buckle by a small projection, but not on the other one. The grooves between the lines along the inner edges are of different widths, the notches of the ladder-like bands of the animal bodies are designed differently and, on one buckle, there is also a hollow instead of the hind leg, which destroys the original pattern. Also the eye parts and the chin dimples of the masks are not completely identical.

It follows, therefore, that the two buckles cannot come from the same mould. The differences in the details can best be explained by the fact that the main design was carved in *intaglio* into a material suitable for cutting, presumably soft wood. From this negative mould an intermediate mould was obtained by reproduction in plastic material, probably wax, which was then used in a *cire perdue* process. The use of this technique has been established exactly in this manner for the manufacture of other forms of jewellery in the Saxon area, among others for the manufacture of the equal-armed brooches with chip-carved decoration which are also found in England.[11]

The two rings, mentioned above, offer no clues for the dating of the grave goods. The pot with the convex base, which is scarcely offset from the body of the pot, can be placed in the period about AD 500. This characteristic is also present on a bowl from a cremation grave at Perlberg, Stade, in which the fragments of a late equal-armed brooch were found.[12] Some of the border animals of this already indicate features of Germanic animal ornamentation. We observe the same phenomenon on our two buckles. Their models are, without doubt, late Roman buckles with biting heads beside the base of the tongue. According to Böhme these last until far into the fifth century.[13] It is difficult to decide whether some of the later examples of this type were still being manufactured in provincial Roman workshops or already by Germanic craftsmen. The transformation of animal heads to bird heads, the design of the thigh as masks, and the entire composition of the loop ornament is, however, only understandable at the beginning of the early Germanic animal ornament. Therefore the grave goods must be dated approximately to the period about AD 500. This date is also possible for the other finds, especially as the combination of wedding ring and spiral disc ring can be quoted in a grave of the Merovingian period.[14] Interesting in this connection is the discovery that attempts at the development of animal ornament can already be observed among the Old Saxons on the Continent, the further development of which can only be established by one find group, a group of gold bracteates, and the workshops of these, according to the centre of distribution, are apparently to be sought in the continental Saxon area.[15]

The author has more than one purpose in the presentation of this list of grave goods. Firstly, the unusual construction of the belt was interesting. When a second buckle has been found in a cremation grave in Liebenau, up to now it has been assumed that one of them belonged to a sword belt, so that the conclusion was suggested that it was a man's grave. When it is a question of two similar buckles this argument is no longer convincing according to the present find. Secondly, attention should be drawn to the details of a distinct workshop also evident in the metal objects, so that it may lead to evidence for the presence of typical Saxon workshops. In this way it will be possible to delineate their marketing areas and even, with luck and skill, to localize these, as Myres has succeeded in doing for definite pottery shapes and their characteristic elements of decoration.

Bibliography

BECKMANN, C., 'Metallfingerringe der römischen Kaiserzeit im freien Germanien', *Saalburg-Jahrbuch* 26 (1969), 5–106.

BÖHME, H.W., *Germanische Grabfunde des vierten bis fünften Jahrhunderts zwischen unterer Elbe und Loire, Münchner Beiträge zur Vor-und Frühgeschichte* 19 (München, 1974).

GENRICH, A., 'Über Schmuckgegenstände der Völkerwanderungszeit im nordöstlichen Niedersachsen', *Neues Archiv für Niedersachsen*, 23 (1951), 221–81.

GENRICH, A., *Der gemischt belegte Friedhof bei Dörverden,* Kreis Verden/Aller (Hildesheim, 1963).

GENRICH, A., 'Einheimische und importierte Schmuckstücke des gemischt belegten Friedhofes bei Liebenau', *Nachrichten aus Niedersachsens Urgeschichte* 36 (1967), 75–96.

GENRICH, A., *Der gemischt belegte Friedhof bei Liebenau, Kreis Nienburg/Weser,* I (Hildesheim, 1972).

GENRICH, A. and FALK, A., *Liebenau, ein Sächsisches Gräberfeld, 2, Wegweiser zur Vor-und Frühgeschichte Niedersachsens,* 3 (Hildesheim, 1976).

GENRICH, A., 'Zur Herstellungstechnik kerbschnitt-verzierter Schmuckstücke', *Die Kunde* NF 28/29 (1977/8), 105–110.

HENKEL, F., *Die römischen Fingerringe der Rheinlande und der benachbarten Gebieten* (Berlin, 1913).

ROEDER, F., 'Neue Funde auf Kontinental-Sächsischen Friedhöfen der Völkerwanderungszeit', *Anglia* 57 (1933), 321–60.

SMITH, R.A., *British Museum Guide to Anglo-Saxon Antiquities* (London, 1923).

Notes

1. Myres, 1969, (No. 158), 120 ff.
2. Roeder, 1933, 37 ff.
3. Genrich, 1977/8, 105 ff.
4. Genrich–Falk, 1976.
5. For the position of these cemeteries compare the general map in Genrich, 1963, and the accompanying legend.
6. Beckmann, 1969, 34 and Taf. 11.
7. Henkel, 1913, 46, paragraph 328; Smith, 1923, fig. 45, information Vera I. Evison.
8. The find spot indication of 'Liebenau' in West Prussia (Poland), Beckmann, 1969, No. 740 is doubtful. In the cited literature there is no evidence of such a ring. Presumably B. has seen a bronze reproduction of the Liebenau ring in Hanover and entered it incorrectly in her catalogue.
9. Henkel, 1913, paragraph 328.
10. Beckmann, 1969, 27.
11. Genrich, 1977/8.
12. Genrich, 1951, Abb. 1.
13. Böhme, 1974, 79 ff.
14. Henkel, 1913, paragraph 328.
15. Genrich, 1967, 86 ff.

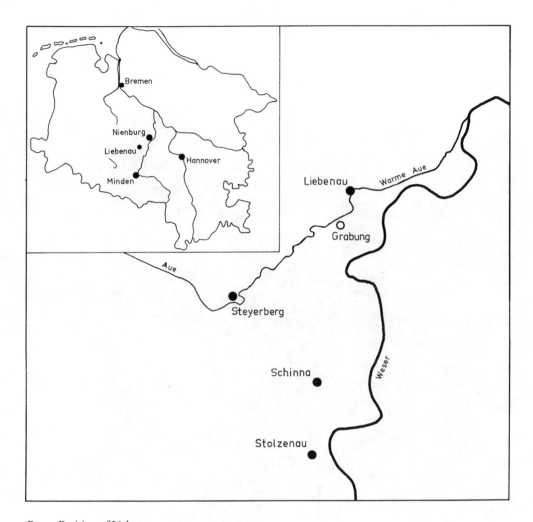

FIG. 1. Position of Liebenau

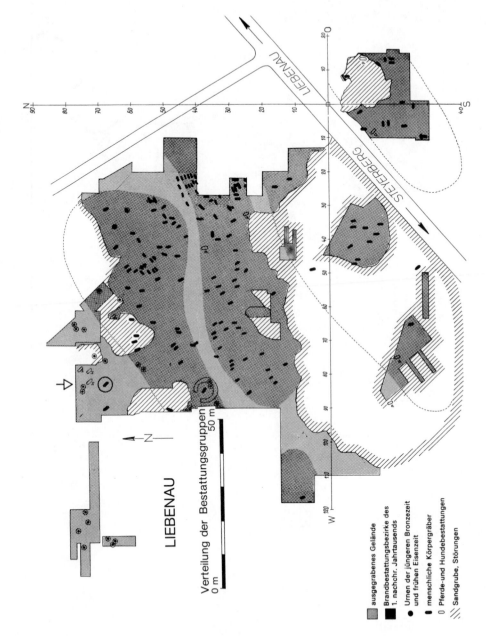

LIEBENAU

Verteilung der Bestattungsgruppen

0 m   50 m

- ausgegrabenes Gelände
- Brandbestattungsbezirke des 1. nachchr. Jahrtausends
- Urnen der jüngeren Bronzezeit und frühen Eisenzeit
- menschliche Körpergräber
- Pferde- und Hundebestattungen
- Sandgrube, Störungen

Fig. 2. General plan of the Liebenau cemetery

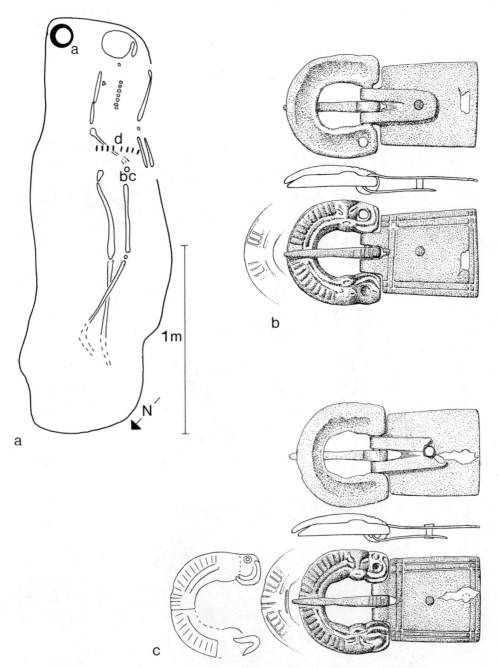

FIG. 3. (a) Plan of grave 119 (A 1)
a = pot
b, c = two finger rings
d = belt mounts   Scale 1/20
(b), (c) The buckles.   Scale 1/1

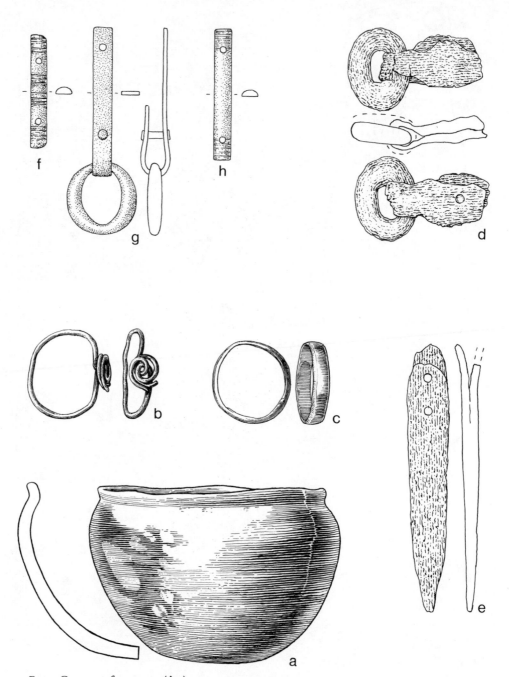

FIG. 4. Contents of grave 119 (A I)

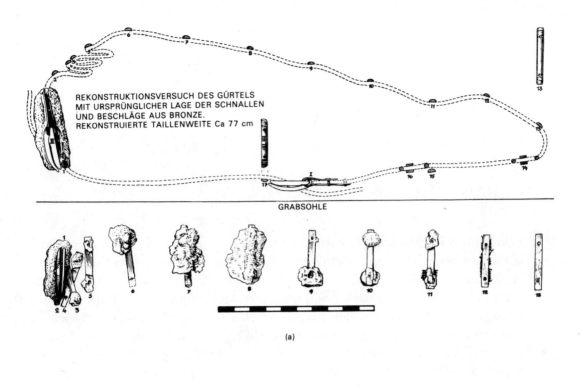

REKONSTRUKTIONSVERSUCH DES GÜRTELS
MIT URSPRÜNGLICHER LAGE DER SCHNALLEN
UND BESCHLÄGE AUS BRONZE.
REKONSTRUIERTE TAILLENWEITE Ca 77 cm

GRABSOHLE

(a)

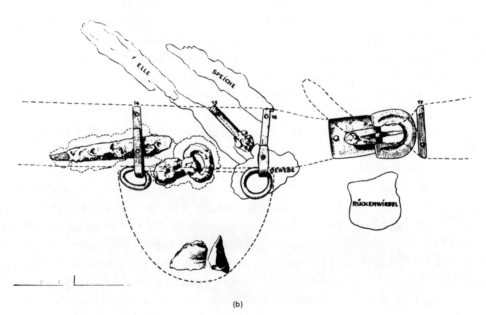

(b)

FIG. 5. a. Belt mounts *in situ*, with attempted reconstruction
b. Purse mounts and contents *in situ*, with attempted reconstruction.   Scale: less than 1/2

71

5

Inlaid metalwork of the late Migration period and the Merovingian period from Lower Saxony*

HANS-JÜRGEN HÄSSLER

While inlaid metalwork is known, sometimes in abundance, from the homelands of the Franks, Alemanni, Burgundians, and Thuringians[1] and also from the graves of the Anglo-Saxon settlement areas,[2] products of this type appear to be missing from the late Migration period and the entire Merovingian period in the Lower Saxon region of the continental Saxon homelands. It must be assumed, however, that works of craftsmanship of this kind are likely to have been known in this area at that time, since among the numerous finds, especially of the early Roman period, a modest number of metal objects with inlaid metalwork has already been known for some time.[3] In addition to this W. Holmqvist[4] published in 1951 various *Tauschierte Metallarbeiten des Nordens,* and for the early examples had been able to deduce dependence for inspiration on late Roman work. The suggestion put forward was that these contacts and flow of ideas between the Germanic North and the Roman empire must have been conveyed, at least to a certain extent, through the metal craftwork operating at that time in what is today the region of Lower Saxony.[5]

By means of intensive excavations in Lower Saxony, especially in the past 25 years, some finds have now been excavated which make it appear worth while drawing attention to these metal objects of the Migration and Merovingian periods. In doing so, the examination must deal, not only with the chronological arrangement of the finds, but also particularly with the question of their cultural assignment, this last question leading up to the subject of to what extent native craftsmanship flourished in the continental Saxon region during the Merovingian period, and what typical Saxon forms and autonomy of style can be distinguished in the finds. The discussions and conclusions expressed concerning this are submitted in the consciousness that they are based on a very small supply of finds.

The previous lack of inlaid metalwork in Lower Saxony depends on two

* Translated from German by Miss Margaret Hardie and V.I.E.

factors: on the one hand on a general gap in the finds of the Merovingian period, on the other on the problem that because of the heavy corrosion of the iron in which the metal inlays are mostly set, they cannot be recognized with the naked eye, or only on rare occasions. It is to be assumed, therefore, that to a large extent they have been lost in the processes of conservation. How great a wealth of information concerning the state of metalworking of that time remains concealed or can be completely destroyed in this way is shown by the examples of Anglo-Saxon material in the article by Vera I. Evison[6] already quoted, in which a considerable number of X-ray photographs of rusted equipment with inlaid metalwork is reproduced. This investigation forcefully elucidates how large the proportion of inlaid metalwork objects originally was, particularly in the sphere of simple objects in daily use.

In north-west Germany there is moreover another very decisive factor in the preservation of metal inlays and the simplest inlaid work, which to a large extent is not present in the above-mentioned areas, i.e. the custom of cremation, which, in the region under examination, prevailed far into the seventh century. The metal inlays of non-ferrous and precious metals with a low melting point, which are normally badly damaged by corrosion even in inhumation graves in so far as they are present, are simply melted out by the fire of the funeral pyre. The iron basis of the objects bearing the metal inlay, which is likewise more or less damaged, then allows recognition of the metal inlay grooves and identification of the object in question as inlaid metalwork only in the rarest cases, particularly since the vast number of urns and funeral pyre finds lie immediately below the present land surface and the objects are consequently susceptible to a climatically stronger effect than, for example, the finds from inhumation graves. Moreover the intensity and completeness of the damage to metal by the funeral pyre is shown by the finds from the cemetery of Liebenau. Usually, larger metal objects such as belt sets, brooches, fittings, or metal vessels but also glass and pottery have been melted down until they are unrecognizable. It is understandable that delicate metal inlays had little chance of survival in the heat.

Although attention has already been drawn to the gap in the finds of the present area of Lower Saxony in the Merovingian period excavations, the processing and analysis at present being carried out of the total material from the cremation and inhumation[7] cemetery at Liebenau, Kreis Nienburg (Weser), have especially brought about a clear improvement in the position regarding data and finds.[8] The abundance of materials recovered there during the twenty-five years of excavation activity already permits today an appreciably more precise judgement of settlement history and foreign cultural contacts, as well as political conditions in the middle Weser region at the time of the Merovingians. Among the numerous finds at this burial place was also some of the metal-inlaid work presented here, which suggests that an increase of such material can be expected when the conservation of all the finds has been completed. Besides the finds from Liebenau, inlaid metalwork has survived from the cemeteries of Bremen-Mahndorf[9] and Dörverden, Kreis Verden.[10] As this list shows, all these objects were recovered from comparatively modern cemetery excavations. Moreover further finds which may lie still unrecognized in the numerous museums of Lower Saxony are not to be excluded. A systematic examination and discussion had unfortunately to be renounced here for reasons of time. Up to the present metal-inlaid objects are completely unknown from settlements.[11] The present known stock of inlaid metalwork objects can be subdivided into the following groups: 1. Buckles; 2. Metal belt and strap mounts; 3. Horse-bits; and 4. Miscellaneous. The finds will be presented in this sequence.

1. Buckles

In SN-Grave 1 of the Mahndorf cemetery, as well as the large type-specimen bow brooch (Mahndorf Type), three silver wire finger rings, one small bronze brooch, a string of beads, and knife fragment, there was also an iron buckle with triangular plate as well as a strap end (fig. 1).[12] Both fittings show inlays of silver strips—even if very badly disintegrated. While only the remains of disjointed, mainly straight-line ornamentation can still be recognized on the buckle plate, on the second fitting spiral patterns, dotting, and a straight linear border can be clearly made out.[13] The grave is dated unanimously to the seventh century by various writers on account of the brooch and not least on the basis of the buckle. While, because of its decayed condition, the inlay on the triangular buckle plate gives no information concerning the possible area of origin of this ornamentation or the possible place of manufacture of these belt fittings, the preserved double spiral pattern on the other fitting indicates a workshop operating in the seventh century in the Bavarian–Swabian region.[14] That far-reaching contacts between individual tribal homelands represent absolutely no exception is shown also by the occurrence of a large whirling animal brooch from the Mahndorf cemetery together with further examples quoted below. This brooch type is mostly concentrated in the Main–Tauber region, but also has a certain concentration in the Thuringian area.[15]

A second buckle with metal inlay comes from horse grave H12/A1 in the cemetery of Liebenau (fig. 2a). This object, 2.7 × 4.8 cm, lay beside a ring–bit (fig. 2b). Broad strips of metal inlay in sets of three, of which four are completely corroded, can be distinguished on the front of the loop. The metal inlay is probably brass (fig. 2a).[16] This single piece belongs to a large group of similar buckles found in relatively numerous early Merovingian *Reihengräbern* on the Continent and in the Anglo-Saxon region of the British Isles.[17]

2. *Belt and strap mounts*

At the east end of the extraordinarily large grave pit of the WE burial 60 of the cemetery at Dörverden, Kreis Verden, A. Genrich recovered[18] several iron objects, which obviously belonged to a belt set, from a hollow permeated with charcoal. The pieces in detail are: a plain oval iron buckle with rectangular plate, a curved strap end of iron, 6.4 × 1.6 cm, the end of which is held together by two bronze rivets, two rectangular plates, an iron clamp, as well as a fragment of an iron knife. The X-ray examination which was carried out after the publication of these finds, showed that the two rectangular fittings displayed silver metal inlay which has been completely unknown up to now in Lower Saxony. Judging from the arrangement of the ornament, one might assume contemporary manufacture of both pieces by one craftsman. In detail, however, the two ornament patterns deviate from one another (pl. VIII, a–c). On the narrower fitting with measurements of 2.4 × 5.2 cm (pl. VIII, a) an interlacing ribbon of broad silver stripes and dots has been carefully inlaid inside a double rectangular framework containing an undulating strip, the space between the rectangular framework and plaited ribbon ornament being filled in with a ladder pattern. Although this piece came from a cremation grave, the carefully executed metal inlay was not destroyed by the effect of the fire but is completely preserved apart from a little damage by rust. This object, like the next one, was fastened with bronze rivets to its correspondingly shaped under-plate.

On the almost square plate (3.7 × 4.1 cm) the four bronze rivets, of which only two are still preserved, were inserted into the metal-inlaid field (pl. VIII, b). Like the first piece, here also the square frame of the metal inlay is formed by two silver strips, in which again an undulating strip has been laid. Inside this on all four sides is a ladder-type border and, only on the narrower sides of the fitting, a row of strip inlay arranged in steps. A composition of rectilinear interlaced dotted bands fills the central field. Unfortunately almost half of the pattern has been destroyed by corrosion or fire (it is not possible to say which), so that the original effect of this metal-inlaid work can only be provisionally described.

Although an exhaustive search has not been made for the closest parallel to our pattern on the fittings from Dörverden, an amazingly similar parallel has come to hand, especially for the rectangular fitting pl. VIII, a, even down to the measurements, among the numerous fittings in Grave 6 of the aristocratic graves of Niederstotzingen, Baden-Württemberg.[19] Here the three long rectangular fittings on Paulsen Taf. 48, 1–3, some of which end in an ornamental semicircular edge, are especially relevant. According to P. Paulsen the fittings found there belonged to the hind part of a horse harness. They had been placed with rich weapons in the grave of a wealthy lord. Unfortunately the context of the two fittings from Dörverden permits no clear assignment of function to the two pieces. They could represent components of a rich belt suite just as well as parts of a horse harness. In any event, in either case the metal remains of the costly furnishing of a cremation was probably badly destroyed by a later intrusion of WE Grave 60. For the second, larger fitting (pl. VIII, b) from Dörverden a parallel similar in form and ornament can be brought forward from the cemetery of Schretzheim.[20] The comparable piece from there is also a component of a horse harness. By means of the two south German grave finds the chronological assignment of the Dörverden pieces also can be established. They must both have been manufactured in the first half of the seventh century.

The question was not pursued further as to whether metal inlay patterns in the form of the two fittings from Dörverden occur mostly in Alemannic territory, which the two parallels from Niederstotzingen and Schretzheim imply to a certain extent, or whether these ornament patterns are distributed over the entire Merovingian region.[21] The extensive work necessary for the distinguishing of various workshop areas cannot be accomplished in the framework of such a small study. That these articles are imports into this locality seems to the writer beyond question. For our two Lower Saxon fittings an exact location of the workshop would be of especial importance in order eventually to obtain more precise ideas of the direction from which imports flowed into Lower Saxony in the seventh century. Apart from whether there are similarly ornamented fittings in the west Frankish region, on the Lower Rhine, in Belgium, or in northern France, a special relationship between the south and middle Lower Saxon region on the one hand and the Alemannic settlement area on the other seems to be emerging slowly. In addition to the buckle with triangular plate from SN Grave 1 at Bremen-Mahndorf and the large whirling animal brooch found there (see above), the brooch find from Rosdorf, Kreis Göttingen, as well as further finds from Middle and Lower Saxony are indications of this.[22]

A third inlaid metalwork object comes from Dörverden cemetery. It is a flat, iron object of pointed oval shape, probably another strap mount, 2.4 × 6.2 cm, the end penetrated by two iron rivets (pl. VIII, c). The metal inlay of silver strips consists of two entwined 'ladder' bands each of which are still surrounded by a silver wire outside. Although the piece is an isolated find and its original function can therefore no longer be determined, the character of its metal inlay resembles so closely that of the two fittings described above that undoubtedly a comparable chronological assessment can be accepted for this piece also.

Among the finds now conserved from the cemetery of Bremen-Mahndorf is also a small rectangular plate of iron (pl. IX, a) which is ornamented with three ring-and-dot motifs of brass.[23] The plate, which at one time had a rivet in each corner, measures 4 × 2.2 cm. The diameter of the rings is 0.8 cm, the thickness of the strip measures 0.1 cm. Fittings of this kind have often been found as plates on belt buckles. An especially closely comparable piece comes from a WE woman's grave from the cemetery at Reuden, Kreis Zeitz, East Germany,[24] but other analogies exist in abundance[25] in the Frankish and Anglo-Saxon settlement areas as well. There is agreement amongst different writers concerning the chronological placing of this kind of plate and buckle in the second half of the fifth century, possibly also the first decades of the sixth century, so that a similar date applies also to the single find from Mahndorf.[26]

Also from the Mahndorf cemetery comes a strap end, 5.6 × 2 cm, the front of which shows carelessly scored grooves of a now completely corroded or melted inlay (pl. IX, b). As in the case of the buckle components from the SN grave 1 of the same cemetery already described above, fine silver strips have been used as the inlay material. Unfortunately this piece too is a single find so that the dating of the object cannot be determined with certainty. Probably a date in the beginning of the seventh century is likely.

3. *Horse-bits*

Apart from the example from Grave 4 of the Bremen-Mahndorf cemetery,[27] the rest of the horse-bits of the Merovingian period in Lower Saxony known to the writer were found in the Liebenau cemetery. While two buckles as well as plates of the head harness were retrieved from the Mahndorf horse grave 4, which was unfortunately already disturbed, one of the four graves with bits at Liebenau held no further burial offerings, one had also a buckle (cf. grave H12/A1), one bit probably came from a cremation grave, while the fourth bit was uncovered along with numerous other associated finds. These, and the example from the possible cremation grave, are ornamented with metal inlay.

What is certainly the most beautiful brass-inlaid horse-bit from N.W. Germany up to the present time was found only a few centimetres under the present land surface (fig. 3). It was probably part of a richly furnished cremation grave, but this cannot be established with certainty, as in this area of the cemetery the sites of the funeral pyres were extensively worn away by medieval cart tracks and deeply eroded waterways. Should it prove true that the find being dealt with here is from a cremation, this would be unique as far as is known. The object concerned is a snaffle which is 13 cm long with a two–part bit joined by means of a link. The two cheek pieces are approximately 12 cm long and taper towards the bent ends. Both bars are ornamented with closely set brass rings and meticulous attention has been paid to maintaining an equal distance between each ring. By this means the craftsmen effected a well-proportioned exact sequence of dark iron colour and bright brass rings. In the middle of the snaffle is fixed a slightly indented ring for the suspension of the bridle and other parts of the head harness. Both rings are ornamented in front with two fairly large ring-and-dot motifs 0.8 cm in diameter.

The second Liebenau bit with inlaid metalwork was recovered from horse grave H11/A3. It was found in connection with various buckles and a small plate of the head harness. On account of the general importance of this bit, the entire find will be briefly presented here.[28]

The horse had been buried with legs bent in a SN direction (head to the south), and the head was found turned nearly vertically downwards. The following objects were uncovered:

1. Iron bit with fine silver strip inlay, which had probably been inlaid into the iron in spiral fashion. The cheek pieces, approximately 15 cm long, are bent at the tapering ends and terminate in ball terminals. The cheek pieces are linked to the looped ends of the two–part bit, the length of which is *c.* 11.5 cm. In the middle of each cheek piece is an indented loop for the suspension of the bridle and the head harness (fig. 4a).

2. Oval iron buckle with heavy, rectangular sectioned loop and tongue rectangular in cross-section, 3 × 4.8 cm (fig. 4b).

3. Oval iron buckle with circular loop cross-section but rectangular tongue cross-section, 2.5 × 3.8 cm (fig. 4c).

4. Small oval iron buckle, 1.4 × 1.9 cm (fig. 4d).

5. Small, nearly rectangular iron buckle with angular tongue, 1.4 × 2.4 cm (fig. 4e).

6. Oval iron buckle with rectangular cross-section, tongue missing; 1.8 × 2.4 cm (fig. 4f).

7. Iron buckle with small rectangular folded plate of sheet bronze with rust-preserved leather remains of head harness adhering; buckle 1.8 × 2 cm, length of plate 1.4 cm (fig. 4g).

8. Small gilt bronze fitting with 4 rivets, of which one is broken off. On the back the remains of an organic substance can be recognized. This piece was probably the setting for a stone which ornamented the head harness. Diameter 0.6 cm (fig. 4h).

9. Fragment of two leather straps rolled into strong cords of which one is bent like a loop; the second cord is threaded through this loop. Present length of the pieces *c.* 5 cm (fig. 4i).

10. A piece of birch bark, 9 × 5 cm. Probably this is the remains of a branch which got into the grave by chance.

The silver strip inlay of the bit had become clearly visible by means of the X-ray examination which followed immediately after the discovery in 1971 of this very badly corroded object. Unfortunately the conservation of the bit was not carried out immediately at that time. Conservation carried out now, on the occasion of this contribution, with further radiography of the object, showed that the metal inlay had completely disappeared in the intervening period and the rust has extensively pervaded the metal inlay grooves and so made them unrecognizable. This reveals a further special difficulty in connection with metal-inlaid objects: unconserved metal inlays can oxidize and corrode so completely during long storage that they can no longer be established by means of X-ray examination.

The classification of the two Liebenau bits as to period and place of origin is not without difficulties. If one looks for parallels, then fairly comparable bits can be found in the Vendel graves of Uppland, Sweden.[29] The bit with fine silver strip ornament from grave H11/A3 at Liebenau especially finds an acceptable counterpart as to shape in a bit from grave 1 from Vendel, unfortunately only incompletely preserved.[30] As in the Liebenau example there, too, the cheek bars are inlaid with spiral silver strip. Chiefly on account of the similarity in shape of the silver–inlaid bit from grave 1 at Vendel to the example from the well-known harness from Gammertingen, W. Holmqvist at that time recommended the assignment of the Swedish piece also to the sixth century. This chronological assessment was made difficult by the fact that small animal heads were attached as terminals to the example from Vendel which, according to their stylization, are to be classified to the period about AD 700, possibly even somewhat later. Holmqvist attempted to explain the discrepancy in time between the shape of the bit and the animal heads by suggesting that the two ornamental heads had been added later, and that the actual bit, consequently earlier, could be approximately contemporary with the example from Gammertingen. In the meantime finds of bits have come to light from graves especially of the south German *Reihengräber* culture, among them the bar snaffle bit from Niederstotzingen,[31] and the unornamented piece from a double horse burial near the prince's grave at Beckum in Westphalia.[32] These finds make possible a date of about AD 600 and clearly also the beginning of the seventh century. Although the associated finds from the bit grave H11/A3 at Liebenau give no actual help in dating, a similar date is also acceptable for the Liebenau example as a rich flow of south or west German imports can be noticed particularly in the sixth and early seventh centuries. The writer considers the workshop in which the Liebenau bit was manufactured to be in that area also.

On the other hand the brass-inlaid bit from Liebenau must be placed chronologically earlier. In the execution of the metal inlay, especially with respect to the ring-and-dot ornament, there are such clear references in technique and style to other early Frankish metal objects (and here one thinks mainly of the above-mentioned buckles with ring-and-dot ornament, rectangular plates and objects like the similarly ornamented fire-steel/purse-mounts cf. below), that it must be concluded that the ideas and techniques of the early Frankish products have been taken over. Moreover, to my knowledge, ornamented bits of this type are not recorded up to the present from the region of early Merovingian metalwork, so that effective dating aids regarding closed finds of similarly ornamented bits are so far lacking. Strangely enough, the nearest parallels to our bit are found once more in Uppland Vendel and indeed, in graves XII and XIV.[33] Ornamented in a similar fashion, but with bronze instead of brass, the pieces from Vendel are, however, more squat in shape, and are far from the elegant, slim form of the bit from Liebenau.

For the bits from Vendel XII and XIV W. Holmqvist used as an analogy the example covered with sheet gold from Grossörner, Kreis Hettstedt, East Germany, which seems admissible, even if in the end the differences in the shape of these pieces are relatively great. As the Grossörner bit is assigned to about AD 500, a date of about AD 500[34] could also be established by means of this long, circuitous route of comparison for our Liebenau example. This would mean that bar snaffle bits are likewise already present in the area under examination about AD 500 and, as the find with the ring bit and the brass-inlaid buckle from horse grave H12/A1 suggests, both types of bit were used concurrently. For the bits from Vendel, however, the find from Liebenau signified that, beside an east German–Thuringian contact for the craft, a contemporary west Frankish one is also quite probable.

4. *Miscellaneous*

Undoubtedly one of the most beautiful metal-inlaid iron objects was retrieved from cremation grave K12/B2 of the Liebenau cemetery (fig. 5). This is one of the objects which are looked upon in turn as fire-steels or purse-mounts. The object is 8 cm long and displays no traces of any kind of striking in possible use as a fire-steel. So much, however, for this relatively unfruitful discussion about the function of this type of object. In the middle of the bar a small iron buckle had been riveted by means of a bronze or brass pin. The ends of the bar are clearly forged as birds' heads. The eyes of the heads are ring-and-dot motifs with a central brass dot. These are in balanced arrangement with the row of seven larger ring-and-dot motifs which are distributed symmetrically along the bar. Traces only survive of a very fine silver wire inlay which enclosed these ring-and-dot motifs in a border. It is easy even today to imagine the original effect of the golden shining brass and the bright silver on the dark iron. As the object is only ornamented on one side, obviously this is the front with which we are concerned here.

As the extremely clear details make it easy to understand the form of this fire-steel, it can be classified without hesitation as a Krefeld type, as has already been noted by David Brown. In fact the example found in Krefeld-Gellep is the closest parallel to our Liebenau piece.[35] In accordance with the numerous and well-dated associated finds in the Krefeld grave, and also on the basis of an assured chronology, the Liebenau example must also be placed in the second half of the fifth century. Unfortunately the cremation grave at Liebenau lacks chronologically determinable associated goods so that dating is not possible from the finds. Because of its good shape and design the Liebenau object belongs to the most beautiful of its type, and can certainly not be a native product of Lower Saxony. Certainly it is to be placed in a series with the early Frankish buckles and plates ornamented in a similar fashion, as briefly discussed above. It would be extremely interesting to discover the workshop or workshops in which these objects ornamented with ring-and-dot motifs were manufactured by means of an exact analysis of workshops. An exact measurement of the ring-and-dot motifs alone could even now give an inkling of this. Probably the west Frankish area would emerge as the area of origin as has often been suggested. The solution to this question can, however, only result from extensive work for which the large amount of similarly ornamented goods in England is also important and would naturally have to be taken into acount.

Summary

As the preceding comments show, inlaid metalwork products are extant in a few examples only within the limits of the area of investigation among the finds of Lower Saxony in the late Migration and Merovingian periods. The probable reasons for this deficiency were pointed out at the beginning. In spite of this small number, however, a series of questions have already been raised, and co-ordination with other cultural phenomena of the period under discussion brings possible answers nearer.

It is remarkable that it appears that all the objects ornamented in this manner can be fitted into an unbroken chain of the predominant ornament patterns of the Merovingian period. As a result two distinctive groupings are clearly revealed according to ornament, type of metal inlay material used, and processing technique, and these groupings also reflect chronological differences.

If the brass-inlaid pieces extant are considered (fire-steel, bit, buckle, plate) then it can easily be established that the manufacture of these products can unhesitatingly be compared with similarly ornamented objects from Thuringia, the Merovingian kingdom, and the Anglo-Saxon region. These objects offer an excellent glimpse into the craft of that time because of their fairly careful production, and on the basis of various securely dated finds in these areas they are to be dated to the second half of the fifth century, or in individual cases, perhaps to the decades around AD 500.

An important point for the judgement of local metalwork is the question of whether the pieces described here are native products or imported goods. As the number of finds is rather small no statistically conclusive answer can be worked out yet concerning this. Every interpretation given till now is only hypothetical in character and will be nullified or verified by the increase in finds in Lower Saxony

The search for parallels for the brass-inlaid products originating in Lower Saxony leads to the west Frankish region, especially through the fire-steel/purse-mount from cremation burial K12/B2. Analogies can also easily be found for the small ring-and-dot ornamented fitting from Bremen-Mahndorf and for the belt buckle from horse grave H12/A1 at Liebenau.

Up to the present the brass-inlaid bit from Liebenau, the closest parallel for which was encountered in the graves of Vendel although with definite reservations, cannot be more exactly placed. Consequently, although definitely comparable pieces are lacking from the west Frankish area, the manner of ornamentation especially points so clearly to this region that, for the writer, the manufacture of this piece also in the Frankish Rhineland is highly probable.

As these finds permit no characteristics to be recognized which are specifically Lower Saxon, it can consequently be accepted that they came from the

Merovingian kingdom to the region of Lower Saxony. This assumption is particularly likely as, after about AD 500 strong influences can be recorded from the Rhineland on the finds of various cemeteries south of the Weser/Aller line, while finds of this kind north of this line, actually in the centre of continental Saxony, are nearly completely lacking. This phenomenon is especially to be seen in the part of the cemetery at Liebenau which has been very carefully excavated. Besides numerous brooches of Frankish type there are a large number of belt buckles, metal vessels, glasses, pottery, and many other chattels (as well as weapons) which must without doubt have been imported from the Merovingian kingdom.[36]

A rather strange conclusion regarding the assessment of native metalwork arises from this situation. Obviously in the period around AD 500, and in the whole of the following century, there is no specific formation of Saxon design and ornament with independent execution, as is clearly established in the late Roman-Migration period.[37] Quite apart from the glass and beads which doubtless represent imports, whatever there is of datable metalwork comes particularly from the graves in the region south of the Weser and Aller, and all, except for the pottery, are to be regarded as Frankish imports. How far the most simple metal products, such as oval iron buckles, knives, fire-steels, pins, fittings of the most varied forms, and doubtless also individual weapons, were manufactured by small native smiths cannot be stated with certainty. These objects in all the geographical areas discussed here resemble one another so strongly that native production of these pieces can hardly be assumed with any certainty. That is to say it is quite possible that these mass-produced objects were also imported from the Merovingian kingdom. It will no doubt be very difficult to find proof of this, however.

For the silver-inlaid objects also there is the question of whether they are native or imported products. Although the search for parallels of the individual pieces is only sketchy it has shown that from the analysis of the ornament patterns, as well as the inlaid-metal technique, there is once again no clear indication of north German metalworking. These pieces must also doubtless be looked upon as products imported into the continental Saxon region.

Most likely all the silver-inlaid products discussed here belong to the seventh century, and the analysis of the total number of Lower Saxon finds of this period although small, indicates no clear native metal craft. The few datable pieces of jewellery of the seventh century from Lower Saxony, as well as some of the amethyst beads from various Liebenau graves and also from burial I from Bremen-Mahndorf (see above), the cast whirling animal brooch from the same cemetery as the above-mentioned brooch, the large millefiori bead, the comb, and also the spearhead from the cemetery at Rosdorf, Kreis Göttingen, point in the seventh century more to an influx of south German or Alemmanic products. Here it is once more remarkable that pieces of this kind are found in Lower Saxony again only south of the Weser/Aller line, and Bremen-Mahndorf, which lies immediately north of the Weser, must be counted in this sphere of influence. The silver-inlaid fittings from the cremation pit at Dörverden, which unfortunately cannot be more closely characterized, and the metal-inlaid products of Bremen-Mahndorf must consequently be assumed to have come from the south German *Reihengräber* civilization.

The metal-inlaid work from the Merovingian period in Lower Saxony can therefore be included in the large quantity of imports which streamed in from the various areas of the Merovingian kingdom into its northern areas of contact, especially from AD 500 until the seventh century. This affinity, partly of the finds but also partly of the layout of the grave,[38] permits it to become more obvious today that at least the area south of the Weser/Aller line was orientated towards the fashion and taste in ornament of the *Reihengräber* civilization zone. At the same time these finds make it clear that a native metal craft in the period from approximately AD 500 until far into the seventh century is not clearly recognizable. Specific 'continental Saxon' material from this area cannot therefore be proved up to the present. Apart from some buckles and a few brooches,[39] which on the grounds of their inferior workmanship may be regarded as products of small native craftsmen, the vast proportion of the extant precious and non-ferrous metal finds, various iron objects, doubtless also weapons and of course also the glasses and beads, were imported. On account of the wide uniformity in central Europe of small objects such as, for example, simple iron buckles, knives, keys, fittings, etc., it cannot be proved whether these are in general native products, and even the question of whether these crude objects in daily use were not also imported from the *Reihengräber* civilization zone must remain open. The derivation of the few metal-inlaid objects from this area does not permit the assumption that a large proportion of these simple objects in daily use were manufactured in Lower Saxony, but rather that they actually entered in fairly large quantity as commercial wares. This would imply that in the Merovingian period in Lower Saxony native metalworkers must only have been active within a limited radius. A high level of technology with independent designs is not discernible. Likewise there is no characteristic style of ornamentation. This may be surprising as the area, particularly that of the Liebenau cemetery, is in the centre of the continental Saxon homeland.[40] Here healthy independent metalworking, which would symbolize an expression of political sovereignty, and also the potency of power politics, is really to be expected. If, instead, a strange and heavy dependence on the handicraft products of the Merovingian kingdom is established, which incidentally coincides in various respects to occurrences in the Thuringian homeland in this period,[41] the question demanding an explanation for this will have to be brought more into the foreground of future investigations, and indeed the question of whether the region south of the Weser and Aller in the sixth, and partly also in the seventh century, was Saxon–controlled territory or whether it was politically dependent on the west and south German *Reihengräber* civilization or, to state it more clearly, whether it was extensively controlled by the Merovingian central power. A letter from Theudebert (AD 583–4) to the Emperor Justinian, in which he names the Saxons among the peoples subject to him,[42] is certainly interesting in this connection. It is probable that the find area closely investigated here was amongst others which came under Theudebert's sphere of power. Further research will have to show whether this appraisal of a historical explanation of the picture given by finds and facts obtained from various groups of objects will permit further conclusions.

Bibliography

BÖHME, H.W., *Germanische Grabfunde des 4. bis 5. Jahrhunderts zwischen unterer Elbe und Loire*. Münchner Beiträge zur Vor- und Frühgeschichte 19 (München, 1974).

BROWN, D., 'Firesteels and Pursemounts again', *Bonner Jahrbücher* 177 (1977), 451–77.

COSACK, E., 'Das Kriegergrab von Hankenbostel aus der älteren Römischen Kaiserzeit', *Studien zur Sachsenforschung* 1 (1977), 35–45.

DANNHEIMER, H., 'Neue Reihengräberfunde aus Bayerisch-Schwaben', *Bayerische Vorgeschichtsblätter* 25 (1960), 179–202.

EVISON, Vera I., 'Early Anglo-Saxon inlaid metalwork', *Antiq. J.* XXXV (1955), 20–45.

FALK, A., 'Der Friedhof Liebenau, Kr. Nienburg/Weser. Bearbeitungsstand und Ausgrabungsergebnisse 1971', *Nachrichten aus Niedersachsens Urgeschichte* 41 (1972), 218–28.

GARSCHA, Fr., 'Fränkische Tauschierarbeiten aus frühen Reihengräbern am Oberrhein', *Badische Fundberichte* 22 (1962), 133–63.

GENRICH, A., *Der gemischtbelegte Friedhof von Dörverden, Kreis Verden/Aller* (Hildesheim, 1963).

GENRICH, A., and FALK, A., *Liebenau, ein sächsisches Gräberfeld. Wegweiser zur Vor- und Frühgeschichte Niedersachsens 3* (Hildesheim, 1972).

GROHNE, E., *Mahndorf, Frühgeschichte des Bremischen Raums* (Bremen, 1953).

HÄSSLER, H.-J., 'Kulturelle Einflüsse aus dem fränkischen Reich', *Sachsen und Angelsachsen Veröffentlichung des Helms-Museums Nr. 32* (Hamburg–Harburg, 1978), 163–77.

HOLMQVIST, W., *Tauschierte Metallarbeiten des Nordens. Aus Römerzeit und Völkerwanderungszeit* (Stockholm, 1951).

KOCH, R., *Bodenfunde der Völkerwanderungszeit aus dem Main-Tauber-Gebiet* Berlin, 1967).

KOCH, U., *Das Reihengräberfeld bei Schretzheim* (Berlin, 1977).

MAIER, R., 'Verzeichnis der Schriften Albert Genrichs 1935–1975', *Studien zur Sachsenforschung* 1 (1977), 467–72.

NOWOTHNIG, W., 'Das merowingerzeitliche Gräberfeld von Rosdorf bei Göttingen', *Göttinger Jahrbuch* 1958 (1959), 20–56.

PAULSEN, P., *Alamannische Adelsgräber von Niederstotzingen (Kreis Heidenheim)*, (Stuttgart, 1967).

PAULYS, *Real-Encyklopädie der classischen Alterums-Wissenschaften*, Neue Bearbeitung von Georg Wissowa (Stuttgart, 1921).

SCHMIDT, B., *Die späte Völkerwanderungszeit in Mitteldeutschland* (Halle, 1961).

SCHMIDT, B., *Die späte Völkerwanderungszeit in Mitteldeutschland (Katalog Südteil)*, (Berlin, 1970).

TRENȚESEAU, B., *La Damasquinure Mérovingienne en Belgique, Dissertationes Archaeologicae Gandenses* IX, (Brugge, 1966).

WEGEWITZ, W., *Das langobardische Brandgräberfeld von Putensen, Kreis Harburg* (Hildesheim, 1972).

WEIDEMANN, K., 'Das Land zwischen Elbe- und Wesermündung vom 6.–8. Jahrhundert', *Führer zu vor- und frühgeschichtlichen Denkmälern* 29 (1976), 227–50.

Notes

1. From the numerous works about early Merovingian metal inlay objects, reference is here made only to the study of Garscha, 1962; in addition for Thuringia, Schmidt, 1961 and Schmidt, 1970.
2. Particularly Evison, 1955.
3. Amongst the finds in Lower Saxony spurs especially have been dealt with, cf. for example Wegewitz, 1972, Cosack, 1977.
4. Holmqvist, 1951.
5. In addition, contacts with the Roman provinces are also documented as they are known concerning the numerous finds of objects decorated with chip-carving, particularly in the north of Lower Saxony. Cf. Böhme, 1974.
6. Evison, 1955.
7. The study of all the finds from the Liebenau cemetery will no doubt throw new light on the question of the continuity of settlement, and also on the still continuing discussion of whether there was a gap in settlement after the second half of the fifth century until *c.* AD 700, especially in the region between the Weser and the Elbe. This will probably come about because in Liebenau the large quantity of native pottery can be arranged in more precise chronological order by means of reliably datable Frankish imports than has been possible up to the present time. It will probably be shown that several of the numerous cremation cemeteries in the north of Lower Saxony also conceal burials of the sixth and seventh centuries which, on account of the lack of datable finds, cannot as yet be determined with certainty.
8. For the cemetery at Liebenau see A. Genrich in this volume, pp. 59–71, and the numerous articles by the same author about this cemetery, which have been assembled by Maier, 1977.
9. Grohne, 1953.
10. Genrich, 1963.
11. Settlements of the Merovingian period in the central Weser region have remained undetected up till now. Since this manuscript was completed a settlement site of the sixth century has been excavated in Barrien, Hoya (Weser) by Dr E. Cosack of Hannover. Thanks are due for this information to Dr Cosack, who will shortly be preparing the material for publication. The few Merovingian settlement sites, e.g. Klein Denkte, Kreis Wolfenbüttel (report by Niquet forthcoming) from east Lower Saxony unfortunately give no decisive insight into the settlement structure of this period in Lower Saxony. The reason that the settlement finds from the Merovingian

period in Lower Saxony are so rare may be that they are the original settlements of the present-day villages, their remains lying, therefore, buried under the still existing settlements.

12. Grohne, 1953, 171–2 and Abb. 70 on p. 203.

13. For the dating of grave E, Grohne, 1953 and most recently Weidemann, 1976.

14. Dannheimer, 1960, especially 201, Abb. 10 with a distribution map of spiral-ornamented objects. I have to thank Professor W. Hübener of Hamburg University for this information.

15. Grohne, 1953, SN grave 39, Abb. 71 on p. 210. A distribution map of this brooch form is given by Koch, 1967, Taf. 87, Abb.5.

16. A metal analysis cannot be carried out on account of the lack of time.

17. Cf. Garscha, 1962; Schmidt, 1961; Schmidt, 1970; Evison, 1955.

18. Genrich, 1963, 30 and Taf. 11.

19. Paulsen, 1967, Taf. 48, 1–3.

20. Koch, 1977, grave 345, especially Taf. 209, 8.

21. Similar decorated mounts from the cemetery of Rosmeer in Belgium (Trenteseau, 1966, pl. 13) have been pointed out to me by V.I. Evison.

22. Nowothnig, 1958; Hässler, 1978.

23. I should again like to thank Dr K.H. Brandt, Focke-Museum in Bremen, for the loan of this and the following find for the purpose of publication.

24. Schmidt, 1970, 43 and Taf. 127, 3. This ornamentation is concerned, however, with a silver metal inlay.

25. Compare the illustrations in Garscha, 1962 and Evison, 1955.

26. Holmqvist, 1951; Garscha, 1962. V.I. Evison suggests that this type of inlay begins in the first half of the fifth century, see pp. 132, 134 of the present work.

27. Grave 4 of the cemetery. The horse-bit probably had cheek-pieces made of organic material. Grohne, 1953, 258 and Abb. 82 on p. 263.

28. The horse-bit was first published by Falk, 1972.

29. Holmqvist, 1951, 124 ff.

30. Ibid. 124, Abb. 67.

31. Paulsen, 1967, 56 ff. and the illustrations given there.

32. *Sachsen und Angelsachsen,* Katalog (Hamburg–Harburg 1978), 673, Abb. 450, 12.

33. Holmqvist, 1951, Abb. 68 on p. 125 and Abb. 70 on p. 127.

34. Schmidt, 1961, 157.

35. Brown, 1977, for literature concerning all the objects of this type found up to the present time.

36. Hässler, 1978.

37. Böhme, 1974 for his discussions and distribution maps of Saxon metalwork of this period.

38. During the excavations in the Liebenau cemetery in 1976 and 1978, amazing parallels were found in the inhumation graves in connection with the methods of wearing

weapons and in the costume of women with jewellery, for example, with the *Reihengräberfeld* at Bülach. The finds are at present being prepared for publication.

39. For example the pair of buckles from an inhumation grave of Liebenau cemetery, published in this volume by A. Genrich (p. 59).

40. Genrich and Falk, 1972, 10 ff.

41. The processing of the find material from Liebenau will probably demonstrate that the individual types of object and also the contexts in which they are found resemble one another in the sixth century in both tribal homelands. The fact that in the Lower Saxon area cremation still prevails, while in the Thuringian homeland inhumation is preferred, makes direct comparison complicated.

42. Pauly, 1921, 320, under 'Saxones'.

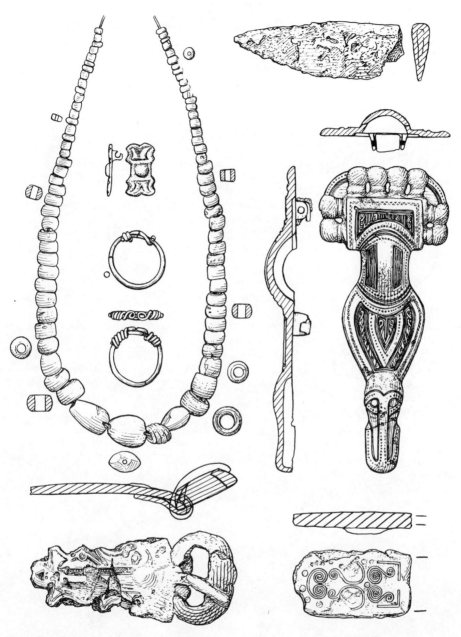

Fig. 1. Bremen-Mahndorf, contents of SN grave 1 with metal-inlaid buckle and plaque
Scale 2/3

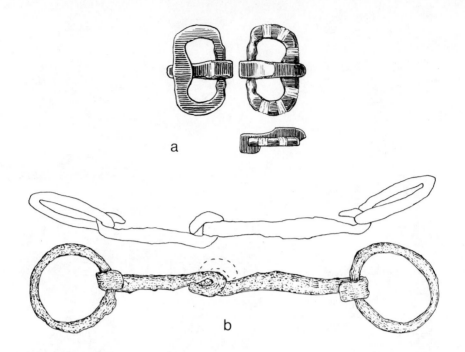

a

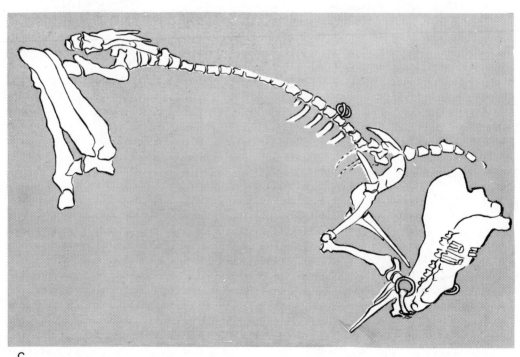

b

c

FIG. 2. Liebenau, Nienburg (Weser). Horse grave H12/A1
    a. Inlaid buckle,   b. Ring bit,   c. Position of the bit and buckle on the skeleton
    Scale a, b 1/2, c 1/40

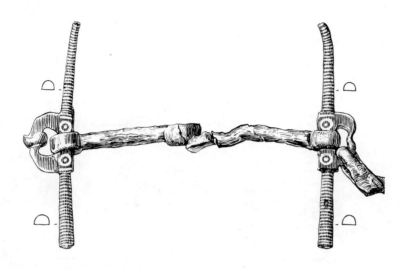

FIG. 3. Liebenau, Nienburg (Weser). Iron bit with brass inlay, possibly from a cremation grave   Scale 1/2

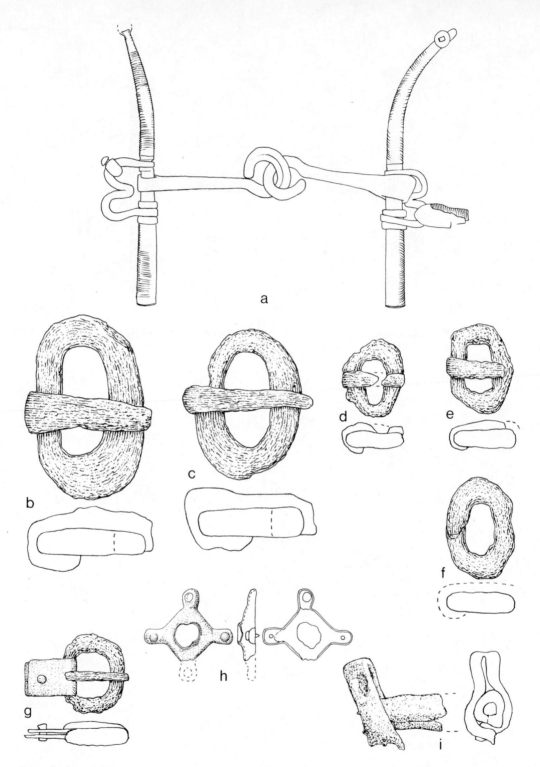

Fig. 4. Liebenau, Nienburg (Weser). Silver-inlaid bit with associated finds from horse grave H11/A3
Scale 1/1 except a = 1/2

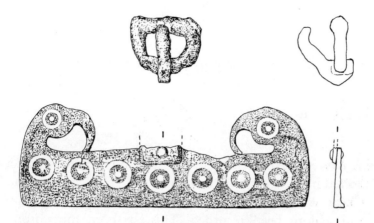

Fig. 5. Liebenau, Nienburg (Weser). Fire-steel/purse-mount inlaid with brass and silver, from cremation grave K12/B2   Scale 1/1

6

Barred zoomorphic combs of the migration period

CATHERINE M. HILLS

When J.N.L. Myres began his study of pagan Saxon cremation pottery few of the pots he collected had closely recorded contexts. Their contents had been either lost or not kept with the pot, and the position of individual pots within the cemetery had seldom been recorded. This has been the reason for Myres's concentration on typological analysis: it was the only approach available. As a result of recent excavations it is now becoming possible to see the pots as parts of assemblages which include a surprising number of grave goods. Even if they are partially burnt, diagnostic fragments often survive. This article is a discussion of one type of grave find, combs, and specifically of the variety of comb which has in the past sometimes been given the name 'Frisian'. These combs are distinguished by their zoomorphic decoration, and by the plano-convex bars which usually form the front of the comb. Thirty-four combs or cases of this type have now been found at Spong Hill, North Elmham, in Norfolk,[1] and the second part of this article is a discussion of these thirty-four combs in the context of the cemetery in which they were found. In the first part, the ancestry of the type is examined.

Any study of combs of the Migration period is complicated by the fact that they were usually made from perishable materials: wood, antler, or bone. Wood may have been more frequently used than now appears, since it is even more perishable than bone, and certainly would not have survived a cremation pyre as some of the bone combs apparently have. Not all combs found with cremations were burnt, and some were also buried with inhumations, but these have often been entirely destroyed by chemicals in the soil. In the whole of the cemetery at Krefeld-Gellep so far only one comb has been recorded from over 2,000 published graves. This was preserved because it had been put in or under a bronze bowl.[2] It is sufficient to show that the practice of putting combs in graves was not unknown to the inhabitants of the Krefeld region, and it may well be that we have lost many more combs from other graves. Even from cremations the numbers of combs recorded are probably far lower than the total originally deposited, because even unburnt combs have often fallen into a great many very small fragments, which can only be recovered by careful and repeated sieving and examination of the cremated bones, a practice which has only recently become standard. Distribution maps, and conclusions based on the small proportion which do have recorded associations, must therefore be regarded with considerable caution. Another problem is that, even when combs are recorded, they are seldom described in detail and, if illustrated, are usually shown at a scale too small for detail to be entirely clear.

Nevertheless, there are a few studies which have provided some useful information on the subject.[3] S. Thomas has published a broad survey and catalogue of European combs of the Migration period.[4] and triangular combs have been discussed in more detail by Böhme.[5] Using these, it is possible to distinguish the elements which went to make up the 'Frisian' type. These are: the plano-convex bars, the zoomorphic decoration, and the shape, i.e. single-sided and rectangular with a handle in the middle of the back.

This shape is one classified by Thomas as Typ III.[6] It has a distribution slightly more eastern than western European, but seems to appear at about the same time, the beginning of the fifth century, in most regions. It was popular in Scandinavia, where it may have remained in use longer than elsewhere. Nerman recorded examples from Gotland which he dated from the fifth to the eighth centuries.[7] A south Russian, Gothic origin has been suggested for this type, but as yet there is little available evidence to substantiate this. It is not a type found often, if at all, in England during either the Roman or the early Saxon period, apart from the 'Frisian' combs themselves.

Plano-convex bars appear on late Roman double-sided combs. Double-sided combs in general are a common late Roman type. They usually have a flat central plaque and indented ends, which are sometimes extended into elaborate patterns, occasionally zoomorphic. Sites as widespread as Wroxeter and Witcombe in the west of England,[8] Colchester,[9] Little Wilbraham,[10] Yverdon Cure in Switzerland,[11] and Valley in Bavaria[12] have all produced zoomorphic double-sided combs. Their dating has been discussed by several authors, including Keller,[13] who gives a list of combs with datable contexts. These all appear to belong to the end of the fourth century: one was found in a grave with a coin of Valentinian I, another in a fort thought to have been constructed during the reign of the same emperor. Even if some of the dates are not entirely secure, their consistency is fairly convincing in giving at least a *terminus post quem* of the latter quarter of the century. Of the double-sided combs with plano-convex bars there is one from Jakobwullesheim in the Rhineland which has been published with three parallels,[14] from Steinfort in Luxembourg and from Abbeville and Vermand in northern France. The Jakobwullesheim comb is especially interesting because it is zoomorphic as well as barred, and because it is very closely paralleled not only by the Steinfort comb, but also by a fragment from Beadlam in Yorkshire.[15] All three are so similar, so far as one can tell from the illustrations, that they might even have been made with the same template and surely in any case were products of the same workshop. Barred double-sided combs are recorded from elsewhere in the Rhineland[16] and from another Yorkshire villa, Langton.[17] Their contexts are again late fourth century or later. The Jakobwullesheim comb was in a grave with late Roman glass and a coin of Valentinian II, the one from Abbeville with a coin of Gratian, and the one from Vermand with a coin of Arcadius. Although such coins can only be used as lower dating limits, it is perhaps significant that none of the combs so far mentioned derives from a purely Germanic context. There is one possible example, from Issendorf near State in northern Germany,[18] but otherwise this does not seem to have been a type popular outside the Roman empire, which may be an argument for its going out of use in the early years of the fifth century.

The other type of comb which is characteristic of western Europe in the late Roman period is the single-sided triangular variety. This has a specifically western distribution as opposed to the more easterly pattern shown by semicircular combs.[19] Thomas distinguishes three categories of triangular comb, and it is her 'variante 3' which is relevant to this discussion. This is a type which has decorative extensions to the centre tooth plates which extend above the triangular outline of the outer back plates. These extensions may take the form of zig-zag or scalloped edges, sometimes pierced, or they may be cut into the form of animal heads. Böhme has separated these into two categories, group D which contains the scalloped and zig-zag forms, and group E to which the zoomorphic combs belong. The latter had already been listed by Koch[20] in a discussion of zoomorphic belt fittings. Both D and E combs are relevant to a discussion of 'Frisian' combs, E because of the zoomorphic detail and D because they are found with cases of the barred zoomorphic variety otherwise associated with 'Frisian' combs.

Böhme's list of D combs[21] can be increased by several English examples. At least six have been found at Spong Hill (in cremations nos. 1407, 1465, 1183, 1534, 1663, 1686, and possibly 2183) and there were at least two at St John's, Cambridge.[22] There may be more than one from Sancton, although the comb from grave 92 which is listed by Böhme as belonging to this group may in fact be part of an E comb.[23] There are two combs from settlement sites, Sutton Courtenay[24] and West Stow.[25] This gives a total of twenty-seven recorded sites, as well as the unspecified sites in the Netherlands which produced the six combs illustrated by Roes.[26] Many of the combs have no close provenances but where there are datable contexts these belong in the latter part of the fourth century and in the fifth century. These include four Roman towns or forts (Alzey, Köln, Trier, and Dittenheim) and five cemeteries which began in the late Roman period (Furfooz, Brény, Thivars, Vert-la-Gravelle, and Rhenen). Three of the graves were included in Böhme's catalogue.[27] Vert-la-Gravelle grave 26 and grave 284 from Vermand both appear to belong to his *Stufe* II, that is, the last third of the fourth century. Rhenen grave 842 contained a coin of Gratian, but on the basis of belt typology the grave could be slightly later than this would suggest, and may date from the first part of the fifth century. There are three other continental graves with combs of group D. One from Mainz has been examined by Werner[28] who puts it in the first half of the fifth century. Another is a rich female grave at Heilbronn-Bockingen[29] which contained a necklace of coin pendants, imitations of late fourth or early fifth-century coins. This grave has been dated variously to the middle and end of the fifth century. At Holzheim a grave was dated purely on the basis of the comb to the late fourth century which may be too early, especially as the rest of the graves in the cemetery appear to be of a later date.[30]

Boeles published one D comb[31] and refers to another from Oosterbeintum[32] which do not appear to correspond with any of the further six shown by Roes. None of these has any published associations. Three north German cemeteries have produced D combs: Perlberg, Gudendorf, and Issendorf, which has so far produced three, from graves 185, 243, and 248.[33] The Gudendorf comb was in a shouldered pot with chevron decoration,[34] and the Issendorf pots had linear and dot patterns. These pots might be fourth or fifth century in date.

In England one D comb was found at Winchester in a pit dug through Roman rubble and sealed by a layer which elsewhere lay above fourth-century cobbles and below seventh-century building traces.[35] At Colchester one was found above late Roman destruction levels but not in a very securely stratified context.[36] The Sutton Courtenay comb was unstratified also, but the one from West Stow was found in a hut which also contained faceted-angled pottery and which belongs to the earliest, fifth-century, phase of the settlement. Combs of this type are recorded from six pagan Saxon cemeteries: Castle Acre, Pensthorpe, Spong Hill, and Caistor in Norfolk; St John's, Cambridge, and Sancton, Yorkshire. Where the associated pots are known, they are, if at all datable, of fifth- and not sixth-century types. These include plain pots from Sancton and Spong Hill, and from Spong Hill a faceted-angled pot, slashed cordons, and chevron patterns.[37] One pot from Caistor has a linear swastika pattern.[38]

Böhme's list of zoomorphic triangular combs needs few additions. There is one comb from Westerwanna, whose associated pot has not yet been published,[39] and a curious comb found in London in the nineteenth century should perhaps be included.[40] At Abingdon in Oxfordshire, the terminal of a zoomorphic bone comb case was recently excavated from the bottom of a *Grubenhaus*.[41] The neatness and naturalism of this horse head suggest it was part of the case from a triangular zoomorphic comb rather than from the usually less carefully shaped 'Frisian' comb type. Associated pottery and finds are not very remarkable, and do not allow of closer dating. A comb fragment from St Johns may be zoomorphic.[42] Combs from Caistor listed by Böhme as belonging to this type are in fact of the 'Frisian' variety.

A few E combs have precise provenances. At Abbeville grave 53[43] contained a coin of Valentinian I, and at Cortrat grave 6[44] contained a tutulus brooch of late fourth-century type and grave 30 a zoomorphic buckle of similar date.[45] Further east on the Danube a zoomorphic comb was found at Lébéni in a layer thought to date from before the arrival of the Huns in AD 433.[46] At Richborough one fragment was unstratified,[47] but another was found in a pit which also contained a Theodosian hoard.[48] Combs from Furfooz mostly no longer have a specific grave provenance, but the whole cemetery belongs predominantly to the latter part of the fourth century.[49]

The contexts of these combs are similar but not identical to those of the D combs. There seem to be none from the Frisian terps, at most three from English Saxon cemeteries (St Johns', Lackford, and Sancton), and one possible fragment from a settlement (Abingdon). So far only the Westerwanna comb comes from a continental Germanic context. Four were found in late Roman sites on the Danube (Dinogetia, Lébéni, Kupinovo, and Szoni) and the remaining fourteen are also either definitely or probably from late Roman towns or forts (Köln, Trier, Lauriacum, Troyes, Strasbourg, Colchester, Richborough, and London), or graves (Furfooz, Abbeville, Balleure, Vermand, Bavai, Cortrat). This contrast in emphasis between Roman and Germanic contexts, in so far as the two can be distinguished, suggests that in general D combs remained in use longer than E combs and were perhaps made by Germanic craftsmen as well as Roman.

The barred zoomorphic combs which form the main subject of this discussion combine various elements, most of which derive from the late Roman comb types described above. Only the basic form of the comb is possibly more Germanic than Roman in character. Both shape and decoration derive from comb types current in the later part of the fourth century, perhaps lasting into the fifth. A date in the early fifth century for the beginning of the use and manufacture of the barred zoomorphic single-sided combs seems to be supported by this examination of their origins, although this gives no very clear indication of an upper date limit. A fifth-century date has been suggested in past discussions of the type by Roes,[50] Green,[51] and Macgregor.[52] This has chiefly depended on the association of a barred comb from Hoogebeintum with a cruciform brooch. The photograph of this brooch published by Boeles[53] shows a fragmentary brooch which might well have been old when buried. It is not even clear to which type of cruciform it should be assigned, since the side-knobs are missing and the foot is corroded. The name 'Frisian' has been given to these combs because the first published examples were found in the Frisian terps. One of these, from Kantens, has a runic inscription[54] and in the discussion of this case another, found at Kastell Deutz near Cologne, was recorded. In the report on the cemetery at Caistor-by-Norwich, Barbara Green published a further four and referred to others from York, Pakenham, Spong Hill, and Lackford. Macgregor republished the original York comb together with a second, new find and added one example from Issendorf to the list, as well as suggesting that a comb case from Girton should belong to this group.

There are several additions to this list. At Pritzier, in Mecklenberg, one cremation contained the remains of what looks like a comb-case of this type,[55] and a fragment of a zoomorphic comb found in Strasbourg also might be included.[56] At Issendorf, as well as the fairly complete example already listed, there seem to be barred comb fragments from another six graves.[57] At Sancton one cremation contained fragments of a comb or case,[58] and a very complete example has recently been found near Peterborough.[59] There may be three combs of this kind from Loveden Hill.[60] At least thirty-four combs or cases have so far been found at Spong Hill. In one or two instances it is not clear whether parts of two combs, or of a comb and case, are present. Since the majority of the type does not now come from Frisia, and the distribution shows a much wider North Sea or indeed northern European pattern, it might be better to find a new name. It is difficult to think of a descriptive, precise name shorter than 'zoomorphic barred single-sided combs' which is cumbersome, but probably preferable to rechristening them 'Spong' combs, since in future that might also come to seem an irrelevant title.

There are no published associations for any of the terp finds, except for the one from Hoogebeintum, nor for the Strasbourg, Kastell Deutz, Girton, and the first York, combs or cases. However, most of the remainder are recently excavated and have recorded contexts. The case from Pritzier was found in a carinated bowl attributed to the later fourth century. At Issendorf the first season of excavation alone produced seven cremations with parts of this type of comb, and there may well be more from the remainder of the cemetery, now excavated but not yet published. The combs so far published are from graves nos. 38, 37, 76, 104, 188, 200, 248. A number of other graves contained scalloped triangular combs or flat zoomorphic comb cases. The best example of a barred comb is the one from grave 200 which is zoomorphic, probably with a mushroom-shaped handle, with a barred case. In grave 248 a barred case was found with a scalloped triangular comb. The other grave goods in these cremations are not very remarkable, nor are they consistent: beads, strike-a-light, tweezers. The associated pots have linear and dot patterns and are of a variety of shapes.

In England, the comb from Pakenham was found in a Saxon *Grubenhaus* together with some not very distinctive pottery and two spindlewhorls. The second York comb was found in a layer dated as 'late Roman or immediately post-Roman'.[61] The Lackford comb was found in a pot decorated with bosses and a slashed cordon.[62] This comb has probably been wrongly reconstructed,[63] since it has been put together with bars at both back and front, a construction not otherwise known for this type. The comb, as it is now, is too long to fit into the case found in the same grave, and is, in fact, much longer than any comparable comb. It seems likely that most of the bars at present attached to the comb tooth fragment should in fact be put together with the flat back of the comb case, to form its front. This would give the case three bars, a feature known elsewhere, from one of the terp finds.[64] The Peterborough comb was found on a site which has produced both late Roman and early Saxon material. It was in a ditch fill, associated with pottery which is described as of Saxon fabric, but imitating Roman forms.[65] Two of the Caistor combs were found in undecorated hollow-necked pots, the third in a pot with linear and dot decoration, and a fourth comb came from a fragmentary pot. The bones from one pot, Y17, have been identified as those of a young child.[66] Only one of the Caistor pots contained any other grave goods apart from the combs, an iron fragment, perhaps part of a pair of miniature tweezers, from Y8. At Sancton, in cremation 166 were found what are described as parts of a bone bracelet.[67] These are almost certainly bars from a comb or comb case. The pot, which also contained two spindlewhorls, melted glass, and a bronze knife, is decorated with vertical bosses and a horizontal row of stamps.

So far, then, the only approximately datable piece of metalwork found with a barred comb remains the Hoogebeintum brooch. The pots do not form a clear cut, well-defined group, and the dating of Migration period pottery is in any case not yet very precise. None the less, it can at least be said that all the pots are of types equally familiar on the Continent and in England, and that none therefore needs to belong to a phase during which development on both sides of the North

Sea was no longer following a common course. There is nothing to contradict a fifth-century dating, even if there is nothing to make that date more precise. The association, at Issendorf and at Spong Hill, of scalloped D combs with barred cases indicates some correspondence in date between the two, but as we have seen in discussion of D combs above (p. 99), this also does not give a more precise date than late fourth to fifth century.

At Spong Hill by the end of 1978, sixty inhumations and 1,268 cremations had been excavated.[68] None of the inhumations contained combs but this may only be the result of the poor soil conditions for organic preservation. Very little of any of the skeletons survived, except for teeth and fragments of jaw bones which had been preserved by being in close contact with bronze brooches. Of the cremations, one hundred and twenty-seven, that is approximately 10 per cent, contained combs or comb cases. Fifty-one of these combs are too fragmentary to be identifiable as of any particular variety. Of the remainder, thirty-six are triangular, thirty-two barred (with a further possible example from cremation 2192 and two from earlier excavations), seven double-sided, four miniature, and one semi-circular. Five of the triangular combs were in the same cremations as five of the barred cases, including cremation 2211, which also contained one of the miniatures. At least three of the triangular combs with barred cases are of the scalloped 'D' group.[69]

The cremations which contain any kind of comb at Spong Hill are distinguished, in general, from the remainder by two characteristics. One is that they tend to contain larger numbers of grave goods altogether. The other is their association with sets of miniature shears, tweezers, and razors.

Approximately 28 per cent of all cremations contained more than one grave find, counting all glass beads from each cremation as a single item, and of these, one hundred and eighty-eight, approximately 15 per cent, contained three or more items. Of the cremations with combs eighty-five, 66 per cent, contained two or more items, and fifty-seven of these contained three or more, which is more than 45 per cent. Triangular combs stand out particularly in this context since twenty-two of the thirty-six had three or more grave goods. Fifteen of the barred combs or cases were found in cremations with three or more items. There are several possible explanations for this. One is that combs belonged to the more prosperous members of the community, who were buried with more objects. Other possible indications of relative wealth amongst the cremations might be imports or precious metals. No gold has as yet been found in a cremation and silver occurred in only two. One of these, 1743, did contain a comb, a double-sided example which is the only comb from Spong Hill to have bronze and not iron rivets. This cremation also contained brooch fragments, glass beads, two silver rings, and a silver pendant,[70] and is clearly an exceptional burial. The obvious imports, glass vessels and ivory rings, do not appear to have any significant association with combs. Forty-two cremations contained glass vessels, but only three of these also produced combs. Of fifty-seven cremations with ivory rings, eleven also contained combs which is a slightly higher but still not very striking proportion.

Another explanation is simply that graves with combs tended to be those with more than one occupant. A bone report has been compiled for the barred combs, but not as yet for the remainder (p. 112). This does show a number of multiple burials higher than might have been expected from the over-all numbers of multiples from already analysed cremations. It also shows that the constant element is the age of those buried, since all the cremations which could be examined included child burials as part or all of the assemblage. This might explain why there is no apparent link between either sex and combs. Combs have been variously attributed to male and female categories of grave goods,[71] but in fact they do not seem, amongst inhumations, to be specific to either. It is not easy to distinguish the sex of a cremated burial either through the bones or the grave goods, but at Spong Hill it is possible to divide associated grave goods into two groups, one possibly representing female, the other less certainly male, burials.[72] Combs are found both with typically female objects such as spindlewhorls and jewellery, and also with the sets of miniatures and playing pieces which may represent the male burials.

Yet there does seem to be a significant relationship between combs and sets of miniatures. From the cemetery as a whole so far twenty-eight sets of three items are known, and of these nearly half, thirteen, were found in cremations which also contained combs. Twenty-five of the seventy-five recognizable combs were associated with sets of two or three miniatures, which is a very high proportion. Unfortunately as yet there is no detailed study of miniatures,[73] although since in Mecklenberg they are given a third-century date and in Schleswig-Holstein they appear to belong to the late fourth–early fifth century, they may well be relatively early in England. Analysis of all the bones from Spong Hill, when complete, may show whether they are an age or sex specific grave object.

The cremations from Spong Hill which contain barred combs or cases are listed and described below (p. 109), together with brief descriptions of the pots and lists of the grave goods associated with each. Fuller descriptions and illustrations of the pots will be found in Hills 1977 and Hills, Penn, and Rickett forthcoming. The four aspects of this group of cremations to be considered are the pottery, the grave goods, the distribution of the cremations within the cemetery, and the bones, which are the subject of a separate report by Glenys Putnam (p. 112).

It is not possible to make a simple equation between cremations containing barred combs and any one category of pottery. However, by comparison between the proportions of types of pot found in association with barred combs and in the cemetery as a whole, it is possible to suggest some significant associations. Six of the pots with barred combs are undecorated. This compares very closely with the 17 per cent of all pots which have no decoration, but it includes none of the wide-mouthed hemispherical pots, usually made from organically tempered fabric, which form a large part of the undecorated pots overall. More than 28 per cent of all pots have stamped decoration, yet only five of thirty-two cremations in this group had any stamped decoration. Of these, 2211 has a pattern which is essentially composed of bosses, lines and dots with the substitution of three stamps for dots in one panel only.[74] A row of stamps is set around the neck of 1216, a pot otherwise decorated with close-set vertical bosses,[75] and on 1556 the pattern includes only isolated stamps set in panels between bosses.[76] No. 1389 has rows of stamps covering most of the upper half of the pot, but it also has a slashed carination and a concave neck.[77] All four therefore, although stamped, also exhibit characteristics familiar from continental sites, and the stamps are not the dominant element in the decoration. Only 1806 looks like the product of an independent local tradition,[78] and may belong to a group of pots attributable to one of the identifiable 'Spong' potters. The remaining pots are all of types which are equally at home on both sides of the North Sea, including seven decorated with linear and dot designs out of the total of fifty of all the cremation pots which have such patterns. This must represent a significant association, since if the pattern of pottery types were the same as that found throughout the cemetery, such a concentration of dot patterns would not have occurred, nor would there have been so few stamped pots. In so far as these pots can be closely dated, they would appear to belong to the fifth century rather than to the sixth. There are no pots belonging to the large stamp-linked groups, none with pendant triangles of stamps and no random-stamped pots, all types which seem to represent stages of evolution within England during the sixth century. The carinated plain bowl, 1475, compares closely with the two similar Caistor pots which also contained barred combs.[79]

A wide range of grave goods is associated with the combs. The incidence of sets of miniatures apparent amongst comb graves in general is repeated: nine of the thirty-two contained one or more items, including four sets of three. Four of the cremations contained brooches. One of these, from 1389, was unidentifiable, but those from 1216 and 1664 definitely, and also that from 1475 possibly, were cruciform brooches of Åberg group I.[80] Another pot, 2017, did not itself contain a brooch, but it appears to have been made by the same potter as 2093, which did contain another definite example of a group I cruciform brooch as well as a fragmentary comb. This means that three of the seven[81] definite examples of this type of brooch found so far at Spong Hill were found directly or indirectly in association with barred combs or cases. This is a strong argument in favour of the contemporaneity of the two classes of grave goods, so that if one could be dated, it would throw light on the chronology of the other.

Cruciform brooches have recently been reconsidered by Reichstein who has produced a far more complex classification than that by Åberg.[82] He has distinguished a series of types, described by the name of one of the sites at which they have been found. On the basis of this typology he has constructed a relative chronology, relying chiefly on associated brooch finds from Norway and on two large excavated cemeteries in Mecklenberg. This relative chronology is fixed fairly firmly at the beginning, in the mid to late fourth century, by the association of the earliest types with late Roman material. The upper end is given by the lack of association between any except the latest English varieties of cruciforms with objects decorated in Style I. For the beginning of Style I, Reichstein accepts Bakka's dating of around AD 500.[83]

The chief problem in using this new typology lies in the fact that nowhere does Reichstein explicitly state which criteria he regards as important for classification and why, nor how many criteria each brooch needs to possess before it is included in one type rather than another. In most cases this is reasonably clear from the illustrations, but unfortunately there is some overlap between the two types which seem closest to the Spong Hill brooches, types Gross Siemz and Midlum.[84] In fact, because he uses the over-all appearance of the brooch, rather than its possession or lack of one or two clearly defined characteristics, it is only possible to apply his system to complete brooches and therefore, strictly speaking, only the larger brooch from cremation 1468 and the one from cremation 1469 should be considered here,[85] neither of which was associated with a barred comb. Both these brooches correspond to the description given to type Gross Siemz[86] in all details except for the fact that they have short pin-catches, whereas Gross Siemz brooches are said to have long pin-catches. From the illustrations it is also clear that the relative length of the lengthwise faceting above the horse-head terminal is greater on the Gross Siemz than on the Spong Hill brooches. Typ Midlum includes several brooches which appear virtually identical with the brooch from cremation 1468, especially those from Yttrup Holmgard, Denmark, and from East Shefford.[87] However, there are other brooches in this group which do not appear very similar at all. The bow and foot of all except two of the group are consistent but the head plates are not. These range from comparatively narrow, with separately cast side knobs (Yttrup Holmgard, Hammoor, East Shefford, Glaston), to wide with half-round cast-in-one side knobs (North Luffenham, Lakenheath, Bradwell, Rothwell). It may be reasonable not to take the formation of the head plate as the sole criterion, but one is left with the suspicion that, in this case at least, it has simply been exchanged for the foot. The difference between separate and cast-in-one side knobs is a change in construction which one might have thought deserved some consideration in a classification, and it would have been helpful if Reichstein had explained why he did not think it important in this case.

If one accepts Reichstein's typology, both of the brooches from cremation 1468, the one from 1469 and probably the one from 1664 would go in his Midlum type. The small size of the brooch from 1216 might put it in the Gross Siemz group, while the rest cannot really be even tentatively divided between the two. Such a division of otherwise similar brooches does seem rather artificial and would not matter were it not for the fact that, according to Reichstein's chronology, Gross Siemz is a comparatively early type, belonging to the first half of the fifth century, while Typ Midlum should be put in the latter half of the century. The reasoning behind this dating depends on a very few examples of associated finds and on the similarity between brooches of Midlum type, Hoogebeintum type (an example of which was found with a Midlum-type brooch), and Norwegian brooch types which Reichstein has dated independently through analysis of associations to his 'Stufe D3', that is, after the middle of the fifth century. Midlum-type brooches, including those from East Shefford and Girton, have been found together with other types of cruciform brooches which might be regarded as typologically later. But amongst the Spong brooches under discussion, the two which were associated with the same kind of comb, from 1216 and 1664, might well belong to the two different categories which Reichstein dates differently. Reichstein himself admits that the English material is not as yet susceptible of independent dating, and in a recently published outline of his work in England Vierck treats all of the fifth century as part of one indivisible first period, which may prove to be the best approach.[88] Recent excavations of several large cemeteries should soon provide a better basis for reassessment of the English material. Provisionally one might suggest that Reichstein's Midlum type should be divided, and those brooches with separately cast side knobs put in a different category, together with the 'group I' brooches from Spong Hill. The typological similarity of such a group to the early Gross Siemz brooches together with their associations with 'later' types might give it a transitional position, perhaps occupying the middle years of the fifth century rather than either extreme. This would fit the evolution of the combs better than a later fifth-century dating, which would leave an unexpectedly long gap between them and their late Roman prototypes.

The distribution of barred zoomorphic combs within Spong Hill confirms their association with early cruciform brooches (fig. 7). Both concentrate in the southern part of the excavated area, especially the south-western part. The north-eastern section, which is occupied by both cremations and inhumations, some definitely and most probably of sixth-century date, has produced neither barred combs nor early cruciforms. There are a few combs and one possible early cruciform from the north-western part of the cemetery, which otherwise produces sixth-century stamped pots,[89] but the majority were found in cremations buried within the angle of the large enclosure ditch which divides the site from east to west and north to south. The picture is slightly complicated by the existence of a second apparently early group in the middle of the excavated site, actually partly in the ditch, but in general terms there appears to be a horizontal stratigraphy in which the burials spread from south to north, during the fifth to sixth centuries. The details of this have not yet been worked out, but in outline the sequence is fairly clear.

In conclusion, one can say that both comparative study of the origins of the type, and analysis of its incidence at Spong Hill, support a fifth-century dating for single-sided barred zoomorphic combs. More precise dating would depend on estimates of the length of time it might take such a type of comb to develop and the time it would remain in use, as well as on more precise dating of early cruciform brooches and sets of miniatures. It would also depend on reassessment of the fundamental assumptions underlying migration period chronology in general, in particular with reference to the date and course of the Anglo-Saxon settlement of eastern England. This is not the place to expand further on such a wide subject. It remains also to be seen whether barred combs are the only type of grave goods to be consistently buried with children. If miniatures proved also to be associated with child burials this would remove the only apparent 'male' grave goods group. The bones so far analysed show a preponderance of female burials,[90] so that, unless a substantial male group does soon appear, we may eventually be forced to the conclusion that in England, as in some parts of the Continent, at some periods there were partially separate male and female cemeteries. Barred combs are just one of a number of subjects, all of which will have to be fully explored before any one can be fully understood.

Catalogue of barred combs and cases found at Spong Hill

Bars are decorated with groups of transverse incised lines unless otherwise stated.

1. Parts of two combs allegedly found together in 'Urn I' in 1954, now in East Dereham Museum. Parts of bars decorated with hatched triangles, comb, or comb and case. Fragment of triangular comb with barred case, also two pairs of miniature shears and bronze tweezers. Assemblage looks unlikely for a single grave, may represent two.

2. Cremation 1079. Small fragment of bar and flat decorated piece. Fragmentary pot, linear and dot decoration.

3. Cremation 1151. Fragment of bar with iron rivet. Also shears, razor, playing pieces. Pot: linear and dot decoration.

4. Cremation 1170, Parts of comb and case (fig. 6). Hatched triangles on case, diagonal hatched zones on comb. Not very carefully executed. Linear outline to back of comb, rows of concentric circle motifs on back of case. Shears, possibly tweezers. Pot: rosette motifs.

5. Cremation 1183. Triangular comb with zigzag edge. (fig. 1, pl. X). Case barred, transverse and sloping lines, one zoomorphic end surviving. Back of case interlocking circle pattern. Set of miniatures, bone head. Pot: linear and dot decoration.

6. Cremation 1184. Fragments of tooth-plates with bars attached. Set of miniatures. Pot: undecorated.

7. Cremation 1216. Fragments of bars, hatched triangles, also flat plate, row of concentric circle motifs (fig. 6). Shaped pieces probably part of mushroom-shaped handle, others might be zoomorphic. Cruciform brooch, Åberg group I. Pot: bossed and stamped.

8. Cremation 1227. Comb and possibly case (fig. 4). Interlocking circles on back, shaped pieces probably handle and zoomorphic detail. Arrow head, shears. Pot: linear and dot decoration.

9. Cremation 1240. Fragment of bar. Pot: fragmentary.

10. Cremation 1389. Comb, possibly case (fig. 6). Hatched triangles on bars, rows of circles on back, pieces of teeth and possible zoomorphic detail. Very like 1216. Bronze fragments, ?brooch, glass beads, ivory. Pot: horizontal rows stamps, dots, slashed carination.

11. Cremation 1407. Triangular scalloped comb, tooth plate fragments. Fragment of bar, sloping lines. Glass beads. Pot: fragmentary, linear and dot decoration.

12. Cremation 1447. Fragment of bar and possible zoomorphic piece. Miniature iron blades, probably tweezers and shears. Pot: fragmentary, linear.

13. Cremation 1450. Parts of comb and case, both barred (fig. 4). Comb has zoomorphic ends and mushroom handle. Part of one zoomorphic terminal of case survives. Back of comb and case missing. Glass beads, spindle-whorl. Pot: chevron pattern.

14. Cremation 1459. Bar, flat plate with linear decoration, end tooth. Pot: lower part only.

15. Cremation 1465. Triangular comb, scalloped, pierced edge (fig. 2). Zoomorphic barred case. Bronze wire ring, iron tweezers, flint flake. Pot: plain, ?globular.

16. Cremation 1467. Triangular comb, bars from case. Pot: plain, globular.

17. Cremation 1470. Comb with case (fig. 3). Comb barred, central wide mushroom handle, parts of one zoomorphic terminal. Case part of one zoomorphic terminal, flat back with central row concentric circle motifs. Very like Peterborough comb. Bronze wire ring, glass ?beads. Pot: plain, globular.

18. Cremation 1475. Most complete example. Barred comb and case (fig. 2). Comb central wide mushroom handle, rudimentary animal heads at each end. Case rudimentary animals. Back of comb dot in circle, back of case concentric circle and dot in circle pattern. Two burnt bronze fragments, one probably foot of cruciform brooch, Åberg I or II. Pot: carinated, hollow neck, plain wide-mouthed bowl.

19. Cremation 1482. Fragment of bar and part of handle. Pot: fragmentary linear and boss pattern.

20. Cremation 1534. Triangular comb, scalloped or zoomorphic with barred case (fig. 1). One zoomorphic terminal, concentric circles on back of case. Bronze buckle, glass bead, Pot: linear and dot decoration.

21. Cremation 1556. Zoomorphic comb end, bars, flat plate, and fragment of case end (fig. 5). Pot: slashed cordon, bosses, stamps.

22. Cremation 1605. Fragment of bar. Bronze tweezers, faceted, with earscoop on wire ring, iron shears. Pot: traces linear and bossed decoration, fragmentary. 1605 and 1610 may be parts of same cremation.

23. Cremation 1607. Fragments bar and flat plate, dot in circle decoration. Base of pot only.

24. Cremation 1610. Bar and tooth fragments. Transverse and lengthwise lines, like 1183. Bronze fittings, iron blade ?miniature shears. Pot: base only.

25. Cremation 1634. Part of barred comb, teeth, bars still attached, part of flat plate separate, linear outline (fig. 3). Pot: plain.

26. Cremation 1664. Part of bar, diagonally hatched triangles, and flat plate, interlocking circles. Bronze brooch, cruciform, Åberg group I. Iron needle and bone needle case. Pot: chevron pattern, wide-mouthed bowl.

27. Cremation 1674. Fragments bar and tooth end plate. Diagonal lines on bar, flint flakes. Base of pot only.

28. Cremation 1765. Comb, possibly case. Hatched triangles on bar, rows of dots in circle on back. Compare 1216, 1389. Pot: vertical bosses alternate with vertical lines.

29. Cremation 1806. Barred fragments. Bronze tweezers and earscoop on ring together. Pot: elaborate stamped and bossed decoration, flat stamped lid.
30. Cremation 2009. Comb and probably case, zoomorphic terminal, two different flat pieces backs of comb and case, dot in circle row along middle one piece. Three glass beads. Pot: large 'T' cordons alternate with small round bosses. Cordons around neck.
31. Cremation 2017. Comb and case, both barred, zoomorphic fragments. Glass, ivory. Pot: chevrons, small bosses around body, wedge indentations in some chevron panels and in zone around neck.
32. Cremation 2160. Various fragments bars with hatched triangles, possibly both comb and case although no teeth, so no clear evidence for comb. Zoomorphic piece either case end or handle of comb. Pot: vertical grooves, bosses, rows dots.
33. Cremation 2211. Miniature triangular comb and full-size triangular comb, dot in circle pattern. Fragment bar and zoomorphic terminal from case. Two pairs bronze tweezers, bronze ring and fragments, two iron knives, iron shears, spindle-whorl, glass ?vessel. Pot: arches around bosses, ring stamps, shouldered.
    Also 2192 which may be barred or double-sided, carinated bowl, chevron decorations.

Acknowledgments

I am grateful to the following for permission to refer to unpublished material: the Scole Committee; Barbara Green, Norwich Castle museum; Mary Cra'ster, Cambridge, Museum of Archaeology and Anthropology; Stanley West, Suffolk Archaeological Unit; Nigel Kerr, University College, Cardiff; R. and E. Henderson, Abingdon; Kate Pretty, Cambridge.

Figs. 1–6 are drawn by K. J. Penn, Norfolk Archaeological Unit, after Hills 1977, figs. 129–32. Fig. 7 is drawn by the author.

APPENDIX

Analysis of cremated bones   Glenys Putnam

The cremations analysed from the Spong Hill series accompanying the barred zoomorphic combs consist of twenty mixed cremations, seven infants or children alone, and one female alone. All of the cremations were well fired and broken deliberately after firing for inclusion in a burial urn which was then itself buried. Evidently the placing of pieces in the urn, and its interment, represent a post-cremation ritual of which we know little, no attempt being made to inter the whole fired skeleton, with the bodies represented only by token bones. Animal bones frequently accompany burial, and are as indicated below. Numbers of individuals in urns seem to vary over time, and a possible change in ritual is beginning to be discernible in this large cemetery.

The number of unaccompanied children in the sample analysed is high, and only one other burial in the series as analysed contains no children. It is difficult to assess the importance of this, a possible conclusion being that the combs were buried as children's grave goods. There is also a disproportion between males and females, since of sexable individuals, twelve are female and only four can definitely be described as male. This may indicate either that barred combs are a female attribute, or that they are, as suggested above, associated with children who may normally be buried with an adult female, probably their mother.

Spong Hill Cremations

1070	No report.
1079	Infant 1 (3–4).
1151	4 individuals. Adult (unsexable); Adolescent; Child (infant); Neonate.
1183	2 individuals. Child *c.*10 years; Infant.
1184	2 individuals (?3rd). Female adult and child (infant).
1216	No report.
1227	1 individual. Child (infant) 6–9 months.
1240	No report.
1389	2 individuals (?3rd). Adult female; Child *c.*6 years. (3rd individual only 4 g, possibly male) and Animal bones, lamb, and bird, probably small partridge, English.
1407	2 individuals. Adult (unsexable); Child (infant); and animal bones, Roe Deer and Bird (small water bird, probably Teal).
1447	1 individual. Child *c.*10 years.

1450   1 individual. Child 4–6 years.

1459   3 individuals. 2 Adults (unsexable); Child (infant) *c*.1 year.

1465   2 individuals (?3rd). 1 Adult female and ?male; Child (?age) and bones from forequarter of Red Deer.

1467   3 individuals. Adult female; Child *c*.12 years; Infant.

1470   2 individuals (?3rd). 1 Adult female and ?male; Child (infant) and piece of cow tibia.

1475   1 individual. Young female *c*.10 years.

1482   1 individual only. Child 8–10 years.

1534   2 individuals. Adolescent female; Child (infant).

1556   2 individuals. 1 Adult; Child 6–7 years.

1605   1 individual. Adult ?female.

1607   2 individuals. 2 Adults (?sex).

1610   3 individuals. Adult female; Adult male; Child (infant) *c*.2 years.

1634   1 individual. Child *c*.7 years; Roe Deer and small water bird.

1664   3 individuals. Adult male; Adult female; Child *c*.6 years.

1674

1743

1765   2 individuals. 1 Adult (unsexed); Child (infant) 1 year; and lamb.

1806

2009   3 individuals. Adult female; Adult male; Neonate; 1 piece unidentifiable bird bone.

2017   2 individuals. Adult (unsexable); Child 6–13 months; Lamb and dog.

2160   3 individuals. Adult female *c*.30 years; Adult male; Child (infant) *c*.2 years.

2192   2 individuals. Adult female; Adolescent *c*.14–15 years.

2211   2 individuals (?3rd). Adult female; ?male; Child.

Bibliography

ÅBERG, N., *The Anglo-Saxons in England* (Cambridge and Uppsala 1926).

BAKKA, E., 'On the beginning of Salin's Style 1 in England', *Universitetet i Bergen Årbok, 1958, Historisk-Antikvarisk rekke* Nr. 3, 1–83.

BIDDLE, M., 'Excavations at Winchester, 1969. Eighth Interim Report', *Antiq. J.* 50 (1970), 277–326.

BOELES, P.C.J.A., *Friesche Terpen* (Leeuwarden, 1906).

BOELES, P.C.J.A., *Friesland tot de elfde eeuw* (The Hague, 1951).

BÖHME, H.W., *Germanische Grabfunde des 4 bis 5 Jahrhunderts zwischen unterer Elbe und Loire* (Munich, 1974).

BUSHE-FOX, J.P., *Third Report on the Excavations of the Roman Fort at Richborough, Kent* (London, 1932).

BUSHE-FOX, J.P., *Fourth Report on the Excavations of the Roman Fort at Richborough, Kent* (London, 1949).

CLIFFORD, E.M., 'The Roman villa, Witcombe, Gloucestershire', *Trans. Bristol and Gloucestershire Archaeol. Soc.,* 73 (1954), 5–69.

CORDER, P. and KIRK, J., *A Roman villa at Langton near Malton* (Hull, 1932).

DÜWEL, K. and TEMPEL, W.D., 'Knochenkämme mit Runeninschriften aus Friesland', *Paleohistoria* 14 (1968), 353–91.

ECK, T., *Les Deux cimetières gallo-romains de Vermand et de Saint-Quentin* (Paris, 1891).

FORRER, R., *Strasbourg-Argentorate* (2 vols., Strasbourg, 1927).

GERMANIA ROMANA V, (Bamberg, 1930).

HAUPT, D., 'Jakobwüllesheim', in Jahresbericht 1968, *Bonner Jahrbücher* 170 (1970), 381–91.

HILLS, C.M., 'The Results of the Excavations at the Anglo-Saxon cremation cemetery at Spong Hill, North Elmham, Norfolk, with reference to cultural and chronological contexts', thesis submitted for the Degree of Ph.D. at Birkbeck College, University of London, 1976.

HILLS, C.M., *The Anglo-Saxon cemetery at Spong Hill, North Elmham, Part 1, East Anglian Archaeology Report No. 6* (Gressenhall, 1977).

HILLS, C.M., PENN, K., and RICKETT, R., *The Anglo-Saxon cemetery at Spong Hill, North Elmham, Part II,* East Anglian Archaeology Report (forthcoming).

HULL, M.R., *Roman Colchester* (London 1958).

JANSSEN, W., *Issendorf,* Teil I (Hildesheim 1972).

KELLER, E., *Die spätrömischen Grabfunde in Südbayern* (Munich, 1971).

KRÜGER, H., 'Die Ausgrabungen der Jahre 1865–7 im merowingisch/karolingischen Gräberfeld des Dorfes Holzheim', *Mitt. Oberhess. Geschichtsver.* N.F. 55 (1970), 9–31.

KOCH, R., 'Die spätkaiserzeitliche Gürtelgarnitur von der Ehrenbürg bei Forchheim', *Germania* 43 (1965), 119–20.

LEEDS, E.T., 'A Saxon village at Sutton Courtenay, Berks., second report', *Archaeologia* 76 (1927), 59–80.

LETHBRIDGE, T.C., *A Cemetery at Lackford, Suffolk* (Cambridge, 1951).

LINDENSCHMIT, L., *Das Römisch-Germanische Central-Museum, Bildlichen Darstellungen* (Mainz, 1889).

MACGREGOR, A., 'Barred combs of Frisian type in England', *Medieval Archaeol.* 19 (1975), 195–8.

MACKRETH, D., 'Orton Hall farm, Peterborough', *Studies in the Romano-British villa*. ed. M. Todd (Leicester, 1978).

MOOSBRUGGER-LEU, R., *Die Schweiz zur Merowingerzeit* (Bern, 1971).

NENQUIN, J., *La Nécropole de Furfooz, Diss. Arch. Gandenses I* (1953).

NERMAN, B., *Die Völkerwanderungszeit Gotlands* (Stockholm, 1935).

NEVILLE, The Hon, R.C., *Saxon Obsequies illustrated by ornaments and weapons* (London, 1852).

PIRLING, R., *Das Römisch-Fränkische Gräberfeld von Krefeld-Gellep 1960–63* (Berlin, 1974).

PILLOY, J., *Études sur d'anciens lieux des sepultures dans l'Aisne* (St Quentin, 1886–1912).

PUSZTAI, 'A Lébényi germán fejedelmi sír', *Arrabona* 8 (1966).

ROEREN, R., 'Ein münzdatierter Grabfund der frühen Merowingerzeit aus Heilbronn-Böckingen', *Fundberichte aus Schwaben* N.F. 16 (1962), 119–46.

REICHSTEIN, J., *Die Kreuzförmige Fibel, Offa-Bücher* 34 (Neumünster, 1975).

ROES, A., *Bone and Antler objects from the Frisian terp mounds* (Haarlem, 1963).

RÖHRER-ERTL, O., *Untersuchungen am Material des Urnenfriedhofes von Westerwanna, Kreis Land Hadeln* (Hamburg, 1971).

SCHULDT, E., *Pritzier* (Berlin, 1955).

SODEN-SMITH, R.H., 'Note on a comb found in London', *Archaeol. J. 34* (1877), 450–1.

STEAD, I.M., 'Beadlam Roman villa; an interim report', *Yorkshire Archaeol. J.* 43 (1971), 178–86.

THOMAS, S., 'Studien zu den Germanischen Kämmen der Römischen Kaiserzeit', *Arbeits und Forschungsberichte zur Sächsischen Bodendenkmalpflege* Band 8 (1960), 54–215.

VIERCK, H., 'Zur relativen und absoluten Chronologie der anglischen Grabfunde in England', in G. Kossack and J. Reichstein *Archaeologisches Beiträge zur Chronologie der Völkerwanderungszeit* (Bonn, 1977).

WALLER, K., *Die Gräberfelder von Hemmoor, Quelkhorn, Gudendorf und Duhnen-Wehrberg in Niedersachsen* (Hamburg, 1959).

WERNER, J., 'Kriegergräber aus der ersten Hälfte des 5 Jahrhunderts zwischen Schelde und Weser', *Bonner Jahrbücher* 158 (1958), 372–413.

Notes

1. Hills, 1977, figs. 129–32, and Hills, Penn, and Rickett, forthcoming.
2. Pirling, 1974, Taf. 84, 10a and b.
3. A large catalogue of bone combs has been compiled by P. Galloway, London, but this is as yet unpublished.
4. Thomas, 1960.
5. Böhme, 1974, 122–6.
6. Thomas, 1960, 104–14.
7. Nerman, 1935, 14–17, 83–4.
8. Clifford, 1954, fig. 19, 1 for Witcombe, and K. Pretty, Cambridge, for information as to the unpublished example from Wroxeter.
9. Colchester Museum annual report for 1974, pl. XIII, 6.
10. Neville, 1852, pl. 23.
11. Moosbrugger-Leu, 1971, Taf. 69, 4.
12. Keller 1971, Taf. 23, 2.
13. Ibid 112, note 636.
14. Haupt, 1970.
15. Stead, 1971, fig. 5, 4.
16. *Germania Romana* V, Taf. XVII; Lindenschmit 1889, Taf. VII, 18.
17. Corder and Kirk, 1932, 73, fig. 20.
18. Janssen, 1972, Taf. 45, 260.
19. Thomas, 1960, Karten 5 and 7.
20. Koch, 1965, 119–20.
21. Böhme, 1974, 123–4, especially notes 564–72.
22. Unpublished. Cambridge Museum of Archaeology and Ethnography cat. no. Z16291.
23. Myres and Southern, 1973 (No. 184), fig. 12, 2579.
24. Leeds, 1927, pl. VII, fig. 2, c.
25. Information S.E. West, Suffolk Archaeological Unit.
26. Roes, 1963, pls. IX–X.
27. Böhme, 1974, Taf. 66, 16; 141, 10 and 145, 5.
28. Werner, 1958, Abb. 19, 6.
29. Roeren, 1962, 121, Abb. 2, 16.
30. Krüger, 1970, figs. 1, 1a.
31. Boeles, 1951, pl. XXVII, 6.
32. Ibid. 336.

33. Janssen, 1972, Tafeln 30, 42, 43.
34. Waller, 1959, Taf. 34, 27.
35. Biddle, 1970, pl. 48, b.
36. Hull, 1958, p. 79, fig. 35, 2.
37. Myres and Southern, 1973 (No. 184), fig. 3, 2350 and Hills, 1977, figs. 12, 35, 48, 54, 85.
38. Myres and Green, 1973 (No. 181), fig. 13.
39. Röhrer-Ertl, 1971, 48, Abb. 2.
40. Soden-Smith, 1877, 451.
41. Information Mr and Mrs Henderson, Abingdon.
42. Cambridge Museum of Archaeology and Ethnography, Cat. No. Z16291.
43. Pilloy, 1886–1912, pl. 5, 24.
44. Böhme, 1974, Taf. 117, 1, 2.
45. Ibid. Taf. 120, 1.
46. Pusztai, 1966, 116.
47. Bushe-Fox, 1932, pl. XII, fig. 1, 35.
48. Bushe-Fox, 1949, pl. LIV, 226 and p. 87.
49. Nenquin, 1953.
50. Roes, 1963, 12–13.
51. Myres and Green, 1973 (No. 181), 91–4.
52. Macgregor, 1975.
53. Boeles, 1906, p. 34, No. 27.
54. Düwel and Tempel, 1968, 356, Taf. I, 1.
55. Schuldt, 1955, fig. 450.
56. Forrer, 1927, 746, fig. 551 H.
57. Janssen, 1972.
58. Myres and Southern, 1973 (No. 184), fig. 30, 2340.
59. Mackreth, 1978, fig. 65.
60. Information N. Kerr, Cardiff.
61. Macgregor, 1975, 195.
62. Lethbridge, 1951, fig. 1, 49.6.
63. Macgregor, 1975, fig. 76, 4, 5, shows this more clearly than Lethbridge.
64. Roes, 1963, pl. XIII, 4.
65. Mackreth, 1978, 219.
66. Myres and Green, 1973 (No. 181), 200.
67. Myres and Southern, 1973 (No. 184), fig. 30.
68. I am grateful to the Scole Committee for permission to refer to material which at time of writing this article is unpublished.
69. Hills, 1977, fig. 132.
70. Hills, Penn, and Rickett, forthcoming.
71. Janssen, 1972 identifies all cremations containing combs as female apparently for no other reason than that they contain combs.

72. Hills, 1977, 23–4.
73. Hills, 1976, 139–43 contains a preliminary discussion of the subject.
74. Hills, Penn, and Rickett, forthcoming.
75. Hills, 1977, fig. 89.
76. Ibid. fig. 91.
77. Ibid. fig. 77.
78. Hills, Penn, and Rickett, forthcoming.
79. Myres and Green, 1973 (No. 181), fig. 28.
80. Hills, 1977, fig. 107; Åberg, 1926, 33–6.
81. Definite examples from cremations Nos. 1034, 1216, 1468, 1469, 1474, 1664, and 2093.
    Possible examples from Nos. 58, 1072, 1160, 1168, 1176, 1214, 1496, and 2195.
82. Reichstein, 1975.
83. Bakka, 1958.
84. Reichstein, 1975, pls. 81–2 Gross Siemz, 84–7 Midlum.
85. Hills, 1977, fig. 107.
86. Reichstein, 1975, 41.
87. Ibid. pls. 84–5.
88. Vierck, 1977.
89. Hills, 1977, fig. 153.
90. Information, G. Putnam.

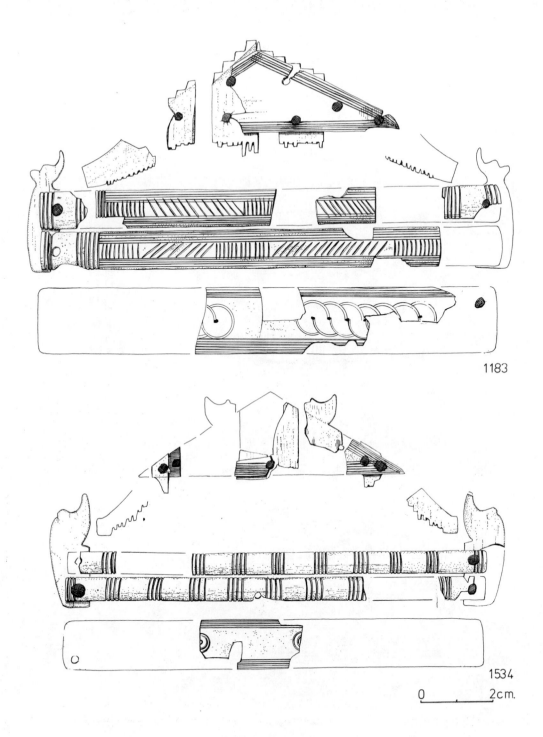

Fig. 1. Triangular scalloped combs with barred zoomorphic cases from Spong Hill (R. Penn after Hills 1977)

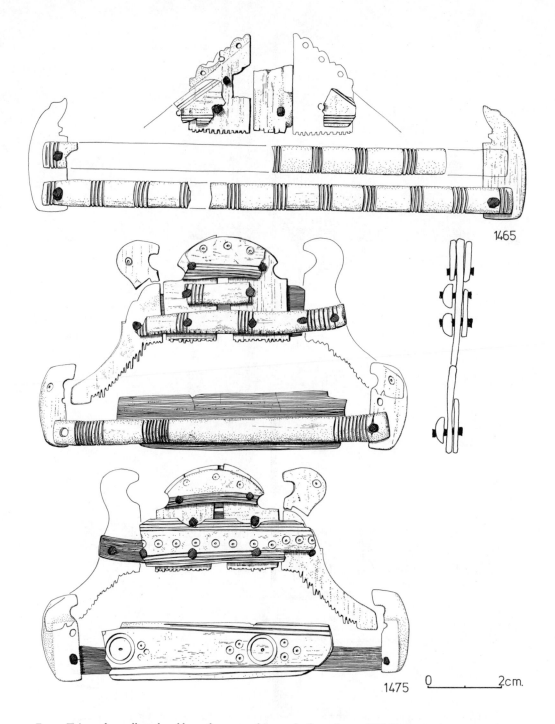

Fig. 2. Triangular scalloped and barred zoomorphic combs from Spong Hill (R. Penn after Hills 1977)

1465

1475

0   2cm.

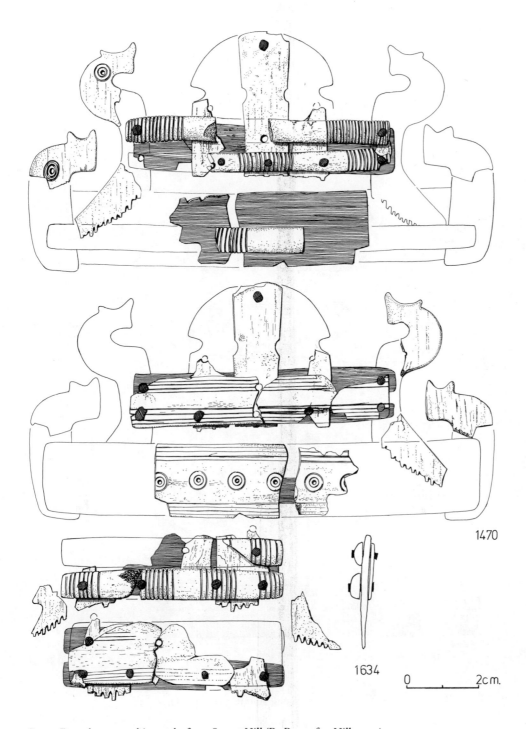

1470

1634

0   2cm.

Fɪɢ. 3. Barred zoomorphic combs from Spong Hill (R. Penn after Hills 1977)

121

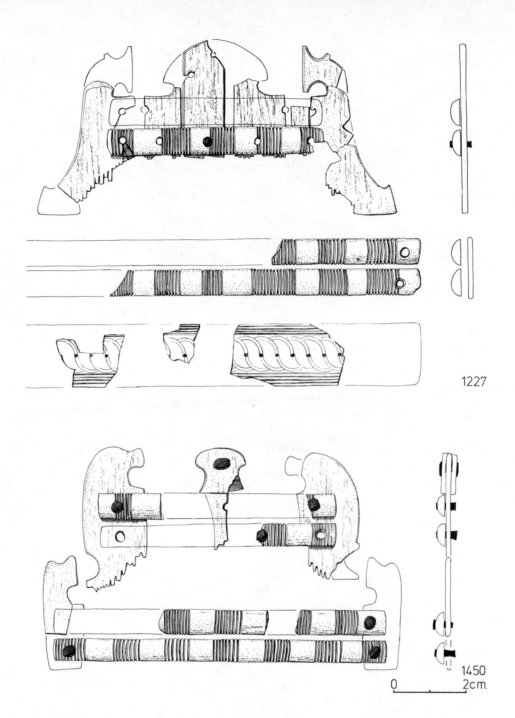

FIG. 4. Barred zoomorphic combs from Spong Hill (R. Penn after Hills 1977)

1227

1450

0   2cm.

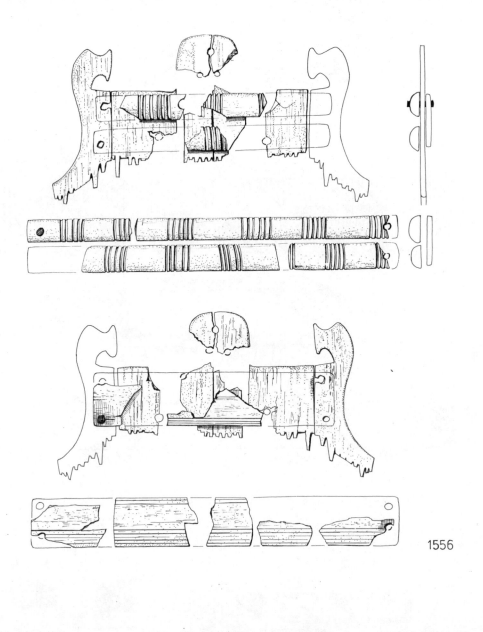

1556

0   2cm.

FIG. 5. Barred zoomorphic combs from Spong Hill (R. Penn after Hills 1977)

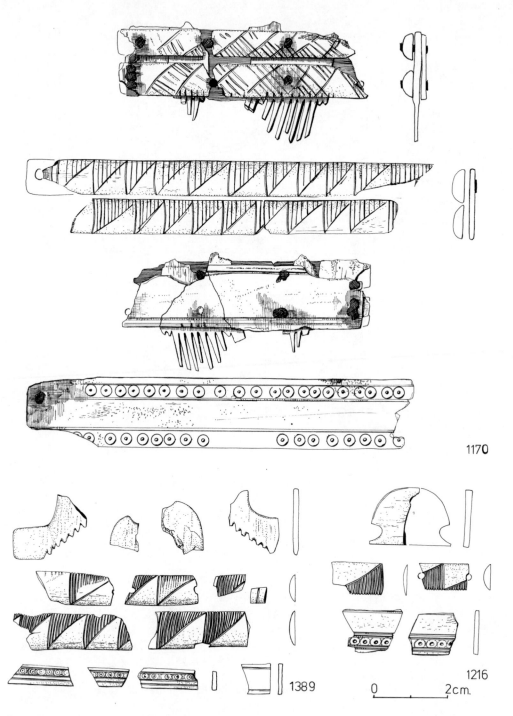

FIG. 6. Barred zoomorphic combs from Spong Hill (R. Penn after Hills 1977)

N

0 ————— 10 m.

● barred comb

▲ early
cruciform
brooch

○ cremation

Fig. 7. Spong Hill, North Elmham, Norfolk 1972–8 (omitting area to east of cemetery): distribution of zoomorphic barred combs and early cruciform brooches

7

Distribution maps and England in the first two phases

VERA I. EVISON

Most of the knowledge of the earliest Anglo-Saxon period in England up to now has been dependent on the study of artefacts, mainly from cemeteries, and their distribution. For a long time Dr Myres's study of early pottery provided almost the only indication of Germanic settlements of the fourth and fifth centuries, and this information was derived almost exclusively from the pots used for cremation burials. Somewhat later, early examples of glass and metalwork were identified, this information being derived almost exclusively from inhumation graves. The distribution maps show the earliest Germanic pottery mainly scattered throughout the area north of the Thames, and the earliest metal and glass in Germanic graves mainly confined to the area south of the Thames, the two sections only meeting along the line of the Thames itself. Interpretations of these maps have tended to be, on the one hand, that as there is little early Germanic pottery south of the Thames there is no substantial early settlement there, and on the other, that glass and metalwork indicate an integrated group of Germanic settlers south of the Thames. Both views are too generalized, and must be reconsidered to take account of a variety of new discoveries.

Material evidence from settlement sites has not yet been retrieved or published in sufficient quantity to be satisfactorily usable as a check on the more plentiful evidence known from cemeteries, so that a balanced view of the situation has been unattainable. It could be that settlement material south of the Thames might include evidence of just as much early pottery as the cremations indicate north of the Thames. Conversely, settlement material north of the Thames might suggest that early glass and metalwork was just as plentiful as found in inhumation graves to the south. The remnants found in settlement sites are not generally very numerous, however, compared with burial sites, and up to now they have not made much impression on distribution maps.

Very important information, however, has been forthcoming from the more recent excavations of cremation cemeteries, where the contents of the pots have been minutely sieved and examined, at Loveden, Lincs., for example, and particularly at the extensive cemetery of Spong Hill, Norfolk. The results already show that far larger numbers of glass vessels were included in the funeral conflagrations than was formerly suspected, so that it is probable that distribution maps show a preponderance of glass south of the Thames simply because the chances of survival or detection are greater in an inhumation than in a cremation. Pointers are that this also applies to metalwork.

It is clear, then, that we must treat distribution maps with caution, and that reliable conclusions will not be possible until much more data is available in the form of well-excavated and published settlements and cremation cemeteries. In the meantime conclusions must be temporary and tentative. One main point which is certain as to distribution is that the ritual of cremation prevails north of the Thames and of inhumation south of the Thames, and it is probable that this was due in the first place to differences of tribal origins and beliefs. Statistical relationships of the contents of urns and graves cannot be assessed with the data at present available, but the impression gained in a cemetery where both rites are present is that the same kinds of objects were likely to be associated with both rituals at any one time.

It is recognized that Germanic tribes were mingled to a considerable extent on the Continent before migration, and correspondences between groups of artefacts, types of burial customs, and identifiable tribes cannot be drawn with certainty. Even more extensive mixture of tribes is evident after their arrival in this country, and the number of times a new party of settlers arrived, the different localities of the many ports at which they landed, and the subsequent movements on land of the immigrants present a complexity of dispersion and amalgamation which can never be clearly followed. However, in spite of this, distribution maps often show definite patterns which invite interpretation. The presence of the same type of object in different places could mean the presence of people of the same tribe because of travel of a temporary nature or permanent settlement, or the marketing area of a product brought about by movement of the craftsman, of the objects, or, in the case of cast metal objects, by the movement of models or moulds. When reduced to the minimum effect, however, whichever of these apply, the distribution map must indicate some connection of one of these kinds between the find spots. There is therefore some value in collecting this type of evidence, but individual distribution maps on their own are likely to be misleading, and no reliable conclusions can be drawn until widespread and accurate examination has been carried out on all available material.

Dr Myres's study of pottery[1] was guided by the recorded historical facts, and has been assembled according to the phases dictated by these facts. The two earliest are of interest here: (1) the phase of overlap and controlled settlement, AD

360–410; (2) the phase of transition, AD 410–50. Objects produced in the first phase are known from datable contexts on the Continent. They have been regarded as scarce or entirely absent in this country, the small number recorded being regarded as long-lasting survivors in Anglo-Saxon contexts. The numbers found are increasing, however, and where they are deposited as part of contemporary grave furniture in a Germanic cemetery in this country, it must be regarded as probable that the grave was dug in the period AD 360–410 or that the person in that grave had been wearing or using those objects in that period although he may have survived to be buried at a later date. Not all objects can be closely dated, and the life of some extends through both periods, but a useful limit can be assigned to some.

Studies concentrated on the fourth and fifth centuries can now be entered into with far more confidence since the publication of the most important Germanic graves of this period on the Continent between the rivers Elbe and Loire.[2] The presence in Gaul of *laeti* of Germanic origin in the third century is known from historical records, but this work makes clear that, quite apart from these early settlers, many Germanic newcomers appeared in this territory during the second half of the fourth century. They can be distinguished from the Gallo-Roman population by their burial customs: they inhumed their dead, providing the men with weapons and belt mounts, and the women with brooches and pins, and both with pottery, glass, and bronze vessels. The total effect is that of a Gallo-Germanic civilization, illustrated by graves which contained both Germanic styles in weapons and ornament, and also the contemporary products of local factories turning out wheel-thrown pottery, glass vessels, and bronze work. These people can only be Germanic men and women, with their own tribal leaders, who were given land in return for military service by treaty. A few of these may have been Saxons, Alemanni, and other Germanic people from east of the Rhine, but the majority were probably Franks. A number of these burial grounds continued in existence without any break into the normal Frankish cemeteries of the sixth century and later, so that the population must have remained much the same, without any major displacements or migrations. Graves containing identical material have been found in Britain, where there are some graves which contain exactly the same groups of objects and which must be contemporary. Some of this material is that which was earlier identified as Frankish and coming from northern France and Belgium.[3]

Connections between northern France and Britain have already been noted for the second half of the fourth century in the metal buckles and other belt fittings associated with the Roman army. A great deal of attention has been lavished on this bronze and silver accoutrement[4] as much of it is accurately dated by association with coins. Many of the buckle loops bear zoomorphic decoration and these fall into two main categories, those with an animal head at each end of the loop at the base of the tongue, and those with a dolphin head on the loop each side of the point of the tongue. The first type is the more common on the Continent by far,[5] and the few provenanced in Britain are no doubt imports. Both types appear in various guises, and sometimes the two are amalgamated so that four heads appear on the loop, the pair near the tongue point sometimes being transformed into an animal by the addition of an ear.[6] The amount of information available on the whole group of related belt mounts is constantly increasing with new finds, and it is evident that any further work on the subject must take into equal consideration finds both British and continental.

The dolphin series is particularly of interest in this country as part of it has a special relationship to Britain, and it may be that a meaningful grouping can be achieved if the following six variants of the dolphin type of loop are considered separately. Illustrations referred to as H/D are from Hawkes and Dunning 1967, and there have been many fresh finds since that publication which could be added.

Variant a[1] Realistic dolphins with curling tails; perforated lugs on the tails to hinge on the bar which also holds the tongue. The curling tails fitted in with volutes on the base of the tongue. (H/D type IIA, fig. 17e), (distribution map fig. 8.)

Variant a[2] The curling tails converted to animal heads. (H/D type IIA), (fig. 5a and distribution map fig. 8.)

Variant b Realistic dolphins, bobbed tails. (e.g. Vermand, H/D fig. 6a.)

Variant c Dolphin bodies merge directly into the hinge bar. (H/D type IA, fig. 13, a–h, k, m–o, 14.)

Variant d Loop and a plate decorated with perforations cast in one piece. (H/D type IIB, fig. 19, a, b.)[7]

Variant e Degenerate, geometric copies with long, narrow plates. (H/D type IA, fig. 13, i, j, l.)

Variant f Degenerate copies with a pair of outward facing horses' heads on the loop with long, narrow plates. (H/D type IB, fig. 15, 16.)

Of these, variants b, c, and d occur abroad as well as in Britain, and it is probable that the larger numbers on the Continent indicate that they were produced there and imported to this country. In fact, none of variant b has been found in England, unless a new stray find of a buckle fragment on the Anglo-Saxon cemetery site at Orpington, Kent, may be allocated to this category. The reason for the cutting-off of the tail was to make room for a double tongue. The largest number of published examples abroad of variant b (seven) come from northern France, so that this may well be where they were produced, as suggested by Martin[8] for buckles of Champdolent type. They do, however, also occur in Germany, Switzerland, and Hungary. Variant c buckles occur in northern France and Belgium, but they are also numerous in Germany. Variant d are too few to have a significant distribution. Variants a, e, and f are peculiar to Britain. A secondary development in Variant a is apparent in the conversion of the tips of the tails into animal heads (a[2]), and three out of the seven of this variety were found in the later context of an Anglo-Saxon cemetery. The a[1] buckles are confined to Roman sites with the exception of the buckle from the Dover cemetery, and occur in more outlying sites to the west and north (fig. 8).

The dating of these buckles has been discussed before.[9] Many were found in Roman contexts of the end of the fourth century, and some were found in Anglo-Saxon graves.

There are other groups of finds which illustrate Germanic presence at this time. To the years around AD 400 belong the knives with inlaid patterns of bronze or silver on the blades which are dated by association with zoomorphic buckles at Landifay, Misery, and Oudenburg, the distribution being mostly in northern France with one in southern England and three in the Rhineland.[10]

The situation is different in regard to glass. Glass vessels at this time were mostly produced in northern Gaul and the Rhineland, and quite a number of 'late Roman' glasses have been recorded in Anglo-Saxon graves.[11] It is not possible, however, to allocate these forms precisely to before or after AD 400. A number of them were in production at the end of the fourth century, but continued to appear at the beginning of the fifth century. It is not insignificant, however, that most of the forms found in the graves of the fourth and fifth centuries between the Loire and Elbe are also to be found in Anglo-Saxon graves in this country.

The small bowl with pinched-out vertical lugs as found at Helle[12] does not occur here, unless one may count the unique specimen with doubled rim from Faversham,[13] which might, in any case, have come from the Roman part of that cemetery. The shallow bowl form with indented walls and unsmoothed rim has been found at Saxon cemetery sites at High Down, Bifrons, Eastry and Milton-next-Sittingbourne;[14] none of them, unfortunately, with identifiable associations. A hemispherical bowl with pushed-in folded foot and rolled-out rim was found in grave 53 at High Down.[15] A hemispherical bowl with unsmoothed rim occurred at Bifrons,[16] and also at Great Chesterford, grave 33,[17] in a grave which could belong to the first half of the fifth century. A mould-blown shallow bowl with unsmoothed rim was found at Selmeston in Sussex.[18]

The type of cone beaker with slightly kicked, just stable base, and unsmoothed rim occurs at Chessell Down, Isle of Wight,[19] Mucking, Essex, grave 992, and with combed trails at Selmeston, Sussex.[20] Another cone beaker with unsmoothed rim, but with indented walls and vertical snicked trails belongs to grave 60 at Alfriston.[21] Also a product of about AD 400 is the claw-beaker from Mucking, grave 843.[22]

Some of the brooch types worn by Germanic women on the Continent from the late fourth to late fifth century have also been found in this country, and a distribution map of two of these types, supporting arm brooches and equal-arm brooches,[23] shows them situated north of the Thames, mainly in the vicinity of the Icknield Way. Another early type, the tutulus form, was found in grave 106 at Abingdon, and there are the possible remains of a pair at Little Wilbraham.[24] A well-preserved example has been noted at Kirmington, Lincs.,[25] and it has also been realized that the backplate in grave III at Dorchester must have belonged to a tutulus and not an applied brooch.[26]

There are a few iron bow brooches, some of which must have been made about AD 400, e.g. Barrington, Cambs.,[27] and two at High Down, Sussex, one with a bronze pin remaining (fig. 1a), and one inlaid with bronze strips (fig. 1b).[28] These resemble iron bow brooches as in graves 546 (no associations) and 968 (with mid fifth-century objects) at Krefeld Gellep, and in a fourth-century cremation pot with a tutulus brooch, etc., at Westerwanna, grave 1654.[29] On the drawing of the Westerwanna brooch parallel lines are shown on the bow; these are suggestive of the presence originally of inlaid strips, and of the probability that inlaid decoration might be more common on iron bow brooches than so far suspected. Another inlaid bow brooch has been found at Altnerding, grave 280, for instance, and a pair in grave 529 at Frénouville, Calvados.[30] An *Armbrustfibel mit Trapezfuss* has been found at Cirencester.[31] There is therefore a considerable amount of glass and metalwork to be added to the witness of pottery for the existence of Germanic people in this country before AD 410.

In the first half of the fifth century, the second phase, forms of personal possessions had changed. One kind of zoomorphic buckle had evolved, for instance, which was cast in one piece with a small trapezoidal plate. It occurred mostly in the Meuse and Rhine valleys, as well as in northern France and between the mouths of the Elbe and Weser, the latter examples presumably taken there by Germanic soldiers returning to their homelands.[32] A few found their way to the south of England, one however, getting as far as Yorkshire (distribution map fig.

9). Böhme distinguished three types of this buckle, and his Trier–Samson type, which is ornamented with animals, is the largest with a loop 6–6.2 cm wide. To this type he ascribes the buckle of unknown provenance in the Douglas Collection at the Ashmolean Museum, although it has no trapezoid plate and is only 5.5 cm wide. A buckle from grave 23 at Bifrons, Kent, found with an early cruciform brooch and a late Roman knife handle (fig. 2a), seems to be a devolved version of the Douglas Collection buckle type, related to the Frilford buckle.[33] To his Haillot type (5–5.8 cm wide) belong the Long Wittenham buckle,[34] one of unknown provenance from Canterbury Museum,[35] and one from Nunburnholme, near Pocklington, Yorks.[36] His Krefeld-Gellep type is smaller (1.5–3.9 cm wide) with degenerate animal heads, and there are five of these known in England so far: Mucking graves 91[37] and 979 (fig. 6c), Alfriston grave 14,[38] Sarre,[39] a second one from Sarre (fig. 2b). Of these contexts, Long Wittenham grave 57 was noted as a woman's grave by the excavators in the nineteenth century, but the accompanying finds of knife and pot are not decisive if the sex is judged by the furniture in the grave. Alfriston No. 14, with a perforated coin, smaller buckle, single disc brooch, bronze tubular belt mount, and a spear, was certainly male, as was Mucking grave 979 described below.

This type of buckle was three times found on the Continent in connection with swords in scabbards decorated with bronze mounts and bronze chape with the motif of a man's head between birds, i.e., the two items presumably constitute a suite of sword and sword belt, and both were produced in the Meuse valley in the first half of the fifth century.[40] The sword scabbard type has occurred in this country at Abingdon and Petersfinger[41] (distribution map, fig. 9).

There is no need to reiterate details of quoit brooch style products which have been fully dealt with elsewhere.[42] They are certainly at a later stage of development than most of the continental examples of metalwork in late Roman tradition, and must begin in the first half of the fifth century. A point which cannot be overstressed is the fact that while a proportion of all other zoomorphic buckle types in this country occur on Roman sites, with some in Anglo-Saxon graves perhaps as survivors from the previous century, not a single fragment of quoit brooch style has been found in any context except that of a grave of Germanic type situated in a cemetery which continued in use as a normal pagan Anglo-Saxon cemetery. There is no doubt whatsoever, therefore, of the Germanic nationality of their owners.

That it was a fighting man among the Germanic settlers who wore the Mucking type of buckle is fairly certain, for the belt on which it was fixed must have been sturdy, being of leather and 4.7 cm wide. Like contemporary buckles from Austria, Yugoslavia, Holland, and France, it comprises familiar and well-tried forms, techniques, and patterns, but also exhibits features not known elsewhere. It makes extensive use of the technique of inlaying silver on bronze which was used on some of the buckles of the period AD 380–420 in northern France and Germany;[43] but which does not seem to have been continued after that time either there or in other regions besides Britain. Nor does the form of the quoit brooch itself appear to have been kept alive except in England, and this particular development of the late Roman animals in a two-dimensional curvilinear form is also peculiarly insular.

The distribution of objects in this style is mainly confined to Kent, the lower Thames valley, Sussex, and the Isle of Wight.[44] The bronze tubular mounts, which are closely connected by reason of the quoit brooch style animals on one of them, follow the same distribution with extension further west into the upper Thames valley and Wiltshire.

Now a few closely related objects have turned up in cemeteries newly excavated in northern France. At Réville in Normandy a Merovingian grave contained the first bronze tube of quoit brooch style[45] found outside this country, and one in fact which is actually ornamented with a pair of backward-glancing animals. It is a strap distributor similar to the example from Croydon, with an oblong opening in the middle of one side and a projection on the other side for some kind of attachment. Other details are very like those of the insular tubes, i.e. division into panels with parallel line decoration, and a triangular projection at one end of the tube, but there are differences in the construction, and, judging from the drawing, possibly also in the animal ornament, so that it is not certain whether it was manufactured in England or whether it is a local copy. However, as the grave in which it appeared, No. 147, III contained, among other things, a shoe-shaped belt rivet, the grave itself cannot be dated before the sixth century.[46]

A quoit brooch, such as has only been found in England, was amongst the grave goods in a cemetery at Bénouville, Calvados,[47] excavated in the early nineteenth century (fig. 3). Its form is nearest to the brooch from Sarre,[48] for the pin was hinged on an inner ring in one piece with the outer band but separated from it by cut-out spaces. Part of the inner ring had broken away on the Bénouville brooch, and it appears from the drawing that another perforation was then made in the outer ring for the pin. At the opposite side of the centre space was the pin slot with a pin stop each side, and probably a second pair of pin stops in the outer zone. There are decorative line borders at the outer and inner edges of the outer band. On the inner ring there are radial double lines dividing it into panels, two of which are ornamented with a diagonal cross. The outer zone is also divided into panels, one blank by the pin slot, but each of the other eight containing a line drawing of a different creature with single contour. Five have the curling tail of the sea-lion,[49] three of them are looking forward and two are backward-glancing. Of the others, two appear to be quadrupeds, one forward- and one backward-looking, and one a bird. The nearest parallel is to be found in the single-line contour animals and diagonal crosses, both in panels, which occur on the quoit brooch at Lyminge, although the outer zone of the Howletts brooch also consists of sea-lions in panels, with masks in between. In the same way as the Réville bronze mount, the Lyminge brooch corresponds closely in form, and design to the products in England, the only difference being that the animals lack their flowing lines and ornamental quality, and are nearer in style to the Frankish animals.

There is a buckle from Amiens in northern France[50] (pl. XI, a) which compares closely with the Mitcham buckle[51] (pl. XI, b) in its over-all shape, cast in one piece except for the tongue, an openwork plate with curvilinear cross motifs, the end ornamented with two pairs of affronted animal heads. The small stamps used to decorate the surface are linked annulets and triangles arranged in 'fir-tree' lines. The curling terminals of the loop are different from those of the Mitcham loop, but find their match in the Orpington and Bishopstone buckles.[52] This is no doubt an import from England.

A similar southern England distribution also applies to wooden vessels with bronze bindings decorated in arcade and dot patterns or Christian motifs,[53] and which must have originated in western France. Iron buckles and purse mounts inlaid with other metals are likewise almost exclusively to be found in this southern area, with corresponding forms in the Seine, Meuse, and Rhine valleys, Switzerland and Thuringia.[54] In England further examples of inlaid iron objects have subsequently occurred at Mucking. Two inlaid iron buckles which have been detected by radiograph at Sewerby, Yorks.,[55] provide interesting additions to the other fifth-century buckle form from a northern site at Pocklington noted above. With few exceptions, all the find spots of the fifth-century objects discussed above occur south of the Thames, and on the Continent in northern France, the middle Meuse and Rhine valleys, Thuringia, and Switzerland.

Some of the glass forms, e.g. the stemmed beaker and the small bowl with constricted neck, span a period from about AD 400 to the end of the fifth century. These conform mainly to a southern distribution, the stemmed beakers coming from Howletts, Kent, Croydon, Surrey, and Burgh Castle, Suffolk, and the bowls from Howletts, Kent, Alfriston, Sussex, and Mucking, Essex.

The Kempston type of cone beaker was also produced during this period, and a number of new finds may be added to the list already known (fig. 10).[56] In grave 63 at Lyminge, Kent, was a version of the type which retains the wider, stable base of late Roman cones, and this, together with the fact that it is in a very light green glass, nearly colourless like the Cassington cone, indicates a date early in the fifth century. The fragments from cremation 1058 at Spong Hill are light bluish-green, also nearly colourless. The light yellowish metal of the cone from Anderlecht, Belgium, suggests that it was made by the producer responsible for the rest of the local group in the same metal, i.e. Pry, St Gillis, and one without provenance in Troyes museum. The olive green colour of the cone from Krefeld-Gellep grave 1850 and the fragments in Spong Hill cremation 1156 is also an early trait. By far the most splendid example has recently been found in the excavation of a house of the early Germanic period at Dankirke, near Ribe, Jutland; this is in a clear blue colour with trails in the same colour, but also embellished with two zones of opaque white trails. A bright colour, and the use of a second colour for decoration, are characteristics more customary for the Roman glass blowers than for their Germanic successors, and as often happens in connection with the glass trade in this period, the most elaborate and expensive version is found furthest from the production centre. The other new finds are in the light-green colour normal to the type which goes on into the sixth century, i.e. Mucking grave 924, Krefeld Gellep grave 1850, fragments in Spong Hill cremation 1602, and possibly a fragment in the fill of grave 2528 at Krefeld Gellep. At Vireux Molhain in the Meuse valley, a well-furnished grave coin-dated to *c*. AD 400 contained a fragment of a brown glass vessel, probably a Kempston-type cone, although as no part of the base was present it could equally well have been an earlier form with a folded foot.[57] It is likely, however, that this fragment is to be connected with the brown cone from Chessell Down which is presumed to be early because of its similarity to the cone in Guildown grave 56 which contained an early spear.[58] With the exception of the addition of the far-flung site in Denmark, the distribution of the Kempston type cone beakers remains much the same, i.e. the Rhine, northern France and Belgium, and isolated sites in Holland, Germany, and Czechoslovakia, while in England the distribution is mainly south of the Thames, with a concentration in Kent, suggesting the possibility of production of some cones at least in that county. The existence of the Danish cone and that in the American Swedish Institute said to have been found in Scandinavia, however, invites speculation on the probability that a re-examination of the Scandinavian glass vessels might increase the find spots in that region.

Britain, with a total of thirty-one, now has the highest number of these cone beakers, and the present distribution suggests two major production areas, in Kent and in the Rhineland. The recent addition of four cones at the one site of Spong Hill, however, illustrates how the balance may be altered at any time by intensive excavation at any one spot.

A distinctive type of spearhead amongst the weapons of these early Germanic men has a leaf-shaped blade and strong mid-rib which continues into a closed socket, and is closely related to the *Saufeder,* a 'winged' type of spear used for hunting. These are allocated to group B2 of Swanton's typology,[59] and noted as Germanic spear types prior to the settlement. An inlaid example with animal-headed 'wings' was found in the Vermand warrior's grave.[60] The distribution map of the *Saufeder* type shows a concentration, and therefore probably the production centre, between the Seine, Marne, and Moselle.[61] The midribbed type without 'wings' occurs in northern France and Belgium, e.g. at Misery,[62] Rhenen grave 833, Vermand grave 284.[63] In England there are graves containing this type of spear, which also contain other objects well represented in the Germanic graves in France and Belgium, e.g. Guildown grave 56 where the spear, tipped with a ferrule, was found with a glass cone beaker of Kempston type of the fifth century.[64] At Fairford, grave 2, such a spear was accompanied by an angular spear and a shield boss, and three repoussé discs on the shield of the type used for early applied brooches.[65] One of these spears, in grave 979 at Mucking, will be noted below (fig. 6f), and another occurred at Mucking in grave 869.

The spear Swanton type B1, which is rather like a spike, is a Nydam type, occurring at Helle, grave 1, and Furfooz.[66] The only early example in this country is at Harwell, which, if my supposition is right, is to be associated with an early fifth-century applied brooch, and not with later material.[67]

Recognized as one of the types of spear used by the Germanic men in France and Belgium is the 'corrugated' blade, occurring at e.g. Rhenen graves 819 and 829, Haillot grave 4, Eprave, Vert-la-Gravelle grave 6, and Abbeville Homblières.[68] A suggested British origin is difficult to support for the examples in England,[69] but if such models existed among the British at the time this would have encouraged the continued use of the similar types brought in by the Germanic mercenaries. The earlier corrugated spears, it has been noted, were frequently deposited with quoit brooch style metalwork. Amongst these are Swanton's type I1, but unfortunately the dates suggested by him for this type are based on a dating for the quoit brooch style to the late fifth century and early sixth century which is no longer sustained, and the middle decades of the fifth century are more likely for graves such as grave 50 at Worthy Park where it was found with an inlaid iron plate of Frankish connections, and in grave 14 at High Down where an inlaid purse mount and glass bowl also came from the Continent,[70] both graves containing a type I1 spear, i.e. a leaf-shaped blade with strickening above and a lunate fuller on the left-hand side of the blade.

The distribution of the I1 type follows the western and northern limits of the quoit brooch milieu.[71] The type I2, i.e. a leaf-shaped blade with lunate fuller, occurs in equally early contexts, still sometimes with Frankish objects, but also in one case with a Saxon hand-made bowl with faceted carination, and it has a distribution along the Thames as well as in counties to the north.[72]

Brooches lend themselves to more precise dating than spears, and with reference to applied brooches, Dr Böhme regards the simple, beaded circle type as belonging to AD 350–400, the geometric types, i.e. spirals, floriate cross, and star which are related to the chip-carving patterns on buckles, to AD 380–420, and the zoomorphic types to AD 400–50. This is certainly the general order in which they developed, but the dating for the zoomorphic types is not very firmly based, and the assumption that the cemeteries of East Shefford and Muids in which they occurred did not begin before the second half of the fifth century is not valid dating evidence. There are none of the earliest simple beaded type in Britain, although there are slightly later developments. Some of the five-scroll or floriate cross type in this country might have been made between AD 380–420, particularly that found at Abingdon with a tutulus brooch, but on the whole the incursion of applied brooches must have begun in the early fifth century. The areas reached by these early varieties of applied brooches correspond in general to the areas indicated by the quoit brooch style milieu.[73]

The saucer brooches ornamented with five running spirals have been regarded as a reliable indication of the presence of fifth-century Saxons, for they occur in a limited area between the mouths of the Elbe and Weser before the migration, and further developments of the species take place only in England. Dating of the development stages cannot be accurate, but it is assumed that brooches with five-scrolls are more or less contemporary, and that six or more scrolls come later. That this may be too facile a conclusion may be inferred from the fact that the construction varies even within the five-scroll series, and coexistence of types can be seen from the one grave no. 100 at Abingdon where a five- and six-scroll variant occurred together. Nevertheless, it seems safe to assume that a five-scroll type, which began on the Continent about AD 400, was not made later than the middle of the fifth century, and the map (fig. 11) shows its distribution in England. This is surprisingly widespread. The route along the Icknield Way is only sparsely indicated, but an example of the early type with applied cast centre does occur at Caistor-by-Norwich. A nucleus of find spots is apparent in the upper Thames area, with the usual occurrences on the periphery of

Andredesweald, but there is also a scatter further north, between the upper Thames and the Wash.

Disc brooches, often ornamented with ring-and-dot motifs, also occur in contexts of the first half of the fifth century, and appear to be related to the saucer brooches in origin and distribution.[74]

The archaeological evidence for the presence of the Jutes in Kent in the fifth century, is based mainly on cruciform brooches and pottery. The comprehensive study of J. Reichstein lists only twelve early cruciform brooches from Kent, and of these only two, both from Faversham, are related to cruciform brooches in the Jutland peninsula. His No. 810 belongs to the Midlum type which occurs mostly in England, in the Midlands, and No. 811 belongs to the Oxbøl type,[75] which however consists of these two brooches only, and is an unusual, undatable type. They therefore suggest no more than a tenuous connection with Jutland, and that more in a direction from west to east than east to west. The other Jutish objects in Kent, square-headed brooches and bracteates, do not make their appearance before the end of the fifth century and the beginning of the sixth, and so fall outside the present enquiry.

The distributions of the objects of periods 1 and 2 considered above therefore constitute an assemblage of data which must contain useful clues to the nature of the earliest settlements, and which will be subjected to a preliminary attempt at analysis at the end of this article. Many of the objects have been found in datable contexts although it is only a percentage which is so firmly documented. Complete closed finds in the form of inhumation graves containing a full set of possessions constitute the most reliable evidence for date and identity of the occupant. Some of the graves at Mucking are well furnished and four have therefore been selected for early presentation here as the contents are particularly interesting and valuable for the establishment of the settlement of Germanic warriors and women in this country at about AD 400.

Amongst the graves excavated in Saxon cemetery II at Mucking are four well-furnished graves which belong definitely to the first half of the fifth century, and probably to the earliest decades. One, a woman's grave No. 987 (fig. 4a–d) contained a bow brooch, a *Stützarmfibel* similar to the Mahndorf type,[76] as well as a crude version of a small-long brooch with square head, flat knobs, spatulate foot, and a knife. Also in the grave was a dolphin and horse's head buckle with a long rectangular plate bearing a pattern of a lozenge in the middle and cross symbols each side. Large, flat pieces of lead were laid over the top of the body. The other woman's grave, No. 989 (figs. 4e–g, 5), contained a dolphin buckle loop with curling tails zoomorphized by dotted eyes, and two bow brooches, one a 'Howletts' type with knob-ended, upturned foot, and the other, with a small rectangular headplate and single top knob, and a slightly upturned foot is related to the *Stützarmfibel*. Both brooches have a ring attached to the head, but do not appear to have been linked together as the first brooch was linked by a bronze chain to an iron pin. Also in the grave was a finger ring, beads, buckle, knife, bronze and silver fragments, and a faceted-angle pot. The third grave, No. 979 (fig. 6), was a man's grave with a closed socket spear with a leaf-shaped blade and pronounced mid-rib (Swanton type B2). A bronze zoomorphic buckle with fixed plate is cast in one with the accompanying mount with tubular belt end, and for the opposite end there is a rectangular bronze mount with tubular edging. This latter mount is slightly narrower, and must have been cut down after damage at the original rivet hole. There is also a faceted bronze strip in the grave which would have been used to fix the buckle strap to the belt. A rosette belt attachment holds a free ring. Besides a pair of tweezers, a knife, a fire steel and other iron fragments also in the grave, there was an iron penannular brooch which was worn on the right shoulder.

Although the buckles in graves 987 and 989 were made in England, the whole of the contents of these three graves is closely related to the contents of graves of Germanic people buried between the Loire and the Elbe in the first years of the fifth century. At Rhenen, for example, one may compare the belt mounts and spear in grave 839,[77] and the buckle in graves 834 and 842. Iron annular and penannular brooches in weapon graves of this period have not attracted much attention, presumably because they were ignored in early finds, but a single one is often present in a man's grave, as may be seen from Rhenen grave 818[78] and grave 819,[79] and some were found in cremations at Spong Hill.[80]

The 'Luton' type of brooch and the bow brooch of similar construction in grave 989 have their origins in the *Stützarmfibel* of the Elbe–Weser coastal region, but the spring support on the brooch in grave 987 and the use of a chain in grave 989 are both characteristics of the *Stützarmfibel* types which are found on the lower Rhine and further south. The bronze bow brooch with upturned foot in grave 989 finds most of its closest parallels in England and northern Gaul,[81] even though the existence of a few versions in iron may mean that the distribution could be wider than so far indicated by the bronze brooches only.[82] All of the brooches, then, in graves 987 and 989 are recognizable as continental types, but the unique character of each proposes a possible maker in this country. The same holds good for the buckle in grave 979, which appears to be the only buckle with fixed plate cast in one piece with its belt end. The plate is unusually small in proportion to the loop. As to size, and the detail of ring stamp on plate and loop, it is most like the buckle in Rhenen grave 834.[83] Others similar, of the Haillot type and all with ring-and-dot stamps, are from Samson, Tongres, and Rahmstorf,[84] and the Haillot type occurs throughout the area between the Loire and Elbe. The spear, penannular brooch, and fire steel no doubt came from the Loire–Elbe region, but the three buckles and probably all the brooches could have been made at the site of Mucking itself.

Another grave (272, fig. 7) of the early fifth century contained significant warrior equipment. As well as a featureless iron pin, rivet, and knife there was an unusual buckle and spear, and a very distinctive shield boss with a concave, conical dome (fig. 7f). This type was discussed by Böhme who groups together variants with straight-sided and concave-sided cones. Some were covered with silver sheet, stamps on two of them establishing them as products of official workshops of the late Roman army,[85] and distribution is mainly on the course of the Rhine and in northern France. The curved conical shape of the Mucking boss is nearest to the shape of the boss in the well-known Vermand warrior grave,[86] and to the boss in Rhenen grave 833,[87] and the contexts of these well-furnished graves gives a date in the decades near AD 400. The Vermand grave contained a military buckle and is allocated to the period AD 380–420, while the Rhenen grave 833 also contained a belt set and is dated to the first half of the fifth century.[88] The spear has an angular blade, stepped section, and closed socket, presumably to be classed in Swanton's type L, although most of these have concave profiles and split sockets. There are, however, two others with straight sides and closed sockets from Droxford, Hants., and Stapleford Park, Leics.[89] It is significant that the buckle in the Mucking grave 272 is of iron, kidney-shaped, and ornamented with inlaid red and yellow metal strips. As neither the spearhead nor this type of shield boss can have been in use after the middle of the fifth century it provides reliable dating for the metal-inlaid work on the accompanying buckle.

It has been argued that the consumer goods which provide most of the evidence for these periods represent products which were available to everyone and do not necessarily indicate Germanic nationality.[90] It may be a reasonable assumption that in the Roman army members of Germanic tribes were not distinguished by special equipment, but in the civilian world in the absence of evidence of the dress of Romano-Britons, Gauls, and others, this is difficult to refute. It is, however, possible to be certain that an individual who wore these brooches, buckles, etc. in Germanic fashion, and was buried with Germanic type ritual in a cemetery that continued in use as a normal Frankish or Anglo-Saxon cemetery was without doubt Germanic.

It has been noted above that a number of types of object belonging to the decades just before and after AD 400 have occurred in graves in this country. At Mucking complete, well-furnished graves of this time have been found, similar in all respects to graves between the Loire and the Elbe, save for the absence of wheel-thrown pottery. Dolphin buckles form one of the groups of objects which show connections with northern Gaul, and they are fairly widespread in England. Of the variety noted here, a[1] buckles occur on Roman sites, some as far west as Wales, but the typologically later a[2] type occurs sometimes in Anglo-Saxon graves.

A distribution almost exclusively along the Icknield Way is shown first by the supporting arm brooches, closely followed by the equal-arm brooches, as it was by the pedestal *Buckelurnen*.[91] With a source in the region between the mouths of the Elbe and the Weser, these possessions clearly denote Saxons, although with the supporting arm brooches there is also a connection with northern France. The same source must originally have been responsible for the spiral-decorated saucer brooches (fig. 11) and some early applied brooches, although the latter also look towards northern France. The spiral-decorated saucer brooches in England follow much the same pattern as the supporting arm and equal-arm brooches, although with fewer find spots near the Icknield Way and more south of the Thames. The applied brooches are also present along the Icknield Way but with a concentration in the upper Thames area, and a number south of the Thames. Although the rest of the groups of objects considered follow a somewhat similar pattern, the emphasis is there on the perimeter of Andredesweald south of the Thames and in the Thames valley, with only a slight scatter further north and along the Icknield Way, i.e. the quoit brooch style, bronze tubular mounts, metal inlaid work, and the Kempston type of cone beaker, all with definite Frankish connections. Here and there is evidence of contact with the Rhineland, Thuringia, Switzerland, and Jutland.

There are no doubt many possible interpretations of these data, and the situation during at least the first fifty years of the fifth century must have been extremely fluid and complex, the various spots on the distribution maps probably reflecting conditions which may have changed dramatically from year to year during the half-century. It is difficult to ignore, however, the pattern of a ring of settlements round Andredesweald, with defensible early hilltop sites at High Down, Bishopstone, and Mucking, with a defended position at Portchester, and it may be that this pattern indicates an early defence plan of a limited area. The positions manned are each side of the Thames, so ensuring vigilance against invaders along the whole of its course to the upper reaches, and in the unforested areas facing the Channel in Kent, Sussex, the Isle of Wight, and Hampshire, the west being protected in the Salisbury area. The evidence suggests that these garrisons were manned in the first place by the invited federates who were issued with equipment based on Roman army models, i.e. the quoit brooch style buckles, bronze tubular mounts, inlaid metalwork, etc.

The types of finds and rite of cremation along the Icknield Way point to a much more exclusively Saxon origin, although they are not completely divorced from the finds south of the Thames, and the two groups mingle in the upper Thames area. Various interpretations regarding the Icknield Way suggest themselves, that it was a Saxon invasion route being one that has already been put forward. That it was selected as a line of defence hardly seems likely as there are no natural features to make this feasible, although it could have been regarded as a demarcation line. The reason for the spread of goods along this line may, however, merely be because it was an easily negotiable highway along which merchants found it convenient and safe to travel.

In the southern area the pattern of goods in common suggests a central source of supply. The character of the buckles and other metal fittings is clearly based on the equipment issued to the late Roman army, and some of it, at least, must surely represent an issue of equipment to Germanic federates financed by the Britons. Some of the equipment shows connections with Christianity (the buckles from Mucking grave 987 and Mitcham, and cf. the buckle from Amiens). This may be no more than a reflection of trade connections with northern Gaul where metal and glass objects were often ornamented with Christian symbols, and with the recorded continued intercourse of the Christian church between the two countries until the Council of Arles in AD 455. There is a possibility, however, of reading a meaning into Christian symbols, and to associate them with one side or other engaged in the battles of the Pelagian controversy. The connections with northern Gaul, however, are more likely to be the result of recruitment of Germanic mercenaries from the area between the Loire and the Elbe, an area where there are inhumation graves of Germanic warriors and women from AD 350 onwards which are identical to the types found at Mucking.

With entry to the country thus effectively blocked by federates along the southern coast and the banks of the Thames, it may be that invasion by Saxons was able to take place along the Icknield Way. Alternatively, the differences in burial rite and possessions could indicate another federate settlement as in the south, but of a different tribe. The ring of defence seems to have been successful in repulsing any invasion by Saxons in the early fifth century, for there is comparatively little trace in the southern counties of cremation, handmade pottery, and their early brooch types.

The beginning of a ring of defences enclosing the southern counties this way in the first half of the fifth century must be connected with the powerful British party seeking to protect the richest part of the country from the threat of invasion from all sides. During the second quarter of the fifth century the few records there are tell of connections between the church in Britain and the church in France, for St Germanus crossed the Channel in AD 429 and 446–7 to combat Pelagianism, and the latest contact was at the time of the Council of Arles in AD 455. It is more understandable why these channels of communication remained open if the theory is acceptable that the mercenary company of Franks and others who came on invitation to Britain had been living in France and Belgium, and not in the lands beyond the Rhine. After AD 455, however, the contacts were severed by these Germanic mercenaries who had rejected a British overlord, presumably Christianity as well, and remained as independent settlers.

It is evident that the area most thickly populated by a variety of Germanic people was the valley of the upper Thames, where the two cultures met. The distribution maps seem to establish two distinct areas, one north of the Thames, settled mainly by Saxons who came directly over the North Sea from the land between the mouths of the Elbe and the Weser, and one south of the Thames, settled mainly by Franks, with a sprinkling of Alamanni and Thuringi, who had come from northern Gaul and neighbouring areas west of the Rhine. Their possessions establish the fact that both parties must have arrived at about the same time in the early part of the fifth century, but whether it was a simultaneous settlement, or whether it was a matter of cause and effect with a short space in between, it is not possible to decipher from the archaeological evidence as dating methods cannot be refined down to months or even to decades.

What it does suggest is that the distributions north of the Thames could represent a main body of Saxons who came, probably by invitation in the first instance, from their homeland in free Germany beyond the Rhine. It may have been on the occasion of their switch from a role as allies to one as predatory settlers, which may not have been long after, that Germanic federate assistance was called in from the surviving authorities of the Roman Empire in northern Gaul. Vestiges of the earlier material culture of the Romans are evident in southern England and on the nearest facing Channel shores in the shape of quoit brooch and associated metalwork and glassware deposited in graves of Germanic type, while these artefacts are mostly absent from the cemeteries north of the Thames where Saxon cremation urns and Saxon metalwork predominate. The condition of part of the country then supports the statement of the Gaulish chronicler under AD 442: 'Britain, distressed by various defeats and other

happenings, becomes subject to the Saxons'.[92] According to Gildas the appeal to
Aetius in 446 was not answered, but he had heard vague reports of earlier appeals,
and it looks as though one of these was answered, hardly by the type of Roman
reoccupation often suggested, but at least by shiploads of Germanic federates,
already stationed in Roman territory on the Continent, to the southern part of
Britain.

Distribution map 1

Dolphin buckle loops with tails

(H/D refers to Hawkes and Dunning, 1961)

Variant a¹

1. Caerwent, Gwent. H/D fig. 17b.
2. Dover, Kent. Evison, 1965, fig. 9e.
3. Dragonby, Humberside. Hawkes, 1974, 387, fig. 3,4; Eagles, 1979, fig. 111, 3.
4. Leicester, Leicestershire. H/D fig. 17i.
5. Lincoln, Lincolnshire. Hawkes, 1974, 387, fig. 3,5; Eagles, 1979, fig. 111, 1.
6. Lullingstone, Kent. H/D fig. 17j.
7. Lydney, Gloucestershire. H/D fig. 17k.
8. St Albans, Hertfordshire. H/D fig. 18d.
9. Silchester, Hampshire. H/D fig. 18g.
10. Water Newton, Cambridgeshire. H/D fig. 18h.

Variant a²

11. Caistor-by-Norwich, Norfolk. H/D fig. 17c.
12. Duston, Northamptonshire. H/D 17f.
13. Lakenheath, Suffolk. H/D fig. 18j.
14. Mitcham, London. H/D fig. 18f.
15. Mucking, Essex, grave 989, fig. 5a.
16. North Wraxall, Wiltshire. H/D fig. 18b.
17. Winchester, Hampshire, grave 37. Clarke, 1970, fig. 4, 92.*

Distribution map 2

Fixed plate buckles, and 'Abingdon'-type swords

(H/D refers to Hawkes and Dunning, 1961)

Buckles

1. Alfriston, East Sussex, grave 14. Evison, 1965, fig. 24d.
2. Long Wittenham, Oxfordshire. H/D fig. 20g.
3. Mucking, Essex, grave 91. Evison, 1968, fig. 3c.
4. Mucking, Essex, grave 979, fig. 6c.

* One more buckle of variant a¹ has now been published from Winchester: Clark, 1979: fig. 100, 603 (not mapped).

5. Numburnholme, nr. Pocklington, Humberside. Bowman, 1855, 62–3, pl. XII. 8; Eagles, 1979, fig. 116, 1.
6. Sarre, Kent. H/D fig. 20h.
7. Sarre, Kent. Maidstone Museum. fig. 2b.
8. No provenance, Canterbury Museum. H/D fig. 19 bis b.

Swords

1. Abingdon, Oxon, grave 42, Evison, 1965, fig. 22 c–f, j, k.
2. Petersfinger, Wilts, grave 21, Evison, 1965, fig. 18 a–d.

Distribution map 3

Kempston-type glass cone beakers

(Numbers preceded by E, in brackets, refer to the numbers given to the cones in Evison 1972.)

England

1. Kempston, Bedfordshire, Light green, ht. 26.2 cm, d.m. (diameter of mouth) 9 cm (E No. 1, fig. 8).
2. Alfriston, East Sussex, grave 39. Light green, ht. 29 cm, d.m. 10 cm (E No. 2).
3. Alfriston, East Sussex, grave 43. Light green, nearly colourless, ht. 27.5 cm, d.m. 9.5 cm (E No. 3).
4. Alfriston, East Sussex, Light green, ht. 22.5 cm, d.m. 8 cm (E No. 4).
5. High Down, West Sussex, grave 27. Light green, ht. 29 cm, d.m. 7.5 cm (E No. 5, fig. 9).
6. Guildown, Surrey, grave 56. Light olive green, ht. 23.5 cm, d.m. 11.8 cm (E No. 6, figs, 2, 16).
7. Guildown, Surrey, grave 109. Light green, ht. 25 cm, d.m. 9 cm (E No. 7, figs. 3, 17).
8. Mitcham, London, grave 201. Light green, ht. 26.4 cm, d.m. 9.2 cm (E No. 8).
9. Ozingell, Kent, Light green, ht. 21.5 cm, d.m. 8.4 cm (E No. 9).
10. Westbere, Kent. Light green ht. 28 cm, d.m. 9.8 cm (E No. 10).
11. Howletts, Kent, grave 18. Light green, fragments, d.m. 8.6 cm (E No. 11).
12. Howletts, Kent, grave 30. Light green, ht. 27.5 cm, d.m. 9.3 cm (E No. 12, fig. 10).
13. Chessell Down, Isle of Wight. Amber, ht. *c.*22 cm, d.m. 10.5 cm (E No. 13, fig. 15).
14. Cassington, Smith's Pit II, Oxfordshire. Light green, nearly colourless, ht. 22.5 cm, d.m. 9.6 cm (E No. 14, fig. 1).
15. East Shefford, Berkshire, grave 24. Light green, ht. 26 cm, d.m. 9.2 cm (E No. 15).
16. East Shefford, Berkshire. Light green, ht. 25 cm, d.m. 8.7 cm (E No. 16, fig. 12).
17. Longbridge, Warwickshire. Base fragment, light green, ht. 11 cm (E No. 17).
18. Lyminge, Kent, grave 63. Light green, nearly colourless, ht. 17.2 cm, d.m. 9.7 × 9.4 cm, base 3.8 cm, Maidstone Museum.

19. Dover, Kent, grave 22. Light green, ht. 30.5 cm, d.m. 9.4 cm (E No. 19, fig. 11).

20. Faversham, Kent. Light olive green, ht. 19 cm, d.m. 9.7 cm (E No. 20, fig. 6).

21. Wye Down, Kent. Light green, ht. 19 cm, d.m. 9 cm (E No. 21, fig. 7).

22. Acklam, North Yorkshire. Light olive green, ht. 23.5 cm, d.m. 9.8 cm (E No. 22, figs. 4–5).

23. Wigston Magna, Leicestershire. Fragments. Nichols, 1807, 377, pl. LV, 18 (E, 55).

24. Barrington, A, Cambridgeshire. Light green fragment, Cambridge Museum (E 55).

25. Rivenhall, Essex. Olive green fragments (E, 56, fig. 18),

26. Mucking, Essex, grave 9. Light green, ht. 28.3 cm, d.m. 9.3 cm. Excavation M.U. and W.T. Jones.

27. Spong Hill, Norfolk, crem. 1023. Olive green fragments. Excavation Catherine Hills.

28. Spong Hill, Norfolk, crem. 1058. Light bluish-green, nearly colourless fragments. Excavation Catherine Hills.

29. Spong Hill, Norfolk, crem. 1156. Olive green fragments. Excavation Catherine Hills.

30. Spong Hill, Norfolk, crem. 1602. Light green fragments. Excavation Catherine Hills.

31. No provenance, Canterbury Museum. Light green, rim only to depth of 9 cm, d.m. 8.5 cm (E No. 18).

Germany

32. Krefeld-Stratum. Light green, ht. 24.5 cm (E No. 23).

33. Rill, Mörs. Ht. *c.*25 cm (E No. 24).

34. Schwarzrheindorf, grave 10. Ht. 28.5 cm, d.m. 8.3 cm (E No. 25).

35. Rittersdorf, grave 125. Light green, ht. 26.5 cm, d.m. 8.5 cm (E No. 26).

36. Monsheim, Rheinhessen. 'Weissem Glas', ht. 27.3 cm (E No. 27).

37. Wenigumstadt, Obernburg, grave 1. Light green, ht. 21.6 cm (E No. 28).

38. Eick, Mörs, grave 75. Light olive green, ht. 21 cm (E No. 29).

39. Mühlhausen, Kepplersche Sandgrube. Ht. 26 cm (E No. 30).

40. Weimar, Nordfriedhof, grave 31. Ht. 29.4 cm (E No. 31).

41. Entringen II. Ht. *c.*20 cm (E No. 32).

42. Wurmlingen, Tuttlingen. Ht. 23.5 cm (E No. 33).

43. Hailfingen, Rottenburg, grave 269. Ht. 25 cm and 28 cm (E No. 34).

44. Sindlingen a.M. ht. 27 cm (E No. 35).

45. Wiesbaden, Dotzheimerstr. Light green (E No. 36).

46. Wiesbaden, Schierstein. Light green, ht. 24 cm, d.m. 8.5 cm (E No. 37).

47. Wiesbaden, Dotzheimerstr. ht. 25.5 cm, d.m. 8.5 cm (E No. 38).

48. Düsseldorf-Oberkassel, grave 4 (E No. 39).

49. Beckum, Westphalia, grave 13 (E No. 40).

50. Quedlinburg, Bochshornschanze, grave 41 (E No. 41).

51. Krefeld-Gellep, grave 1850. Olive green, ht. 24.2 cm. Pirling 1974, Taf. 59.23.
52. Krefeld-Gellep, grave 2528 in fill. Fragments. Excavation R. Pirling.
53. Pommerhof, Plaidt, Mayen-Koblenz. Colourless, ht. 17 cm, d.m. 8.7 cm. Ament 1976, Taf. 59.34.
54. Liebenau, Niedersachsen, fläche VIII/19. Genrich 1975, Abb. 2, 9.
55. Hüfingen, Schwarzwald. Yellowish, nearly colourless, Fingerlin 1977, front cover.
56. No provenance, Völkerkunde Museum, Berlin (E No. 42).

Belgium

57. Sint Gillis bij Dendermonde. Yellowish, nearly colourless, ht. 21.5 cm, d.m. 8 cm (E No. 43, fig. 21).
58. Pry. Yellowish, nearly colourless, ht. 22 cm, d.m. 8.5 cm (E No. 44, fig. 20).
59. Samson. Light green, ht. 22.7 cm, d.m. 8.5 cm (E No. 45, fig. 19).
60. Anderlecht. Light yellow, ht. 21 cm. Roosens 1973, 47.

Holland

61. Aalden, Zweeloo. Ht. 25.7 cm, d.m. 9.7 cm (E No. 46).
62. Maastricht, St. Servaaskerk, grave 72. Light olive green, ht. 12.5 cm, d.m. 6.7 cm (E No. 47).

France

63. Herpes, Charente. Light green, ht. 20 cm, d.m. 8.5 cm (E No. 48, fig. 13).
64. Marchélepot. 'Verre blanc', ht. 22.5 cm (E No. 49).
65. Saint Nicolas, Arras (E No. 50).
66. No provenance, Troyes Museum 4583. Yellowish, nearly colourless, ht. 25 cm, d.m. 9.6 cm (E No. 51, fig. 22).

Czechoslovakia

67. Veleslavin, Prague, grave 3. Greenish, lost (E No. 52).
68. Kobylisy, Prague, grave IV. Yellow-green, ht. 27.5 cm, d.m. 9.7 cm (E No. 53).
69. Kobylisy, Prague. Brownish fragments (E No. 65).
70. Certova-ruha, Masov, near Turnov. Greenish fragments (E No. 65).

Denmark

71. Dankirke, Ribe. Blue with white trails, ht. *c*.23 cm. Thorvildsen 1972, colour plate opp. 48.

Scandinavia

72. No provenance. Ht. 24 cm, d.m. 7.9 cm (E No. 66). American Swedish Institute, Minneapolis.

Distribution map 4

Saucer brooches decorated with five spirals   England

1. Abingdon, Oxon., grave 60. Leeds and Harden 1936, pl. XII. (1).
   Abingdon, Oxon., grave 100. Leeds and Harden 1936, pl. XVII. (1).
2. Alfriston, Sussex, grave 46. Griffith and Salzmann 1914, pl. VII, 1, 1a. (2).
   Alfriston, Sussex, grave 87. Griffith 1915, pl. XXIII, 1, 1A. (2).
   Alfriston, Sussex, grave 60. Griffith and Salzmann 1914, pl. VII, 3, 3a. (2).
   Alfriston, Sussex, grave 65. Griffith and Salzmann 1914, pl. VII, 4. (1).
3. Alton, Hants, crem. 1. Excavation V.I. Evison. (2).
4. Beckford A, Hereford and Worcester, grave 12. Excavation V.I. Evison. (1).
5. Beddington, London. Meaney 1964, 237. (2).
6. Berinsfield, Oxon., grave 22. Excavation D. Miles and P.D.C. Brown. (2).
   Berinsfield, Oxon., grave 73. Excavation D. Miles and P.D.C. Brown. (2).
7. Caistor-by-Norwich, Norfolk. Myres and Green 1973 (No. 137), 90, Text fig. 2. (1).
8. Cassington, Purwell Farm, Oxon., grave 2. Leeds and Riley 1942, 65, pl. V, c. (2).
9. Dover, Kent, grave 48. Excavation V.I. Evison. British Museum. (1).
10. Droxford, Hants. BM Reg. No. 1902 7–22 5. (1).
11. Duston, Northants. Brown, 1915 III, 317, pl. LIX, 3. (1).
12. East Shefford, Berks., grave 18. Smith 1906, fig. 6 opp. p. 240. (1).
13. Great Chesterford, Essex, grave 2. Excavation V.I. Evison, British Museum. (2).
    Great Chesterford, Essex, grave 126. Excavation, V.I. Evison. British Museum (2).
14. High Down, Sussex, Wilson N.D., 4, pl. 3, 3, Worthing Museum 3406, 3407. (2).
15. Hornton, Oxon. Meaney, 1964, 209, BM Reg. No. 1836 3–23 11 and 12. (2).
16. Kempston, Beds. BM Reg. No. 91 6–24 245. (1).
17. Leighton Buzzard, Beds. BM Reg. No. 82 8–24 1. (1).
18. Lewes, Malling Hill, Sussex. Norris, 1956, 10–12. (1).
19. Long Wittenham, Oxon., grave 111. BM Reg. No. 75 3–10 290. 291. (2).
20. Marston St Lawrence, Northants. Dryden, 1885, 338, pl. XXIII, 13. (1).
21. Mitcham, London, grave 66. Bidder and Morris, 1959, pl. VIII. (2).
22. Orpington, Kent, grave 75. Excavation Mrs Palmer, Orpington Museum. (2).
23. Reading, Berks. Smith 1906, 240. (1).
24. Spong Hill, Norfolk, crem. 2376. Excavation C. Hills. (2).
25. Welbeck Hill, Lincs. Wilson and Hurst, 1967, 267. (1).
26. Wheatley, Oxon., grave 20. Leeds, 1916, 53, fig. 2, 20. (1).
27. Woodstone, Peterborough, Cambs. Abbott, 1920, pl. opp. p. 40, No. 4. (1).

Acknowledgments

I am very grateful to Mrs M.U. Jones and Mr W.T. Jones for permission to publish material from their excavations at Mucking, Essex, to Miss Valerie Cooper for assistance with the bibliography and distribution maps, to Mr J. Thorn for the maps figs. 7–10, to Mrs E.M. Fry-Stone for the drawing fig. 2, and to Miss J. Dobie for the drawings, figs. 4–7.

The photograph pl. XIa, is published by permission of the Ashmolean Museum.

Bibliography

ABBOTT, G.W., ' "Further discoveries in Anglo-Saxon cemeteries at Woodston, Hunts", and details of a Bronze Age burial', *Precis of the Forty-Ninth Annual Report of the Peterborough Natural History, Scientific and Archaeological Society* (1920), 34–40.

AMENT, H., *Die Fränkischen Grabfunde aus Mayen und der Pellenz Germanische Denkmäler der Völkerwanderungszeit* ser. B *Die Fränkischen Altertümer des Rheinlandes* Bd. 9 (Berlin, 1976).

BAYNES, E.N., 'Notes on two small urns and a glass beaker and bowl of Saxon date, found at Buttsole, Eastry, Kent', *Proc. Soc. Antiq.* ser. 2, 22 (1907–9).

BEHRENS, G., 'Spätrömische Kerbschnittschnallen', *Schumacher Festschrift* 285–94 (Mainz, 1930).

BIDDER, H.F. and MORRIS, J., 'The Anglo-Saxon cemetery at Mitcham', *Surrey Archaeol. Collect.* 56 (1959), 51–131.

BÖHME, H.W., *Germanische Grabfunde des 4. bis 5. Jahrhunderts, zwischen unterer Elbe und Loire. Münchner Beiträge zur Vor- und Frühgeschichte* 19 (München, 1974).

BOWMAN, W., *Reliquiae antiquae Eboracenses* (Leeds, 1855).

BROWN, G.B., *Saxon Art and Industry in the Pagan Period; The Arts in Early England* 3 (London, 1915).

BULLINGER, H., *Spätantike Gürtelbeschläge, Dissertationes Archaeologicae Gandenses* 12 (Brugge, 1969).

CLARKE, G., 'Lankhills School', in M. Biddle, 'Excavations at Winchester: eighth interim report', 292–8 *Antiq. J.* 50 (1970), 276–326.

CLARKE, G., Winchester Studies 3: *Pre-Roman and Roman Winchester*, Part II, 'The Roman Cemetery at Lankhills' (Oxford, 1979).

DICKINSON, T.M., 'On the origin and chronology of the early Anglo-Saxon disc brooch', *Anglo-Saxon Studies in Archaeology and History 1*, BAR British Studies 72, 1979, 39–80.

DURAND, M., l'Abbé, 'Notice sur des tombeaux découverts à la Hogue, près le port dit Bénouville', *Mémoires de la Société des Antiquaires de Normandie* ser. 2, 2 (1841), 325–36.

DRYDEN, H., 'Excavation of an ancient burial ground at Marston St. Lawrence, co. Northampton', *Archaeologia* 48 (1885), 327–39.

EAGLES, B.N., *The Anglo-Saxon settlement of Humberside, British Archaeological Reports* 68 (Oxford, 1979).

EVERSON, P. and KNOWLES, G.C., 'A tutulus brooch from Kirmington, Lincolnshire, (S. Humberside)', *Medieval Archaeol.* 22 (1978), 123–7.

EVISON, V.I., *The Fifth-century Invasions south of the Thames* (London, 1965).

EVISON, V.I., 'Quoit brooch style buckles', *Antiq. J.* 48 (1968), 231–49.

EVISON, V.I., 'Five Anglo-Saxon inhumation graves containing pots at Great Chesterford, Essex', *Berichten van de Rijksdienst voor het Oudheidkundig Bodemonderzoek* 19 (1969), 157–73.

EVISON, V.I., 'Glass cone beakers of the "Kempston" type', *Journal of Glass Studies* 14 (1972), 48–66.

EVISON, V.I., 'An Anglo-Saxon glass claw-beaker from Mucking, Essex', *Antiq. J.* 54 (1974), 277–8.

EVISON, V.I., 'Supporting-arm brooches and equal-arm brooches in England', *Studien zur Sachsenforschung* 1, ed. H.-J. Hässler (Hildesheim, 1977), 127–47.

EVISON, V.I., 'Early Anglo-Saxon applied disc brooches, part II: in England', *Antiq. J.* 58 (1978), 260–78.

FINGERLIN, G., *Neue alamannische Grabfunde aus Hüfingen, Texte zu einer Ausstellung* (Freiburg, 1977).

FOSTER, W.K., 'Account of the excavation of an Anglo-Saxon cemetery at Barrington, Cambridgeshire', *Cambridge Antiquarian Communications* 5 (1880–4), 5–32.

GENRICH, A., 'Der Friedhof bei Liebenau in Niedersachsen', *Ausgrabungen in Deutschland gefördert von der Deutschen Forschungsgemeinschaft 1950–75, Römisch-Germanisches Zentralmuseum zu Mainz Forschungsinstitut für Vor- und Frühgeschichte Monographien* 1, 3 (Mainz, 1975), 17–40.

GODFREY-FAUSSETT, T.G., 'The Saxon cemetery at Bifrons', *Archaeol. Cantiana* X (1876), 298, 315.

GRIFFITH, A.F., 'An Anglo-Saxon cemetery at Alfriston, Sussex. Supplemental paper'. *Sussex Archaeol. Collect.* 57 (1915), 197–210.

GRIFFITH, A.F. and SALZMANN, L.F., 'An Anglo-Saxon cemetery at Alfriston, Sussex', *Sussex Archaeol. Collect.* 56 (1914), 16–53.

HARDEN, D.B., 'Saxon glass from Sussex', *Sussex County Magazine* 25 (1951), 260–8.

HARDEN, D.B., 'Glass vessels in Britain and Ireland, A.D. 400–1000', *Dark Age Britain*, ed. D.B. Harden (London, 1956), 132–67.

HAWKES, S.C., 'Some recent finds of late Roman buckles', *Britannia* 5 (1974), 386–93.

HAWKES, S.C. and DUNNING, G.C., 'Soldiers and settlers in Britain, fourth to fifth century: with a catalogue of animal-ornamented buckles and related belt-fittings', *Medieval Archaeol.* 5 (1961), 1–70.

HILLS, C., *The Anglo-Saxon Cemetery at Spong Hill, North Elmham Part I, East Anglian Archaeology, Report No. 6, Norfolk* (Gressenhall, 1977).

ISINGS, C., *Roman glass from dated finds, Archaeologica Traiectina* 2 (Groningen/Djakarta, 1957).

LEEDS, E.T., 'An Anglo-Saxon cemetery at Wheatley, Oxfordshire', *Proc. Soc. Antiq.* ser. 2, 29 (1916–17), 48–63.

LEEDS, E.T. and HARDEN, D.B., *The Anglo-Saxon Cemetery at Abingdon, Berkshire* (Oxford, 1936).

LEEDS, E.T. and RILEY, M., 'Two early Saxon cemeteries at Cassington, Oxon.', *Oxoniensia* 7 (1942), 61–70.

LEEDS, E.T. and SHORTT, H. de S., *An Anglo-Saxon Cemetery at Petersfinger, near Salisbury Wilts* (Salisbury, 1953).

MARTIN, M., 'Zwei spätrömische Gürtel aus Augst/BL', *Römerhaus und Museum Augst Jahresbericht* (1967), 3–20.

MEANEY, A., *A Gazeteer of Early Anglo-Saxon Burial Sites* (London, 1964).

NENQUIN, J.A.E., *La Nécropole de Furfooz, Dissertationes Archaeologicae Gandenses* 1 (Brugge, 1953).

NEVILLE, R.C., *Saxon Obsequies* (London, 1852).

NICHOLS, J., *The History and Antiquities of the County of Leicester* 4 Part I (London, 1807).

NORRIS, N.E.S., 'Romano-British cremations and Anglo-Saxon inhumations at South Malling, Lewes', *Sussex Archaeol. Collect.* 94 (1956), 10–12.

NOWOTHNIG, W., 'Einige frühgeschichtliche Funde aus Niedersachsen', *Nachrichten aus Niedersachsens Urgeschichte* 39 (1970), 126–43.

PILET, C., 'Le Mobilier Anglo-Saxon de la Nécropole de Frenouville', *Actes du Colloque International d'Archéologie, Rouen 1975* (Rouen, 1978), 441–63.

PIRLING, R., *Das Römisch-Fränkische Gräberfeld von Krefeld–Gellep, Germanische Denkmäler der Völkerwanderungszeit* ser. B *Die Fränkischen Altertümer des Rheinlandes* 2 (Berlin, 1966).

REICHSTEIN, J., *Die kreuzförmige Fibel, Offa-Bücher* 34 (Neumünster, 1975).

RÖHRER-ERTL, O., *Untersuchungen am Material des Urnenfriedhofes von Westerwanna, Kreis Land Hadeln* (Hamburg, 1971).

ROOSENS, H., 'Glas', *Archéologie* (1973), 47.

SAGE, W., 'Das Reihengräberfeld von Altenerding', *Ausgrabungen in Deutschland gefördert von der Deutschen Forschungsgemeinschaft 1950–1975, Römisch-Germanisches Zentralmuseum zu Mainz Forschungsinstitut für Vor- und Frühgeschichte Monographien* 1, 2 (Mainz, 1975), 254–77.

SCHMIDT, B., *Die späte Völkerwanderungszeit in Mitteldeutschland, Katalog (Südteil) Veröffentlichungen des Landesmuseums für Vorgeschichte in Halle* 25 (Berlin, 1970).

SCUVÉE, F., *Le cimetière barbare de Réville (Manche) (VI et VII siècles) Fouilles, 1959–1966* (Caen, 1973).

SIMPSON, C.J., 'Belt-buckles and strap-ends of the later Roman Empire: A preliminary survey of several new groups', *Britannia* 7 (1976), 192–223.

SMITH, R.A., 'Anglo-Saxon remains', *The Victoria History of Berkshire* 1, ed. P.H. Ditchfield and W. Page, 229–49 (London, 1906), 229–49.

STRAUSS, J., *Glass Drinking Vessels from the Collections of Jerome Strauss and the Ruth Bryan Strauss Memorial Foundation* (Corning, 1955).

SWANTON, M.J., *The Spearheads of the Anglo-Saxon Settlements,* Royal Archaeological Institute (London, 1973).

THORVILDSEN, E., 'Dankirke', *Nationalmuseets Arbejdsmark* (1972), 47–60.

VIERCK, H., 'Bemerkungen zum Verlaufsweg finnisch-angelsächsischer Beziehungen in sechsten Jahrhundert', *Suomen Museo* (1967), 54–63.

WERNER, J., '*Fränkische Schwerter des 5. Jahrhunderts aus Samson und Petersfinger*', *Germania* 34 (1956), 156–8.

WERNER, J., 'Römische Fibeln des 5. Jahrhunderts von der Gurina in Gailtal und vom Grepault bei Truns (Graubünden)' *Der Schlern* 32 (1958), 109–12.

WILSON, A.E., *A Guide to the Anglo-Saxon Collection,* N.D. Worthing Museum Publications no. 1, Second Edition.

WILSON, D.M. and HURST, D.G., 'Medieval Britain in 1966', *Medieval Archaeol.* 11 (1967), 262–319.

Notes

1. Myres, 1969 (No. 158), and Myres, 1977 (No. 209).
2. Böhme, 1974.
3. Evison, 1965.
4. e.g. Behrens, 1930; Hawkes and Dunning, 1961; Bullinger, 1969; Martin, 1967; Nowothnig, 1970, etc.
5. Böhme, 1974, 80–1, Texttafel A and B and distribution maps 11–16.
6. Hawkes and Dunning, 1961, fig. 13,0, Ash, Kent; Böhme, 1974, Taf. 120, 1, Cortrat grave 30, Taf. 22, 9, Hemmoor Warstade grave 80.
7. Classed as II B by Hawkes and Dunning, 1961, and regarded as a development of the curling tail dolphin type—II A, because both were found with perforated plates. However, it does not seem useful to endorse this grouping because the form is much nearer to the bar type, and openwork plates occur with other forms of loop also, e.g. with a composite bar and lug loop at Vermand (Hawkes and Dunning, 1961 fig. 6b). A further reason for relating the bar (c) to the fixed plate (d) types is that both occur on both sides of the Channel, while the curling tails (a) do not.
8. Martin, 1967, distribution map Abb. 7.
9. Hawkes and Dunning, 1961; since the completion of this article further dating evidence has been published from Winchester: Clarke, 1979, 273–6 where the two dolphin buckles are confusingly listed under 'Buckles with animal-heads confronted at the top of the loop'.
10. Böhme, 1974, 129, distribution map Abb. 49.
11. Evison, 1965, Map 5.
12. Böhme, 1974, 138; Werner, 1958, Abb. 11, 1.
13. Strauss, 1955, 28, No. 49, included by Harden among Anglo-Saxon types, but with strong reservations (Harden, 1956, 143). There is one of the Helle type with no provenance in the British Museum, Reg. No. 1900 7–19 8.
14. Böhme, 1974, 139; Isings, 1957, form 117; High Down, Harden, 1951, fig. 5; Bifrons, Harden, 1956, pl. XV, f.; Eastry, Baynes, 1907–9, 365, fig. 2; Milton-next-Sittingbourne, British Museum Reg. No. 1905 4–18 13.
15. Böhme, 1974, 139; Isings, 1957, form 115; Harden, 1951, fig. 8.
16. Harden, 1956, pl. XV, e.
17. Böhme, 1974, 136; Evison, 1969, fig. 2,2.
18. Lewes Museum.
19. Böhme, 1974, 139; Taf. 119, 12; Evison, 1972, fig. 14.
20. Lewes Museum.
21. Harden, 1951, fig. 3.

22. Evison, 1974, pl. LVI.

23. Evison, 1977, fig. 6.

24. Leeds and Harden, 1936, pl. XVI; Neville, 1852, pl. III, grave 22.

25. Everson and Knowles, 1978, fig. 1,1.

26. Böhme, 1974, 21.

27. Foster, 1880–4, pl. V,3.

28. I am grateful to Mr D. Leigh for the radiograph of the High Down brooch.

29. Pirling, 1966, Taf. 50, 1, Taf. 78, 15, 16; Röhrer-Ertl, 1971, Taf. 6.

30. Sage, 1975, Abb. 20; Pilet, 1978, 444, fig. 2.

31. Cirencester Museum, information P.D.C. Brown.

32. Böhme, 1974, Karte 16.

33. Buckle from Douglas Collection: Evison, 1968, fig. 3, b. Bifrons buckle: Godfrey-Faussett 1876, 307–8. Frilford buckle, Evison, 1968, fig. 3, d.

34. Hawkes and Dunning, 1961, fig. 20,g.

35. Ibid. fig. 19 *bis* b.

36. Bowman, 1855, 62–3, pl. XII,8. I am grateful to Mr M. Pocock for bringing this buckle to my notice.

37. Evison, 1968, fig. 3,c.

38. Evison, 1965, fig. 24,d.

39. Hawkes and Dunning, 1961, fig. 20,h.

40. Böhme, 1974, 100; Werner, 1956.

41. Leeds and Harden, 1936, pl. XIX, 42 and 49; Leeds and Shortt, 1953, pl. I, 61.

42. Evison, 1965, Chapter V; Later evidence, supporting the dating of the quoit brooch style fifty years earlier to the first half of the fifth century, was given in Evison 1968. A recent addition to the group is Swanton 1973, fig. 83,f, and others have been found at Mucking.

43. Evison, 1965, map 11.

44. Ibid. map 4.

45. Scuvée, 1973, 51, 137–8, fig. 42. The bronze tube noted at Loima, Ksp. Huittinen, Satakunta, Finland (Vierck, 1967, Abb. 1,3) was in a migration period grave, but a belt mount associated with it is late Roman in type, a date which is also quite likely for the bronze tube.

46. Ibid.—other grave contents: knife fig. 17, buckle fig. 20, rivet fig. 25, beads fig. 41, key fig. 46.

47. Durand, 1841, fig. 9 opp. p. 328. Fig. 3 here is a reconstruction based on Durand, 1841, fig. 9.

48. Evison, 1965, pl. 12,c.

49. cf. ibid. fig. 30 a–e.

50. Ashmolean Museum 1909, 571, brought to my notice by Mr P.D.C. Brown.

51. Evison, 1968, pl. LV,c.

52. Ibid. pl. LV, a and b.

53. Evison, 1965, map 8.

54. Ibid. maps 2 and 3.

55. Excavation P. Rahtz and Susan Hirst.
56. Evison, 1972.
57. Information from the excavator, M.J.-P. Lemant.
58. Evison, 1972, figs. 15 and 16. Also in Lower Saxony, see chapter 5 above.
59. Swanton, 1973, 24 and 39 ff.
60. Evison, 1965, fig. 1,f.
61. Böhme, 1974, Abb. 40, note 391.
62. Evison, 1965, fig. 3,7.
63. Böhme, 1974, Taf. 63, 14, Taf. 140, 14.
64. Swanton, 1973, 42, fig. 58,a; an earlier date is preferred in Evison, 1972, 55.
65. Evison, 1978, pl. LIV, i.
66. Böhme, 1974, Taf. 21, 11; Nenquin, 1953, 83, fig. 18, J.15.
67. Swanton, 1973, 38, fig. 57,a; Evison, 1978, 261.
68. Böhme, 1974, 101, Taf. 60, 13, Taf. 62, 15, Taf. 143, 12.
69. Swanton, 1973, 117 ff.
70. Ibid. fig. 83.
71. Ibid. fig. 46.
72. Ibid. fig. 84.
73. Evison, 1978, fig. 4. No further comment is made here on the saucer brooches of similar date and designs, as this is a field in which complete and organized data is not yet available.
74. Dickinson, 1979.
75. No. 810 Faversham, Reichstein, 1975, Abb. 11, cf. No. 492, Yttrup Holmgård, Rybjerg, Salling Nørre, Viborg, and No. 811 Faversham, Reichstein, 1975 Taf. 114, 5, cf. No. 472, Oxbøl, Å1, Vester Horne, Ribe, Taf. 114, 4, Abb. 19.
76. Böhme, 1974, 13, Karte 4.
77. Böhme, 1974, Taf. 65, 2–4, Taf. 64, 1, Taf. 66, 1–3, 10.
78. Ibid. Taf. 59, 10.
79. Ibid. Taf. 60, 7.
80. Hills, 1977, fig. 110, 1469.
81. Evison, 1965, 23–5, fig. 10; Werner, 1958; Pirling, 1966, 162, Taf. 68, 22.
82. Pirling, 1966, Taf. 46, 9–10; Schmidt, 1970, Taf. 40, 2,e. Mr S.E. West informs me that an iron version has been found in the West Stow settlement.
83. Böhme, 1974, Taf. 64, 1.
84. Ibid. Taf. 100, 8, Taf. 106, 9, Taf. 34, 11.
85. Ibid. List and distribution map, 114, Abb. 46.
86. Ibid. Taf. 137, 10 and 11; Evison, 1965, pl. Ie,f.
87. Böhme, 1974, Taf. 63, 15.
88. Ibid. 83.
89. Swanton, 1973, 137.
90. Simpson, 1976.
91. Myres, 1957 (No. 105), fig. 1.
92. Myres, 1937 (No. 31), 301.

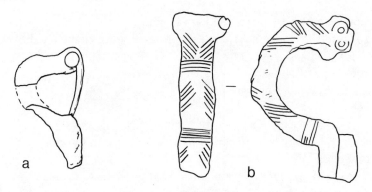

FIG. 1. a. High Down, Sussex: iron bow brooch with bronze pin.
b. High Down, Sussex: iron bow brooch inlaid with bronze strips.

Scale 1/1.

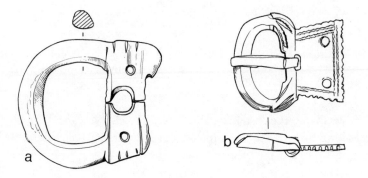

FIG. 2. a. Bifrons, Kent, grave 23, buckle.   b. Sarre, Kent, buckle with
fixed plate.   Scale 1/1.

Fig. 3. Bénouville, France, quoit brooch.
Scale 1/1.

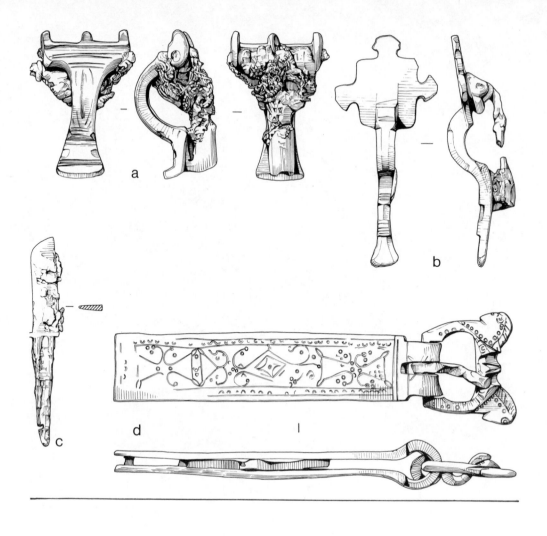

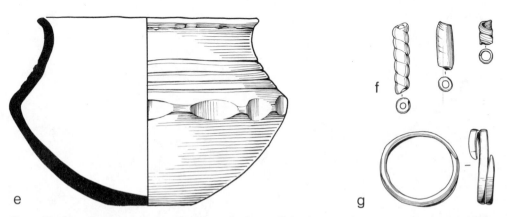

FIG. 4. Mucking, Essex, grave 987: a. bow brooch, *Stutzarfibel*.　b. small long brooch.　c. knife.　buckle.
Mucking, Essex, grave 989 major items: e. pot.　f. beads.　g. finger ring.

Scale 1/1, except c and e 1/2.

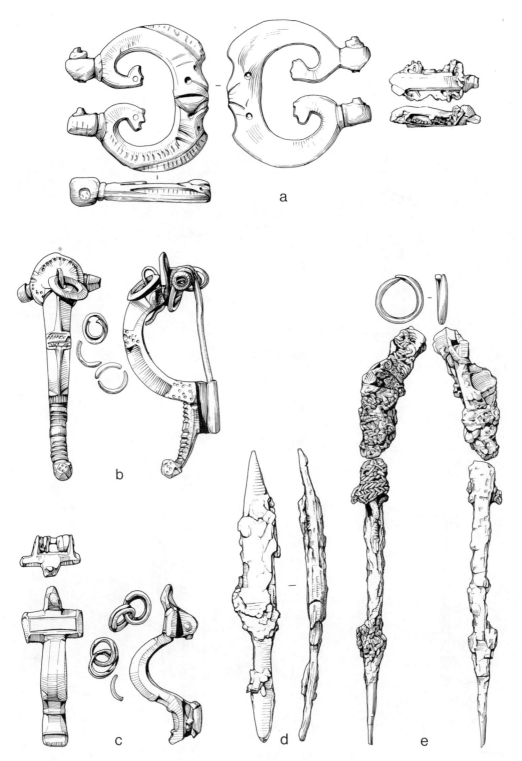

Fig. 5. Mucking, Essex, grave 989 major items: a. dolphin buckle.   b. bow brooch with upturned foot.
c. bow brooch.   d. knife.   e. iron pin and bronze ring.   Scale 1/1, except d 1/2.

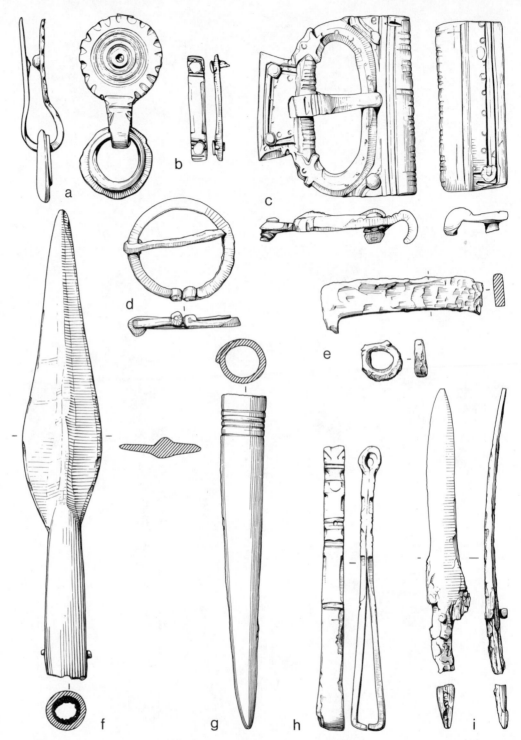

Fig. 6. Mucking, Essex, grave 979 major items: a. rosette belt fitting.   b. belt mount.   c. buckle with fixed plate and counter plate.   d. iron penannular brooch.   e. strike-a-light.   f. spearhead.   g. spear ferrule.   h. tweezers.   i. knife.   Scale a–c, h 1/1, d–g, i 1/2.

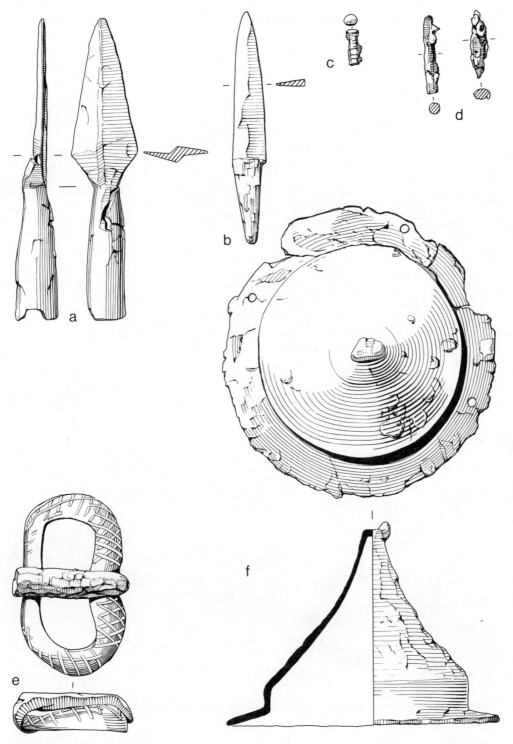

FIG. 7. Mucking, Essex, grave 272: a. spearhead.　b. knife.　c. iron rivet.　d. iron pin.　e. metal-inlaid iron buckle.　f. shield boss.　Scale a–d, f 1/2, e 1/1.

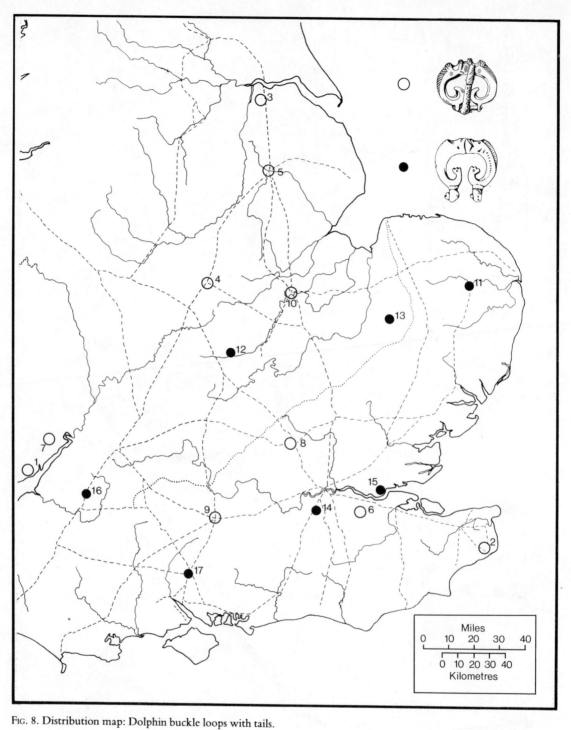

Fig. 8. Distribution map: Dolphin buckle loops with tails.

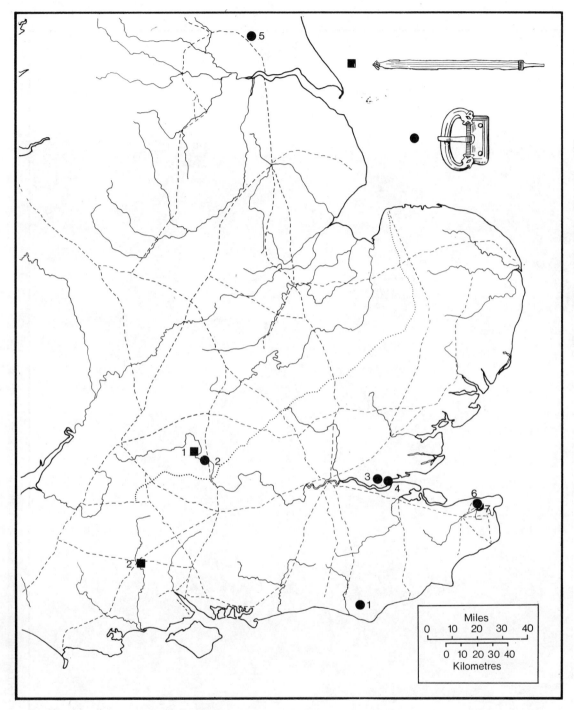

Fɪɢ. 9. Distribution map: Fixed plate buckles and 'Abingdon'-type swords.

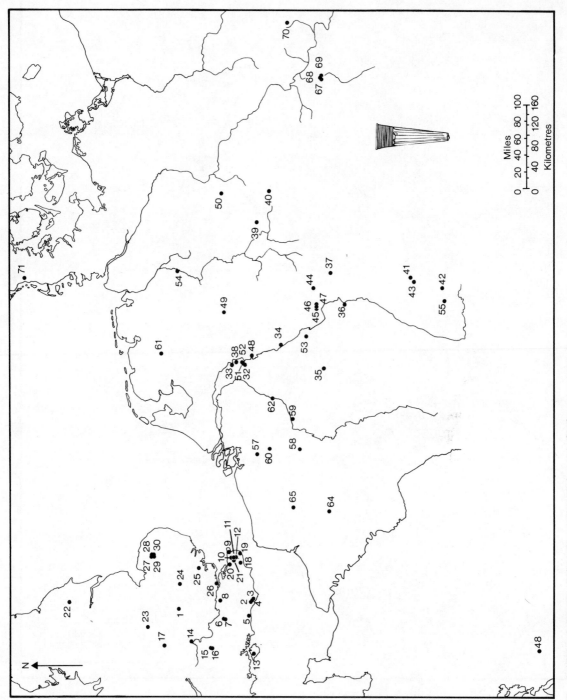

FIG. 10. Distribution map: 'Kempston'-type glass cone beakers.

166

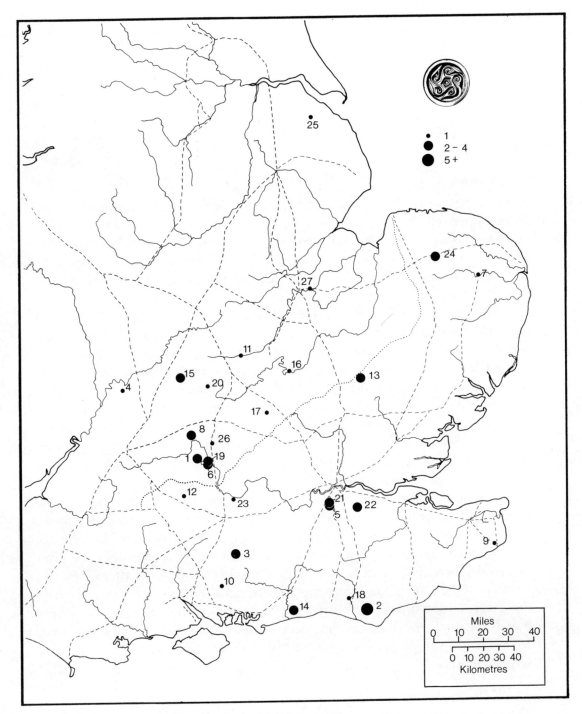

FIG. 11. Distribution map: Saucer brooches decorated with five spirals.

8

Quantity or quality: the Anglian graves of Bernicia[1]

LESLIE ALCOCK

1. Introductory

It has long been a commonplace that, in Bernicia, Anglian graves are distinguished only by their scarcity and poverty. This was expressed most starkly by Hunter Blair in 1959. Assessing, in a mere footnote, 'the entire body' of early Anglo-Saxon material from Northumberland, he declared that it 'would be scarcely equivalent to the contents of six well-furnished graves from, for example, the Cambridge region'.[2]

Given the power of Bernicia to resist combined British attacks in the third quarter of the sixth century, and its even more remarkable expansion towards the end of the century under Ethelfrith,[3] the scarcity of pagan burials has presented an enigma. Various explanations have been proffered, some in historical terms, some looking rather to the hazards of archaeological discovery. Perhaps the settlers were indeed few in number. Perhaps the major Anglian settlement did not begin until the end of the pagan era, and hence furnished graves should not be expected; this explanation, however, leaves the paradox of the late sixth-century expansion. Perhaps the lack of gravel-digging,[4] or arable farming,[5] or other soil-disturbing mechanisms, has left pagan cemeteries largely undiscovered.

There may be an element of truth in each of these explanations. But it is the central purpose of this paper to argue that, in so far as they are addressed to the supposed poverty, as well as scarcity, of Anglian graves in Bernicia, they are misconceived. Bernician graves may be few, but they are frequently rich. Their quality first became evident in 1976, with the proper publication, after a lapse of a century, of the Darlington cemetery;[6] for here, in a cemetery of only six burials, there were two swords as well as rich jewellery. This prompted a reassessment of burials and cemeteries between the Tees and the Forth, which is offered to Nowell Myres as a token of gratitude for all his work on grave goods as a basis for settlement studies.[7]

2. The gradation of pagan graves

The starting-point for the present discussion of Bernician graves is the common observation that there is a graded series among at least the weapon-bearing graves of the pagan English. At one extreme are graves which include not only weapons, but body armour as well: helmets and mail coats. These are so rare that they may be disregarded here. Next are graves which contain a sword, and with it probably a scabbard, sword-harness fittings, and also perhaps a spear and a shield. Less well furnished are graves in which the only military gear is a spear, with or without a shield as well. At the bottom of the range are male graves (where the sex can be distinguished) which have only an iron knife and perhaps an iron belt buckle. These scarcely merit consideration as weapon-graves, but must be mentioned to complete the range.[8]

Without at present entering into questions of social stratification (below, Part 4, pp. 175–7), it can be accepted that this graded series marks differences in the value of the weaponry deposited in the grave, reckoned as a factor of the skill and effort needed for its manufacture. In terms of the labour theory of value, a sword-grave is rich; a grave with only a knife is poor; shield plus spear is richer than spear only. In broad terms, the gradations objectively determined in this way may be signalled by calling sword-graves alpha, spear-graves beta, and knife-graves gamma. In the present state of study, this is more helpful than numerical markers. In particular, it could lend itself to refinement: a grave with a sword, ornamented scabbard, jewelled hangings, and other weapons, might be alpha plus, whereas one with only a sword and poor scabbard fittings would be alpha minus.

It is also a commonplace that sword-graves are rare while spear-graves are common.[9] In some cemeteries swords are entirely lacking. A preliminary report on Bishopstone, Sussex, refers to 112 inhumations: 'weaponry in the graves included spears and three shield-bosses but no swords'.[10] At Snell's Corner, Hants, five graves yielded spears, but there were no swords.[11] A single sword is recorded at Finglesham, Kent, in a cemetery with two spear-graves: the sword-grave, G2, is a typical alpha burial, with a spear, shield, and elaborate belt-fittings.[12] At Holywell, Cambridgeshire, there were twenty spear-graves (a small majority also containing a shield), but only one sword-burial was found.[13] At Bergh Apton, Norfolk, there was only one sword in a cemetery with twelve spearmen.[14] Abingdon, Berkshire, exhibits two alpha minus deposits: swords accompanied with little other than scabbard fittings. In addition there were seventeen spear-graves, of which no fewer than nine lacked a shield (beta minus).[15] A variant on the alpha grave is suggested at Petersfinger, Wilts, where, in addition to eleven spear-graves, there were three sword-graves, of which grave XXI contained an iron battle-axe as well.[16]

It is not considered worth attempting to quantify the gamma graves. Without other diagnostic features, a knife may belong to either a male or a female grave. It seems possible, too, that some burials found without grave goods may formerly have contained small iron knives which have disappeared through corrosion.

While the grading of male, weapon-bearing graves is simple and relatively objective, it is far more difficult to put forward a scheme for women's graves, because of the much wider range of objects in female burials. An iron knife or buckle, or two or three beads, may well mark a gamma grave. But at what point in the proliferation of beads, brooches, chatelaines, work-boxes, and so on do we place the change from beta to alpha? At Holywell, Cambridgeshire, Grave 11 contained, apparently, the body of a child accompanied by a gilt-bronze square-headed brooch; silver bracelets, pendants, and ring; bronze girdle-hangers, buckles, and other belt-fittings; two bronze bowls; beads of amber, crystal, glass, and jet; and an iron weaving batten. Lethbridge reasonably describes this as 'the finery of a young East Anglian lady'.[17] For comparable finery from Kent, we might turn to Finglesham grave D3. Here again was a weaving batten, described by Chadwick as 'clearly a wealthy woman's prerogative'.[18] In Finglesham D3 it was associated with a glass claw-beaker, fifty–two beads of glass and amber, three gold bracelets, five silver brooches further embellished with gilding and garnet inlay, an iron buckle plated with silver, and several minor objects. It would be impossible to grudge an alpha classification to either Holywell 11 or Finglesham D3.

Finglesham E2, with a silver-gilt great square-headed brooch, two other silver-gilt square-heads, a silver disc brooch with garnets, and other trinkets, might be considered alpha minus. So might Holywell 48, with two large and two small cruciform brooches and various beads and pendants; or Holywell 79, with three cruciforms, two small-long brooches, wrist-clasps, girdle hangers, and other miscellanea. At Petersfinger, it would be difficult to assign a grade higher than alpha minus to any female burial: from grave XXV came a gilt-bronze bow brooch, three gilt saucer brooches, two Roman coins, fifty-nine beads of amber, crystal and glass, a buckle, and odd rings, discs, and rods of bronze or iron. Finally, in the case of Abingdon, where two brooches and a string of beads are the height of female display, it is doubtful if any female graves merit alpha at all.

It may be thought that the argument so far has been founded on a very eclectic use of grave-associations. It should therefore be stressed that its basis was a wholly casual collection of cemetery reports, satisfying merely the two criteria that the report should be accessible, and that it should assign objects unequivocally to individual graves. The next part of the discussion is admittedly subjective, and probably tendentious as well. It is not essential to the over-all argument of the paper, but it is included in the hope that it might stimulate or provoke some researcher with adequate resources of time to test it fully.

What is now claimed is that, if individual burials can be graded on an alpha-beta-gamma scheme, then so can whole cemeteries. Ideally this should be done by grading each burial, adjusting the grades to a points system, and averaging for the cemetery as a whole. Clearly this would be a lengthy procedure, certainly far more so than the scope of the present paper allows. On the other hand, it should lend itself to analysis by automated methods of information retrieval. For the present what has been done is to take the summary lists of grave goods from Wiltshire and Berkshire in Meaney's *Gazetteer*.[19] and assign grades to the cemeteries. These two counties were chosen as representing, so far as any modern counties can, the heartland of pagan Saxon Wessex.

In the larger cemeteries, all three grades may be assigned if, for instance, there are a couple of sword-graves, many spear-burials, and some graves containing only a knife. Using summary lists, it is certain that the gamma element is massively underrepresented. It is also possible, since the presence of swords and rich jewellery stands out in the lists, that the alpha grade is overrepresented. With these warnings, the results may be tabulated.

	Berks.	Wilts.	Total
alpha	8	9	17
beta	28	33	61
gamma	4	9	13

The figures for alpha and beta cemeteries seem consistent enough from one county to the other to give some credibility to the scheme. On the other hand, the ratio of alpha to beta, about 1:3.6, when compared with the sword to spear ratio in any one cemetery, demonstrates how far the alpha element is favoured by the method.

3. *The Bernician graves*

With this information about the relative richness of southern English burials in the background, it is now possible to examine the Bernician graves in detail, and attempt to grade them. Two problems arise at the outset: one of definition, the other of the quality of our information.

Firstly, where are we to draw the boundaries of Bernicia? To the south, many distribution maps of the period coyly evade this issue by leaving a gap, roughly between the Tees and the Tyne, separating the names of Bernicia and Deira.[20] Sometimes it is suggested that this was a wilderness, barren of settlement and communications. For the present paper, however, Jackson's bold lead is followed, and the southern boundary of Bernicia is placed on the Tees.[21] On the north, at the very end of the pagan period, the siege and capture of Edinburgh *c.*AD 638 took Bernician power to the shores of the Firth of Forth.[22] Consistent with this, one of the finest, and also one of the latest, objects of filigree and garnet work comes from Dalmeny in West Lothian.

As for the quality of the information available about pagan burials in Bernicia, it scarcely needs saying that not a single cemetery has been reported to the standards considered normal for Wessex or East Anglia. For some of the major finds, the circumstances of discovery are totally unknown. An account of the richest cemetery, that at Darlington, has had to be pieced together from newspaper reports and auctioneers' catalogues.[23] Even the best reported graves, those at Howick Heugh, were uncovered in quarrying operations; and though records were made during periodic visits by R.C. Bosanquet, it was only after his death that the cemetery and grave goods were written up by G.S. Keeney.[24] It is even more regrettable that in this case, where we can attribute objects to individual graves, the over-all grade is gamma, with a few beta elements.

Given the inadequacy of our primary information about find circumstances, we might well feel little confidence in any conclusions to be drawn from it. Despite these reservations, it is worth listing the Bernician burials, and assigning grades to them. In the sequel, the graves are listed alphabetically, with a reference either to Meaney's *Gazetteer,*[25] or to fuller documentation.

BARRASFORD (NTB)   *alpha*

Secondary inhumation in barrow, with abundant grave goods, including a sword, and silver–ornamented shield boss.

Meaney, 198.

BENWELL (NTB)   *beta (? alpha)*

Probably one or more inhumations, with a cruciform and a square-headed brooch, also a glass vessel. If the latter is associated, then alpha would be appropriate.

Meaney, 198.

BOLDON (DRH)   *alpha*

Inhumation burial, with bronze buckle having three bosses ornamented with gold filigree and garnet carbuncles.[26] Although the buckle is the only object known from the grave, the use of gold and garnet argues for the alpha grade.

Meaney, 83.

CAPHEATON (NTB)   *alpha (?)*

Apparently many burials (perhaps not all of this date) secondary in a barrow, from which was also recovered a bronze hanging bowl with two out of three escutcheons present but detached. The hanging bowl suggests at least one alpha-grade burial.

Meaney, 198.

CASTLE EDEN (DRH)   *alpha*

Inhumation burial with a glass claw-beaker.[27] For alpha contexts for claw beakers, compare Finglesham (KNT) grave D3[28] and Coombe (KNT).[29]

Meaney, 83.

CORBRIDGE (NTB)   *beta (perhaps alpha ?)*

Anglo-Saxon objects, potentially from inhumation burials, include two cruciform brooches (not strictly a pair, but apparently intended to be worn as such) and some beads.[30] There is also a mount for a sword-scabbard which, if it was indeed with an Anglian burial, implies an alpha element.

Meaney, 198.

CORNFORTH (DRH)   *beta*

Eight or nine skeletons in cists, two of them with iron spearheads, marking a beta element. The presence of a horse in one cist could even be interpreted as denoting an alpha grave, but this point is not pressed.

Meaney, 83.

DALMENY, WEST CRAIGIE FARM (WLO)   *alpha*

Some time before 1853, a pyramidal sword ornament was found on the land of West Craigie Farm, Dalmeny, West Lothian (not, as recent accounts claim, in Dalmeny churchyard, nor in Roxburghshire).[31] The pyramid, ornamented with gold filigree and plate garnets[32] was curiously overlooked by Baldwin Brown; this may partly account for claims that no pagan Anglo-Saxon jewellery has ever been found in northern Bernicia. Although we have no information about find circumstances, a rich warrior-grave seems the most likely occasion for the burial in the Lothians of this fine jewel. Certainly, the presence of a sword, scabbard, and harness may be inferred.[33]

DALMENY, HOUND POINT (WLO)   *beta (?)*

An inhumation burial in a cist produced a necklace of glass beads, with a centre-piece of Roman glass. Baldwin Brown seems unreasonably hesitant about an Anglian attribution,[34] while Laing even more unreasonably rejects it as 'not a pagan Saxon deposit, nor is the character in keeping with a Christian grave'.[35]

                                                                    Meaney, 304

DARLINGTON (DRH)   *alpha*

The full publication of the finds from this small inhumation cemetery by Miket and Pocock have amply demonstrated its alpha quality.[36] Because of the character of the records, it is not possible to attribute grave goods to individual burials. It is none the less clear that among six skeletons of both sexes, both adult and children's, there were two sword-bearing warriors, and perhaps one spearman. Two great square-headed brooches, two cruciforms, two small-longs, and two circular brooches are to be distributed among the womenfolk, implying at least one alpha-grade lady. A chatelaine may also symbolize matronly authority.

GALEWOOD (NTB)   *beta*

Apparently two inhumations, one a woman with a pot, two bronze rings, and a bead, the other male, with two iron spearheads.

                                                                    Meaney, 198–9.

GREAT TOSSON (NTB)   *beta*

Secondary burials in a barrow, with a bronze buckle and an iron spearhead.

                                                                    Meaney, 199.

HEPPLE (NTB)   *beta*

An uncertain number of burials found with knives, beads, toilet articles, a bronze chain: all very undistinguished.

                                                                    Meaney, 199.

HOWICK (NTB)   *gamma (beta ?)*

Keeney's reconstitution of the evidence of burials and grave goods found in quarrying in 1928–30 demonstrated that they had come from a cemetery of about 15 burials.[37] The only common objects were iron knives which, together with three glass beads, would suggest a gamma grade for the cemetery. Only one burial is raised to the beta level by a spearhead; though an iron horse-bit, if it truly belongs with a burial, may hint at a higher grade.

The grades assigned above may now be tabulated as follows:

alpha	alpha ?	beta	beta ?	gamma
5	1	6	1	1

Even if we ignore the queried alpha and beta, the alpha:beta ratio of 5:6 is obviously dramatically different from that observed in Berkshire and Wiltshire. This point is reinforced by consideration of the ratio of sword to spear burials. If we infer that at Darlington there were two sword-burials and one spear-grave, and if we accept the presence of a sword at Dalmeny but not at Corbridge, then we have a 4:6 ratio. Now it can easily be objected that we are dealing with a small sample, and that these ratios could easily be upset by new discoveries. But before too much weight is given to this criticism, it can easily be calculated that to bring the Bernician ratio into line with that for Abingdon (2:17), the next twenty-eight weapon-burials in Bernicia would all have to produce spears, without a single sword. In other words, the number of spears would have to be multiplied nearly five times without any additional swords. Faced with the need for a numerical manipulation of this order, it can scarcely be objected that our Bernician sample is unusably small.

In brief: it can reasonably be inferred that pagan burials in Bernicia, though scant in number, are rich in quality compared with those of Wessex. It can certainly be demonstrated that the proportion of sword-burials to spear-burials is significantly higher. So far as the evidence of weapon-graves can take us, our picture of Wessex, and of East Anglia too, would be of a community of spearmen, with only a small leaven of swordsmen. But for Anglian Bernicia, we see relatively few warriors, and those as likely to be armed with a sword as with a spear. So far as the weapons go, this is the observed evidence: its implications, in terms of social patterns and settlement history, are another matter.

4. *The social implications of cemetery-gradation*

Although the pioneers of pagan Saxon archaeology, such as Faussett and Akerman,[38] do not seem to have concerned themselves with apparent differences in wealth between one grave or cemetery and another, it has long been accepted that weapon-graves reflect gradations of rank in early English Society.[39] In particular, Davidson has shown that the cost of forging a sword, so well demonstrated by Anstee and Biek,[40] must imply that a sword-grave reflected great wealth, and the corresponding social status of the warrior with whom it was buried.[41] Anthropologically oriented prehistorians are, of course, working towards similar equations between grave goods and social structure,[42] not always without opposition.[43] Fortunately, in the protohistoric field of pagan England, enough retrospective light is cast by the documents of early history for us to be reasonably certain, firstly, that society was stratified, and secondly, that there is some correlation between the status of the living and the equipment of the dead.

Both these propositions are implicit in poetic sources, and especially in *Beowulf*.[44] We may, however, have reservations, because the poet's picture of pagan society and its customs, although ultimately founded in fact, is none the less idealized or romanticized. Fortunately, no such doubts attach to those legal documents which bring wealth, status, and death into common focus, namely, wills and the payment of heriot on a warrior's death. Brooks has shown that the evidence of wills confirms that of law codes: by the Late Saxon period, the payment due from a lesser thegn to his lord consisted of a horse with its gear, a helmet, a mail-coat, a sword, a spear, and a shield.[45] Some two centuries earlier, the capitularies of Charlemagne required a vassal to be equipped with a horse, sword, scramasax, lance, and shield; but the same sources likewise defined the arms of a free man as *scutum et lanceam*: shield and spear.[46] The capitularies reflect here the pattern of Germanic warrior society in the late eighth and early ninth centuries, and equally clearly, the furnishing of our alpha and beta graves two centuries earlier still.

The parallel between warrior status as determined by heriot payments and as reflected in grave goods can be stated even more precisely. Brooks quotes Stein (1967) for the German view that the heriot derived from the pagan practice of burying weapons in the graves of noble warriors, adding that 'the weapons found in the Alemannic aristocratic graves of the seventh and eighth centuries correspond particularly closely with the arms specified in medieval heriots'. In England 'it is certainly possible that the practice of paying a heriot of weapons and treasure to the lord from the goods of a dead noble follower emerged in England . . . from the opportunities provided by the abandonment of pagan burial practices'.[47] Finally, we must note his view that 'the evidence of pagan Saxon graves strongly suggests that . . . the ubiquitous spear and shield were the basic equipment of free men'.[48]

In sum, then, the documentary evidence encourages us to see a three-fold division of the early Anglo-Saxons into thegns, *ceorls* or free warriors, and the unfree. This social stratification is represented in the grave furniture by the three classes of alpha, beta, and gamma graves.

Even if this picture is correct only in broad terms, it could ultimately provide a basis for assessing the relative numbers of the three classes in any one community, in so far as that community is represented by its cemetery. Already we can see in

Wessex a society comprising a few sword-bearing thegns, probably under-represented in the graves because of the practice of handing swords down from generation to generation;[49] a large mass of yeoman-warriors, the *ceorls*; and a substratum of the unfree, difficult to quantify at present because of the poverty of their graves. This view, derived from our analysis of the Wiltshire and Berkshire cemeteries, agrees reasonably with the picture of Wessex society which we gain, for instance, from the Wessex law codes and other documentary sources.

But if the arguments deployed here about the correlation of grave furniture with social status are reasonable, and if the analysis of the Bernician graves in Part 3 above is sound, then the social structure of Bernicia ought to be different from that of Wessex. Such a conclusion need not surprise us, for it is already implicit in Bede's account of the Northumbrian king's thegn, *minister regis*, Imma (HE, IV, 22).[50] Wounded and captured in a battle against the Mercians, Imma attempted to escape death by claiming to be not a soldier, *miles*, but a *ceorl* or yokel, *rusticus*, who was poor and recently married, and had merely come to the battlefield to bring supplies for the troops.

It is difficult to reconcile Bede's antithesis of peasant and soldier with the military obligations of the Wessex *ceorl* as set out, for instance, in Ine's Laws (Ine 51).[51] It is true that Finberg, while accepting that the *ceorl* was liable for military service, claims that 'the story of Imma shows conclusively that the husbandman's place was in the commissariat, not in the fighting line'.[52] Given that the Wessex *ceorl* was a free man with military obligations, and that 'the bearing of arms was in Germanic society a symbol of legal freedom',[53] such an interpretation seems perverse. It is certainly impossible to reconcile with the presence of spears, and frequently shields as well, in the generality of Wessex male graves. Archaeological evidence and documentary sources concur in presenting the mass of Wessex peasants as warriors too.

But the contrast between *miles* and *rusticus*, soldier and husbandman, may be explained if we remember not only that Imma was a Northumbrian thegn, but also that our source, Bede, was Northumbrian, and a man of literally cloistered experience at that. If the high ratio of sword- to spear-graves in Bernicia really has social implications, then it must surely imply a society in which warrior-peasants were thin on the ground, and warrior-aristocrats relatively numerous. This is the social background which Bede's account of Imma requires in order to appear credible.

5. *The Anglian element in Bernicia*

It is agreed that Anglian burials are scanty in Bernicia. In Part 3 it has been shown that, among the few graves, sword burials are commoner in relation to spear burials than is the case in Wessex. In Part 4, it is argued that this implies a different social structure too: one in which the class of spear-bearing freemen was unimportant as compared with the sword-bearing thegnly class. If, in this respect, the graves accurately reflect the character of Anglian society in Bernicia, then the further point may be advanced that in its social structure Anglian society must have differed little from the British society which it supplanted.

We have, of course, no cemetery evidence for the structure of British society, but there is at least helpful documentary evidence. The Welsh law books,[54] though strictly relevant only to early medieval Wales, have echoes in Northumbria which reveal the character of the pre-Anglian arrangements there.[55] By contrast, the *Gododdin* poem is absolutely relevant to Bernicia on the very eve of the Anglian takeover; if, that is, we can believe that its core is the authentic work of the poet Aneirin, composed in the decades around AD 600. The arguments in favour of this are not beyond question, but they have recently been strongly reaffirmed from a historian's point of view.[56]

The law books reveal a sharply tapered pyramid: at the top, the king; immediately below him, a small group of officials, and the rather larger *teulu,* the king's bodyguard or war-band;[57] and then, as a very broad base, the bondmen, tillers of the soil and suppliers of the services and renders in kind which supported king, *teulu,* and officials.[58] There is no sign here of the free, spear-bearing peasantry of Wessex.

Taken at face-value, the evidence of the *Gododdin* is in agreement, for the poem, itself a series of elegies on fallen warriors, incorporates the story of a force of only 300 warriors: the war-band of Mynyddog Mwynfawr of Edinburgh, augmented from other kingdoms for a special campaign. This small band consists principally, if not entirely, of mounted warriors, armed with swords and spears, we cannot say in what ratio. Jackson has argued, however, from general military probabilities, from one express mention of infantry, and from the fact that parts of the action at Catraeth were fought on foot, 'that "three hundred" means three hundred picked chiefs, each of whom would have with him a sufficient complement of supporting foot-soldiers'. He has suggested 'anything up to three thousand or more would perhaps be reasonable' for the whole army.[59]

Jackson's figure was rejected by Alcock,[60] partly on the basis of the social analysis advanced above, partly from a wider examination of the size of Dark Age armies. In reviewing Alcock 1971, Jackson modified his original figure: 'perhaps only two or three [retainers to each mounted noble], making the army total about 1,000, would be acceptable'.[61] On present evidence, the hypothesis that the mounted warrior aristocrats of the Gododdin were accompanied by unsung infantry retainers can neither be proved or disproved. What is certain is that, as a class, such men have left no evidence of their existence in the law codes. From other documentary evidence, Davies has concluded that in another British area, south-east Wales, 'the existence of untied completely free peasantry is neither demonstrable nor deniable'.[62]

The British evidence would seem, then, to point to a society in which free, weapon-bearing peasantry were not prominent. The Bernician graves indicate a similar social structure: one very different from pagan Wessex, and equally different from our general picture of Germanic society. Jolliffe showed long ago that the administrative arrangements of Northumbria owed much to British pre-Anglian organization.[63] Taken altogether, evidence of varied kinds suggests that a very few Anglian thegns, supported by a small number of retainers, took over the territory and organization of the British Votadini as a going concern.

There are other pointers in the same direction. The 'E' recension of the Anglo-Saxon Chronicle, s.a. 547, describes Ida's building of Bamburgh in terms reminiscent of the fortification of a Late Saxon *burh*: 'first enclosed with a stockade, and afterwards with a wall'.[64] This would seem to reflect a tenth- or eleventh-century source,[65] rather than a sixth-century one. Indeed, if Ida really had built Bamburgh, this would be highly remarkable, for we have no other evidence that the early English built fortified places.[66] On the other hand, *Historia Brittonum* provides us with a British name for Bamburgh: Din Guaroy or some such.[67] This British, and therefore pre-Anglian, name, clearly implies a pre-Anglian *din* or fort. We may reasonably see Bamburgh, therefore, as a British promontory fort, which came into the possession of the Bernician dynasty, whether by gift or seizure, in the mid-sixth century. In other words, as a royal city (*urbs regia*) of Bernicia, Bamburgh results from the Anglian take-over of a British centre of power.

The same seems to be true of another Bernician royal site, the *villa regia* . . . *Adgefrin,* Yeavering. The entrance arrangements of the remarkable palisaded fort here—bulbous rampart terminals containing a rectangular timber structure—mark it as a Votadinian work, with antecedents in Harehope II, and probably Hogbridge, Peeblesshire, as well.[68] On this evidence alone, it would be possible to postulate that the Bernician dynasty had taken over a British fortified political centre at Yeavering. This conclusion, already tenable before the full publication of the Yeavering excavations, has now been strongly reinforced by the very varied evidence of Bernician indebtedness to the Britons at Yeavering.[69] Moreover, the succession of royal or thegnly halls at Doon Hill, East Lothian, also argues for an Anglian take-over, perhaps by force, of a prestigious British site.[70]

Finally, there is a distinct probability that the Bernician Angles inherited from the Britons a major military technique: the use of cavalry. The earliest reference to a mounted force among the Anglo-Saxons appears to be in Eddius' *Life of Wilfrid*.[71] He tells us that, about AD 672, Ecgfrith of the Bernician dynasty, in the face of a Pictish rebellion, *statim equitatui exercitu praeparato . . . invasit,* 'having got together a cavalry force, immediately invaded'. I know of no earlier reference to the use of cavalry in battle among the Angles or their continental ancestors. On the other hand, as we have seen, mounted warriors formed the core, if not indeed the whole, of the army of Gododdin. It seems likely, therefore, that the Angles of Bernicia learned this new technique of warfare, which must have included the breeding and training of horses for battle, from the Britons. They may have done so, of course, by contact on the field of battle. But given the clear social implications of this expensive new technique,[72] it is altogether more probable that it was part of the over-all package of social and administrative organization which they acquired from the Britons.

6. *Epilogue*

Parts 4 and 5 of this paper have taken us a long way from the original study of the Bernician graves, on an exploration of the sociological significance of grave-archaeology: a significance which is often hinted at,[73] but all too rarely pursued. It is no doubt appropriate that this exploration should have been attempted in an area of considerable interplay between German and Celt; for over the past two decades most of the progress in combining archaeology with varied documentary sources in order to write a richly textured economic and social history has been made in Celtic areas. At a time, too, when a major survey of Anglo-Saxon archaeology[74] gives little weight to cemeteries and grave-goods, it may have been useful to reassert the historical potential of the traditional materials of pagan archaeology.

At the end of the journey, we are very close to Myres's position in 1936. He then wrote: 'in Bernicia a far greater proportion of the native lands were at first left for tributary British subjects of the new military aristocracy than was the case in those parts of Britain where the invaders were rather seeking habitable lands for themselves than to live on the rents of a dependent native population'.[75] This seems to represent very well the balance of Angle and Briton in Bernician society. To it we would only add that, increasingly, the evidence leads us to believe that the Anglian aristocracy took over the political, military, social, and economic arrangements of the Votadinian Britons as a going concern.

Bibliography

ADDYMAN, P., 'Archaeology and Anglo-Saxon Society', in G. de G. Sieveking, I.H. Longworth, and K.E. Wilson (eds.), *Problems in Economic and Social Archaeology* (London, 1976), 309–22.

AKERMAN, J.Y., *Remains of Pagan Saxondom* (London, 1855).

ALCOCK, L., *Arthur's Britain: History and Archaeology AD 367–634* (London, 1971).

ALCOCK, L., 'Her . . . gefeaht wiþ Walas: Aspects of the Warfare of Saxons and Britons', *Bulletin Board of Celtic Studies* 27, iii (November 1977), 412–24.

ALCOCK, L., 'The North Britons, the Picts and the Scots', in P.J. Casey (ed.), *The End of Roman Britain (British Archaeological Reports)* (Oxford, 1979).

ANSTEE, J.W. and BIEK, L., 'A Study in pattern-welding', *Medieval Archaeol.* 5 (1961), 71–93.

BALDWIN BROWN, G., 'Notes on a necklace of glass beads found in a cist in Dalmeny Park, South Queensferry', *Proc. Soc. Antiq. Scotland* 49 (1914–15), 332–8.

BALDWIN BROWN, G., *The Arts in Early England, 3 and 4, Saxon Art and Industry in the Pagan Period* (London, 1915).

BELL, M., 'Excavations at Bishopstone', *Sussex Archaeol. Collections* 115 (1977).

BROOKS, N., 'The development of military obligations in eighth- and ninth-century England', in P. Clemoes and K. Hughes (eds.), *England Before the Conquest, Studies in primary sources presented to Dorothy Whitelock* (Cambridge, 1971), 69–84.

BROOKS, N.P., 'Arms, Status and Warfare in Late-Saxon England', in D. Hill (ed.), *Ethelred the Unready: Papers from the Millenary Conference (British Archaeological Reports British Series 59)* (Oxford, 1978), 81–103.

BROWN, J.A., (ed.), *Approaches to the Social Dimensions of Mortuary Practices (Memoirs of the Society for American Archaeology, No. 25),* (1971).

BRUCE-MITFORD, R., *Aspects of Anglo-Saxon Archaeology, Sutton Hoo and other discoveries* (London, 1974).

CHADWICK, H.M., *The Origin of the English Nation* (Cambridge, 1907).

CHADWICK, S.E., 'The Anglo-Saxon Cemetery at Finglesham, Kent: a reconsideration', *Medieval Archaeol.* 2 (1958), 1–71.

CHAPMAN, R.W., 'Burial Practices: an area of mutual interest', in M. Spriggs (ed.), *Archaeology and Anthropology: Areas of Mutual Interest (British Archaeological Reports Supplementary Series 19)* (Oxford, 1977).

CHARLES-EDWARDS, T.M., 'The Authenticity of the *Gododdin*: an Historian's View', in R. Bromwich and R.B. Jones (eds.), *Astudiaethau ar yr Hengerdd* (Cardiff, 1978), 44–71.

CLARKE, D.L. and CHAPMAN, B., *Analytical Archaeology*, 2nd edn. (London, 1978).

COLGRAVE, B. (ed. and trans.), *The Life of Bishop Wilfrid by Eddius Stephanus* (Cambridge, 1927).

COLGRAVE, B. and MYNORS, R.A.G. (eds. and trans.), *Bede's Ecclesiastical History of the English People* (Oxford, 1969).

CRAMP, R.J., 'Beowulf and Archaeology', *Medieval Archaeol.* 1 (1957), 57–77.

CRAMP, R.J., 'The Anglo-Saxon Period', in J.C. Dewdney (ed.), *Durham County with Teesside* (Durham, 1970), 199–206.

DAVIDSON, H.R.E., *The Sword in Anglo-Saxon England, its Archaeology and Literature* (Oxford, 1962).

DAVIDSON, H.R.E. and WEBSTER, L., 'The Anglo-Saxon Burial at Coombe (Woodnesborough), Kent', *Medieval Archaeol.* 11 (1967), 1–41.

DAVIES, W., *An Early Welsh Microcosm: Studies in the Llandaff Charters* (*Royal Historical Society Studies in History Series*, No. 9), (London, 1978).

DUMVILLE, D.N., 'Palaeographical Considerations in the Dating of Early Welsh Verse', *Bulletin Board of Celtic Studies* 27, ii (May, 1977), 246–51.

EARLE. J. and PLUMMER, C., *Two of the Saxon Chronicles Parallel*, 2 vols. (Oxford, 1892, 1899).

FAUSSETT, B., *Inventorium Sepulchrale: an Account of Some Antiquities dug up . . . in Kent from A.D. 1757 to A.D. 1773* (London, 1856).

FINBERG, H.P.R., *The Formation of England 550–1042* (London, 1974).

GREEN, B. and ROGERSON, A., *The Anglo-Saxon Cemetery at Bergh Apton, Norfolk: Catalogue* (*East Anglian Archaeology Report* No. 7), (Gressenhall, 1978).

HARDING, D.W. (ed.), *Archaeology in the North* (Durham, 1976).

HOPE-TAYLOR, B., *Yeavering, An Anglo-British centre of early Northumbria* (*Department of Environment Archaeological Reports,* No. 7), (London, 1977).

HUNTER BLAIR, P., 'The Bernicians and their Northern Frontier', in N.K. Chadwick (ed.), *Studies in Early British History* (Cambridge, 1954), 137–72.

JACKSON, K.H., 'Edinburgh and the Anglian occupation of Lothian', in P. Clemoes (ed.), *The Anglo-Saxons* (London, 1959), 34–42.

JACKSON, K., 'On the Northern British Section in Nennius', in N.K. Chadwick (ed.), *Celt and Saxon: Studies in the Early British Border* (Cambridge, 1963), 20–62.

JACKSON, K.H., *The Gododdin* (Edinburgh, 1969).

JACKSON, K., Review of Alcock 1971, *Antiquity* 47 (1973), 80–1.

JOLLIFFE, J.E.A., 'Northumbrian Institutions', *English Historical Review* 41 (1926), 1–42.

JONES, G.R.J., 'Post-Roman Wales', in H.P.R. Finberg (ed.), *The Agrarian History of England and Wales*, I, ii, AD 43–1042 (Cambridge, 1972), 281–382.

KEENEY, G.S., 'A Pagan Anglian Cemetery at Howick, Northumberland', *Archaeol. Aeliana* 4th series 16 (1939), 120–8.

KNOCKER, G.M., 'Early Burials and an Anglo-Saxon Cemetery at Snell's Corner, near Horndean, Hampshire', *Proc. Hants. Fld. Club and Archaeol. Soc.* 19 (1958), 117–70.

LAING, LL., 'The Angles in Scotland and the Mote of Mark', *Trans. Dumfries & Galloway Natur. Hist. and Antiq. Soc.* 3rd ser., 50 (1973), 37–52.

LEEDS, E.T. and HARDEN, D.B., *The Anglo-Saxon Cemetery at Abingdon, Berkshire* (Oxford, 1936).

LEEDS, E.T. and SHORTT, H. de S., *An Anglo-Saxon Cemetery at Petersfinger, near Salisbury, Wilts.* (Salisbury, 1953).

LETHBRIDGE, T.C., 'Recent Excavations in Anglo-Saxon Cemeteries in Cambridgeshire & Suffolk', *Cambridge Antiq. Soc. Quarto Publications* NS 3 (1931).

MEANEY, A., *A Gazetteer of Early Anglo-Saxon Burial Sites* (London, 1964).

MEANEY, A.L. and HAWKES, S.C., *Two Anglo-Saxon Cemeteries at Winnal* (Society for Medieval Archaeology Monograph Series: No. 4), (London, 1970).

MIKET, R. and POCOCK, M., 'An Anglo-Saxon Cemetery at Greenbank, Darlington', *Medieval Archaeol.* 20 (1976), 62–74.

ORDNANCE SURVEY, *Map of Britain in the Dark Ages* 2nd edn. (Chessington, 1966).

REES, W., 'Survivals of Ancient Celtic Custom in Medieval England', in *Angles and Britons; O'Donnell Lectures* (Cardiff, 1963), 149–68.

REYNOLDS, N., 'Dark Age Timber Halls', *Scottish Archaeol. Forum* 10 (1980), 41–60.

RICHARDS, M., *The Laws of Hywel Dda* (Liverpool, 1954).

STEIN, F., *Adelsgräber des achten Jahrhunderts in Deutschland* (Germanische Denkmäler der Völkerwanderungszeit, No. 9), (Berlin, 1967).

SWANTON, M.J., *The Spearheads of the Anglo-Saxon Settlements* (London, 1973).

SWANTON, M.J., *A Corpus of Pagan Anglo-Saxon Spear-types* (British Archaeological Reports 7), (Oxford, 1974).

TAINTER, J.A., 'Social inference and mortuary practices: an experiment in numerical classification', *World Archaeology* 7 (1975), 1–15.

UCKO, P.J., 'Ethnography and archaeological interpretation of funerary remains', *World Archaeology* 1 (1969), 262–80.

WHITELOCK, D., *English Historical Documents c.500–1042* (London, 1955).

WILSON, D.M. (ed.), *The Archaeology of Anglo-Saxon England* (London, 1976).

WORMALD, P., 'Bede, "Beowulf" and the Conversion of the Anglo-Saxon Aristocracy', in R.T. Farrell (ed.), *Bede and Anglo-Saxon England* (British Archaeological Reports 46), (Oxford, 1978), 32–95.

Notes and References

1. This essay has been extracted from my O'Donnell lecture, delivered in the University of Edinburgh on 21 April, 1978. I am grateful to the University, and especially to Professor Kenneth Jackson, for inviting me to read the paper. Some or all of the present version has been discussed with or read by E.A. Alcock, N.P. Brooks, A.A.M. Duncan, V.I. Evison, M. Miller, N. Reynolds, and P. Wormald; I am most grateful to them all.
2. Hunter Blair, 1959, 149, n.1.
3. Myres, 1936 (No. 25), 422.
4. Harding, 1976, 44.
5. Swanton, 1973, 12.
6. Miket and Pocock, 1976.
7. For other recent, less optimistic, surveys, see Cramp, 1970, 199–200; Harding, 1976, 44.
8. There is a preliminary, more tentative statement in Alcock, 1971, 291–2.
9. Swanton, 1973, 2–4; Swanton, 1974.
10. Bell, 1977, 193.
11. Knocker, 1958.
12. Chadwick, 1958.
13. Lethbridge, 1931, 1–45.
14. Green and Rogerson, 1978.
15. Leeds and Harden, 1936.
16. Leeds and Shortt, 1953.
17. Lethbridge, 1931, 9.
18. Chadwick, 1958, 32.
19. Meaney, 1964.
20. e.g. Ordnance Survey, 1966.
21. Jackson, 1969, 7.
22. Hunter Blair, 1959; Jackson, 1959.
23. Miket and Pocock, 1976.
24. Keeney, 1938.
25. Meaney, 1964.
26. Baldwin Brown, 1915, 349, with pl. lxxi, 5.
27. Baldwin Brown, 1915, 484, with pl. cxxiv.
28. Chadwick, 1958, 12, with pl. iv, C.
29. Davidson and Webster, 1967, 21, with pl. ii.

30. Baldwin Brown, 1915, 811–12, with pl. clviii, 9.
31. Report of Curators, National Museum of Antiquities of Scotland, *Proc. Soc. Antiq. Scotland* 1 (1851–4), 217–18. I am grateful to Mr J.L. Davidson, Archaeology Branch, Ordnance Survey, for advice on the correct location.
32. Laing, 1973, 46, with pl. ii; Bruce-Mitford, 1974, 268, with pls. 86 e, f, 87.
33. Davidson, 1962, 85–8; for 'Dalmey Church, Linlithgow' read 'West Craigie Farm, Dalmeny, West Lothian'.
34. Baldwin Brown, 1914–15.
35. Laing, 1973, 45–6.
36. Miket and Pocock, 1976.
37. Keeney, 1938.
38. Faussett, *c*.1773, but published 1856; Akerman, 1855.
39. Baldwin Brown, 1915, 196–7; 205–7.
40. Anstee and Biek, 1961.
41. Davidson, 1962, 211.
42. For instance: Brown, 1971; Chapman, 1977; Tainter, 1975; also Clarke and Chapman, 1978, 140.
43. Ucko, 1969.
44. Cramp, 1957; Wormald, 1978.
45. Brooks, 1978, 81.
46. Brooks, 1978, 82–3.
47. Brooks, 1978, 90–2.
48. Brooks, 1978, 83.
49. Davidson, 1962, 118.
50. Colgrave and Mynors, 1969, 400–5.
51. Whitelock, 1955, 370; Brooks, 1971, 69.
52. Finberg, 1974, 68.
53. Brooks, 1978, 83.
54. Most easily accessible in Richards, 1954.
55. Jolliffe, 1926; Rees, 1963.
56. Jackson, 1969; Dumville, 1977; Charles-Edwards, 1978.
57. Alcock, 1971, 324–5.
58. Jones, 1972, 299 ff.
59. Jackson, 1969, 15.
60. Alcock, 1971, 336.
61. Jackson, 1973, 80.
62. Davies, 1978, 47.
63. Jolliffe, 1926.
64. Earle and Plummer, 1892, 16–17.
65. For which, indeed, there are other arguments, as Professor D. Whitelock kindly informs me.

66. Alcock, 1977.
67. Jackson, 1963, 27–8.
68. Alcock, 1979.
69. Hope-Taylor, 1977 (but not actually published until 1979).
70. Reynolds, 1980.
71. As Colgrave pointed out in 1927, 165; text, ibid. 40–3. But Chadwick (1907, 159, n.1) took a less rigid line.
72. Brooks, 1978.
73. e.g. Meaney and Hawkes, 1970; Addyman, 1976.
74. Wilson, 1976.
75. Myres, 1936 (No. 22), 422.

Addendum

Much of relevance to the evidence and interpretations discussed above may now be found in Rahtz, P., Dickinson, T. and Watts, L. (eds), *Anglo-Saxon Cemeteries 1979* (*British Archaeological Reports British Series* 82) (Oxford, 1980).

For the problems of inferring social status from grave goods, see also Shephard, J., 'The social identity of the individual in isolated barrows and barrow cemeteries in Anglo-Saxon England', in B.C. Burham and J. Kingsbury (eds), *Space, Hierarchy and Society* (*British Archaeological Reports International Series* 59) (Oxford, 1979), 47–79.

9

The Illington/Lackford workshop

BARBARA GREEN, W.F. MILLIGAN, AND S.E. WEST

In a seminal paper published in 1937, Myres drew attention to a number of groups of Anglo-Saxon pots which, from a careful study of their stamped decoration, he suggested were the products of individual potters or workshops. Among the vessels discussed were three in the Ashmolean Museum from the cemeteries at Lackford and West Stow, Suffolk, and a fourth, then unprovenanced, urn, in the Moyse's Hall Museum, Bury St Edmunds.[1] Myres considered '. . . they raise the possibility of something like a miniature commercialized industry, even perhaps of mass production on a limited scale'.[2]

Reporting on his 1947 excavations on the Lackford cemetery, Lethbridge discussed further this group of stamped vessels which he designated the 'Icklingham' type, as he considered they had probably been made across the river Lark at Icklingham, from clay deposits which had been exploited by Romano-British potters. He defined the type as '. . . a globular jar or bowl, ornamented with several fine neck-grooves. It has often one or more horizontal zones of stamped ornament separated by three or four fine grooves and below that either a zone of pendant shield-shaped panels filled with stamped ornament or a similar zone of incised chevrons . . . It can be shown that identical stamps were used on many of these vessels, not only at Lackford but also at Little Wilbraham, West Stow Heath, and the St John's College cemetery at Cambridge.'[3]

In 1950, Group Captain Knocker excavated part of a predominantly cremation cemetery at Illington, Norfolk. Over forty urns or sherds from this workshop have been identified from the site, forming about one-fifth of the decorated pottery and about one-seventh of the total. When Myres discussed the workshop in 1969, he renamed it the Illington/Lackford workshop or potter after the two cemeteries which had produced the majority of finds.[4]

Lethbridge found one unusually large and elaborately decorated urn at Lackford (CN 931). It has a raised collar, vertical bosses, applied swastikas in the panels between the bosses and stamped decoration. He compared it with an even larger urn from St John's, Cambridge (CN 286). These two urns were linked to the Illington and Lackford urns by the stamps, but otherwise were unlike any other products known from this workshop.[5] Between 1957 and 1972 Evison and West excavated the Anglo-Saxon settlement site at West Stow Heath, Suffolk, and recovered sherds from a further twenty vessels of this type from this workshop.

The reports on the West Stow settlement and the Illington cemetery are well advanced. Rather than duplicate the study of this workshop in both reports, the present authors felt that a separate article would be more satisfactory. This volume presented an appropriate opportunity to publish the results to date, even though the detailed evidence from these sites has not yet been published.

DISTRIBUTION

The products of this workshop have been recovered from nine sites in a comparatively small area of south-west Norfolk, north-west Suffolk, and east Cambridgeshire, with a single outlier from north-west Norfolk at Castle Acre.[6] Since Myres published his distribution map[7] two new find spots have been added (fig. 1). The Norfolk sites are the Illington cemetery in Wretham parish, the Rushford cemetery (Brettenham parish), Castle Acre cemetery,[8] and a sherd from Redcastle, Thetford. In Suffolk, finds are recorded from the West Stow settlement and from the West Stow cemetery,[9] from the Westgarth Gardens cemetery at Bury St Edmunds, from the Lackford cemetery,[10] and from Icklingham, this latter being a stray find from a late Roman site. The two Cambridgeshire sites are the Little Wilbraham and St John's College, Cambridge, cemeteries.

Except for the Castle Acre cemetery which lies close to the river Nar, the sites lie near rivers which form part of the Ouse river system which at this period flowed into the Wash at or near Wisbech. All lie on, or in the case of the Cambridgeshire cemeteries close to, the chalk ridge which runs from north Norfolk through western East Anglia and eventually becomes the Chilterns. The Norfolk and Suffolk sites lie north of the system of Dykes which cut across this chalk ridge, along which ran the Icknield Way. Little Wilbraham lies between the Devil's Dyke which cuts across the ridge at Newmarket Heath and the Fleam Dyke, some six miles to the south-west,[11] while the St John's cemetery lies about six miles north-west of the chalk ridge.

It is difficult to be certain how far these sites truly reflect the distribution of the products of this workshop. Over sixty isolated burials and cemeteries have been recorded from this area of south-west Norfolk, north-west Suffolk, and east Cambridgeshire,[12] the largest concentration in the whole region. Of these, six are predominantly cremation cemeteries, ten are mixed cemeteries and twenty-nine are inhumation cemeteries, while a further nineteen sites have produced between one and three inhumation or cremation burials. The majority are old discoveries, and few objects survive from them or are otherwise recorded. For instance, out of over a hundred urns said to have been found at Rushford, only four survive. The single Illington/Lackford pot was identified by Dr Myres from a manuscript in the Maidstone Museum.[13] Out of over five hundred urns recovered by Lethbridge from the Lackford cemetery, only seventeen vessels from this workshop have been identified, while even at Illington only forty-three out of over three hundred pots can be attributed to the same source. The chances therefore of Illington/Lackford workshop pots being recovered and preserved from sites which have not been excavated under modern conditions are small. This is particularly true of finds from inhumation cemeteries, from which usually only the more attractive objects, e.g. the brooches, buckles, wrist clasps, spears, and swords tend to be preserved or published. It is interesting that vessels from the Illington/Lackford workshop have been recovered from three out of the six predominantly cremation cemeteries in the area (Illington, Lackford, and Rushford, and two of these have been excavated since the Second World War), three out of the ten mixed cemeteries (West Stow Heath, Little Wilbraham, and St John's), and one out of twenty-eight predominantly inhumation cemeteries (Westgarth Gardens excavated in 1972). Two of the finds are stray sherds (Red Castle, Thetford, from the western edge of the late Saxon town and Icklingham, from a late Roman site). The largest number of finds recorded from a single site is from the West Stow settlement (150), the only settlement in the area which has been fully investigated.

The evidence for the dating of these vessels has been deliberately omitted as it will be dealt with in full in the West Stow and Illington cemetery reports. But studies so far confirm the general late sixth-century date attributed to them by Lethbridge[14] and Myres.[15] A study of the associated grave goods and cremated bone from the Illington vessels show that they were used for both sexes and for children, adolescents, and adults.

METHOD OF STUDY

This survey has been based upon a detailed comparison of the stamps and decorative schemes, and upon a macroscopic examination of the pot fabrics. As far as possible the stamps on any pot or sherd have been compared directly with other vessels, rather than relying on drawings or photographs. In a few cases this was not feasible, and in these cases rubbings of a number of impressions from each vessel have been used.[16] The importance of such a direct confrontation became increasingly obvious as the study progressed.

Some stamps could be identified with certainty, either because of their size or certain details (see pp. 194–6 and Table 1, p. 193 for the detailed classification of stamps). With others it was more difficult, and it is possible that some of the stamps classified separately reflect, in fact, two or more states of the same stamp. For instance, it is possible that the D2 stamp impressions could have been made with a single stamp whose minute variations resulted from use, either by the development of flaws or by the clogging or wear of small details. On Illington CN 2140, the majority of the stamps could be classified as A8b, but a few clearly show the small hook used as the diagnostic feature of class A7. It is arguable therefore that some, at least, of the A8b impressions on other pots were made with the A7 stamps.

Experiments carried out by S.E. West with a bone stamp of type A (the cross stamp), and using a fine potting clay, have confirmed the reservations raised by other writers about the use of a single stamp on several vessels.

1. The appearance and size of a stamp varies with the depth of the impression.

  (a) A deeply impressed stamp was found to be up to a mm larger than a shallowly impressed stamp.

  (b) A stamp which appeared open (i.e. the ends of the cross arms reached the edge of the impression) in a shallow impression appeared closed in a deep impression.

2. The appearance and size of a stamp varies according to the angle at which the stamp is held.

3. The degree of dryness of the clay affects the depth to which the stamp could be impressed, so that if the critical stage was missed an impression could hardly be made.

4. Observations show that different fabrics shrink differently on firing; a further factor which could affect the size of an impression.

There are occasional examples among the urns where surface treatment after stamping, by smoothing or burnishing, has distorted both the shape and detail of an impression. It seems likely that most smoothing and burnishing was carried out before the stamped decoration was added. This argues therefore that the potters had a considerable technical skill as it was essential that a pot should reach a degree of dryness before burnishing, so that the vessel was not distorted, but it should not be so dry that the decoration could not be added.

Several bone or antler stamps have been found in this part of East Anglia. Although some produce impressions similar to those on the Illington/Lackford vessels none could be shown to have been used by this workshop.

POT FABRICS

Ten main fabrics have been identified by macroscopic examination. Illington urns were used to establish types 1 to 9, a West Stow vessel was the type specimen for 10.

Fabric

1. Close paste with sparse, small, rounded quartz grains (Type vessel CN 2144).
1 var. As 1 but with the addition of sparse small mica (Type vessel Illington 327(i)).
2. Yellow mica, visually glittery in break, and sub-angular quartz grains (Type vessels CN 2142, 2143).
2 var. As 2 but more grit (Type vessel CN 2147).
3. Rare mica, common angular grits, rather larger than in Fabric 2 (Type vessel CN 2146).
3 var. As 3, but less grit (Type vessel CN 4075).
4. White mica, common, fairly large angular grit (Type vessel CN 2152).
5. Large angular grits, common; white and yellow mica, the yellow mica is larger and more abundant than the white (Type vessel CN 2141).
6. Close paste with rounded sparse grit; sparse red inclusions; both surfaces pitted (Type vessel CN 2149).
7. Close paste with rounded sparse grit; common small to large red inclusions; sparse yellow mica; pitted surfaces (Type vessel CN 2125).
8. Very fine close paste all through; common small white mica; rare angular grits (Type vessel CN 4072).
9. Surface with small 'chaff'; break also 'chaffy'; large quartz grit and small grains (Type vessel CN 2138).
10. Close paste, very hard, common angular grit (Type vessel: West Stow Hut 50 (2)).

Although the type specimens were compared directly with all the vessels handled by the writers there were a number of difficulties. In the event of a disagreement a majority decision was taken. The sherds with weathered fractures were especially difficult to assign to a fabric type, as the detail was often obscured. This was found particularly when there was a suspicion of chaff or grass tempering. There were examples among the broken pots, for which much of the profile could be established, of a distinct variation in the proportion of inclusions visible in the different fractures. The fabrics of some complete or restored pots could not be established. Despite these problems it was felt worth attributing vessels to these fabric types and considering the stamps and decorative schemes in relation to them. Some interesting results have been obtained, see pp. 209–11.

Clearly one of the critical questions raised in any study of an Anglo-Saxon pottery workshop is whether the pots were produced in a single centre and traded from there to surrounding settlements, or whether itinerant potters travelled from settlement to settlement, producing vessels to order. The writers are certain that such a problem cannot be solved by the macroscopic examination of the pastes. Before this present comparative study began samples were taken from Illington, Lackford, and West Stow for examination by X-ray diffraction.[17] A random selection of samples was made from incomplete vessels or those which had not been fully restored for display purposes. Vessels represented only by small sherds were also excluded. The present fabric types had not been established but care was taken to include fabrics which contained red inclusions (fabrics 6 and 7) as well as those without. To date no pattern has emerged. It is clear that a more systematic study, perhaps using a different technique, must be carried out. This is under consideration at the time of writing.

In the main the pots attributed to this workshop are hard, and give the impression of being well fired. Almost without exception, the Anglo-Saxon sherds excavated from the West Stow settlement (not just those attributed to this workshop) were hard when found, and could be washed immediately. In contrast, S.E. West remembers that, during the excavation of the Lackford cemetery, which is situated on soils similar to those at the West Stow settlement site, much of the pottery had to be allowed to dry off before being lifted. Today many of the urns give the impression of being well fired. It is possible, therefore, that many of the Lackford urns, including perhaps those from the Illington/Lackford workshop, were made specifically for funerary purposes and would not have stood up to domestic use.

THE STAMPS

Sixteen categories of stamps are recognized on the basis of shape;[18] some are divided into sub-classes where there are significant differences, or into varieties where there are differences but of a minute kind. The possibility of two stamps being defined which may in fact be the same has already been discussed above (p. 190).

Table 1: Illington/Lackford stamps

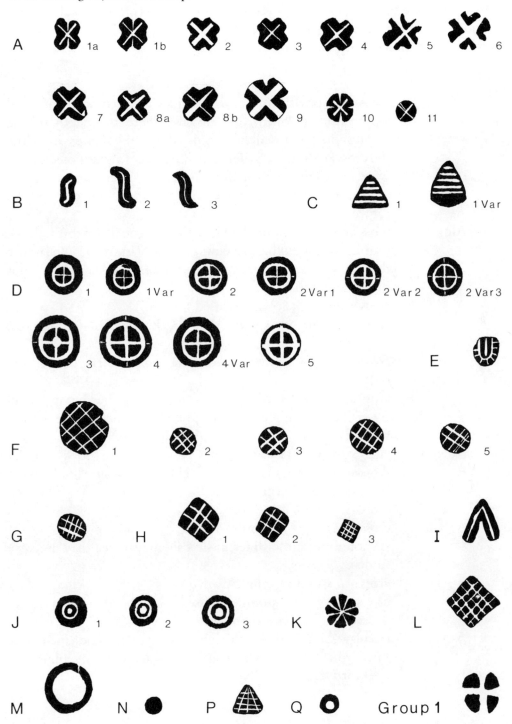

Table 1 Stamps: The style of drawing used was chosen after considerable comparison, and the blacked-in areas represent the hollows on the vessel. It is not intended that these should be used to confirm the identity of Illington/Lackford finds, without direct comparison on a stamp to stamp basis.

Definitions:

Class A	Cross stamp with arms at right angles, approximately of equal length, either 'open', or 'closed' where the depth of the impression has caused the outside edge of the stamps to enclose the cross arms entirely. The tiny differences in size noted below were sufficiently consistent to justify the statements.
A1a	cross arms 7 × 7 mm; closed, with a diagonal line through the centre.
A1b	cross arms 8 × 8 mm; closed, with a diagonal line through the centre. Although these two differ slightly in size, in appearance they are very similar. It cannot be certain that A1a and b are not the same stamp.
A2	cross arms 7.5 × 8.5 mm; closed.
A3	cross arms 6.5 × 7.5 mm; closed. The smallest of the cross stamps.
A4	cross arms 9 × 8 mm; closed. One arm thickens toward the centre.
A5	cross arms 9 × 8.5 mm; just closed. Arms rather broader than A1–4. Few examples, poorly preserved; may not be a valid type.
A6	cross arms 10 × 11 mm; open. Cross arms very broad.
A7	cross arms 10 × 8.5 mm; closed. There is a distinct hook on the end of one cross arm.
A8a	cross arms 8 × 9 mm; closed.
A8b	cross arms 9.5 × 10.5 mm; closed. Although 8a and b differ in size, in appearance they are very similar.
A9	cross arms 12 × 12 mm; closed.
A10	cross arms 7.5 × 7.5 mm; a crossed cross, the main cross closed; the second, fainter cross open.
A11	circular stamp with simple right-angled cross. One arm double lined, diameter 5.5 mm. Not classified as an Illington/Lackford stamp.

Class B	An 'S' stamp, normally reversed; with medial bar.
B1	real S.
B2	reversed S; both ends rounded.
B3	reversed S; both ends pointed.

Class C	Barred triangle.
C	Four bars.
C var.	Five bars; this may well be the same stamp, the variation due to rocking, thus giving an additional bar and a rounded base.

Class D	A cross in circle, the diameters used are to the outer edge of the raised circle, not the edge of the stamp.
D1	diameter 6.5 mm, fine cross arms.
D1 var.	diameter 6.5 mm, as for D1, but the outline is slightly pear-shaped, with a slight thickening of the raised circle on one side. This could be the D1 stamp which had developed a flaw.
D2	diameter 8 mm. No outer bars between the raised circle and the edge of the stamp.
D2 var. 1	diameter 8 mm, with one bar.
D2 var. 2	diameter 8 mm, with two bars.
D2 var. 3	diameter 8 mm, with four bars.
	By size these could all be the same stamp. The presence or absence of the outer bars may be due to clogging, as these are extremely fine.
D3	diameter 10 mm, with central hub and one outer bar.
D4	diameter 11 mm, with four outer bars and broad cross arms.
D4 var.	diameter 10 mm, with no outer bars. This was lightly impressed and could therefore be the D4 stamp.
D5	diameter $c.9$ mm, with four outer bars, the same thickness as the cross arms.

Class E	Horse-shoe shaped stamps, length 7 mm.

Class F	Round gridded stamp.
F1	diameter $c.14$ mm, 3×4 bars.
F2	diameter 6.5–7 mm, 3×2 bars.
F3	diameter 8 mm, 2×2 bars.
F4	diameter 9 mm, 2×4 bars.
F5	diameter 8.5 mm, 2×4 bars, but 2 bars are very close.

Class G	Oval gridded stamp; 6.5 × 7.5 mm, 4 × 2 bars.
Class H	Square gridded stamp.
H1	*c*.8.5 mm, 2 × 2 bars.
H2	*c*.8 mm, 2 × 2 bars (only one stamp found).
H3	*c*.5 mm, 3 × 3 bars.
Class I	Inverted V stamp. Height 11.5 mm.
Class J	Raised dot-in-circle stamp. Diameters given are to outer edge of circle, not to the border of the stamp.
J1	diameter 4.5 × 5 mm, central dot 1.5 mm.
J2	diameter 5 × 5.5 mm, central dot 2 mm.
J3	diameter 6.5 mm, central dot 3 mm.
Class K	Rosette stamp. Diameter 8.5 mm.
Class L	Lozenge gridded stamp. 13 × 14.5 mm across points. 4 × 4 bars.
Class M	Broken circle. Diameter of inner circle *c*.9 mm.
Class N	Dimples.
Class P	Triangular gridded stamp. Height *c*.7.5 mm. 4 × 3 bars. Marginal, does not occur with other Illington/Lackford stamps.
Class Q	Raised dot in broad groove. Dot off centre. Diameter to outer edge of impression *c*.5 mm. Marginal, does not occur with other Illington/Lackford stamps.
Group 1	Large circular stamp with simple right-angled cross. Classified as a Group 1 stamp in the West Stow settlement series.

THE DECORATIVE SCHEMES

Six decorative schemes can be defined among the existing complete material, using the numbers of horizontal lines of stamps, the use of swags, bosses, and panels. Within these broad categories, schemes 3, 4, 5, and 6 are further subdivided by matters of detail. Further subdivisions could be made with regard to the numbers of horizontal lines, but this would unnecessarily complicate the main issues.

With the exception of the type figure for Scheme 5a, the type figures for the decorative schemes are reprinted here from Myres's Corpus[19] as figs. 2 and 3.

Table 2: The use of Illington/Lackford stamps by site, including marginals

Stamp	C. Acre	Ill.	Rush.	Thet.	W. S.	Lkd.	Ick.	WG. G.	L. W.	St J.
A1a					4	3				
A1b					2	3				1
A2		2								
A3					10	1				
A4					24	4				
A5					7	2+1?			1	
A6					7+2?					
A7		1			1					
A8a		8			1	1?				
A8b		10+1?			4			1		
A9		1								
A10		1								
A11		1								
A?			1		12	2				
B1		1								
B2		4+1?		1	9					
B3		3								
C		5			8					
C var.		3								
D1		6		1						
D1 var.		2								
D2		5								
D2 var. 1		5+1?			1	1				
D2 var. 2		1								
D2 var. 3						1				
D3					3	4?				
D4					7+1?					1 var.
D5		2								
D?					7					
E		1			13	1				
F1		1								
F2		2								
F3					1					
F4		5+1?								
F5		2								
G		8								
H1										1
H2					1	1				
H3		1								
H?		1				1				
I		1	1?							
J1					31	8+2?	1			
J2		1			23+1	5		2	1	1
J3					1					
J?			1?		8	2				
K						1				
L					1					
M		4								
N					2	1				1
O										
P						1				
Q						1				
Group 1		1								

In all cases the description of the decorative schemes run from the upper part of the pot, and are set out in the text to read from left to right in order to save space.

Scheme 1 Two horizontal lines of stamps, alternating with three groups of lines. Type pot: Illington, Urn No. 147B, Corpus No. 2144.

Scheme 2 Three horizontal lines of stamps, alternating with four groups of lines. Type pot: Illington, Urn No. 141, Corpus No. 2145.

Scheme 3 One horizontal line of stamps between two groups of lines, with, below, swags or pendent triangles defined by 1–3 lines and filled with stamps.
3a. Swags. Type pot: West Stow, Corpus No. 2060.
3b. Pendent triangles. Type pot: Little Wilbraham, Corpus No. 2625.

Scheme 4 Two horizontal lines of stamps alternating with three groups of lines, with, below, swags or pendent triangles, defined by 1–3 lines and filled with stamps.
4a. Swags. Type pot: Illington, Urn No. 229, Corpus No. 2131.
4b. Pendent triangles. Type pot: Lackford, Corpus No. 938.

Scheme 3a or 4a Fragments which show one line of stamps above swags; but which are not complete enough to determine the presence or absence of a second line of stamps above.

Scheme 3b or 4b Fragments which are not complete enough to determine swags or triangles.

Scheme 5 Three horizontal groups of lines separated by an upper line of stamps and a lower zone of empty swags or chevrons.
5a. Swags. Type pot: West Stow, Feature 104(1), no Corpus No.
5b. Chevrons. Type pot: Lackford, Urn No. 49.3, Corpus No. 929.

Scheme 6 Elaborately decorated panel pots with vertical bosses and raised collars.
6a. With swags below panels. Type pot: St John's. Corpus No. 286.
6b. With raised swastikas in panels. Type pot: Lackford. Corpus No. 931.
    The detailed analysis of each decorative scheme, giving the types of stamps identified on each vessel, is set out below with all the examples known from each

site, together with the Corpus Number or other site identification. No account has been taken of the number of horizontal lines. For full details of each vessel or sherd see catalogue.

DECORATIVE SCHEMES: ANALYSIS

Scheme 1. Total: 8 pots

Illington:

1 × D2–A8a	Corpus No. 2144
3 × D1–A8b	Corpus Nos. 2142, 2143, 2147
2 × A8b–B2	Corpus Nos. 2149, 4074
1 × C–D2	Corpus No. 2146
1 × G–C. var.	Corpus No. 4076

Scheme 2. Total: 4 pots

Illington:

1 × A8a–C–D2	Corpus No. 2145
1 × A8a–D2 var. 1–C	Urn No. 375
1 × D5–F1–B1	Corpus No. 2152
1 × H3–D2–D5	Corpus No. 2141

Scheme 1 or 2. Total: 1 pot

1 × A8b–I	Corpus No. 2150

Scheme 3a. Total: 18 pots

Illington: 6 pots

1 × A7 with E in swags	Corpus No. 2140
1 × A8a with H? × ? stamp in swag	Urn No. 327(i)
1 × A8b with D1 in swags	Corpus No. 2125
1 × A8b with D1 var. in swags	Corpus No. 2126
1 × A10 with M in swags	Corpus No. 2139
1 × D2 var. 1 with D2 var. 1 in swags	Corpus No. 2124

West Stow: 5 pots

1 × A4 with J2? in swags	Corpus No. 2060
1 × A8b with J1 in swags	Hut 45 (3)
1 × A3 with J1 in swags	Pit 64
1 × A4 with J? in swags	Above Hut 50(1)
1 × A? with J1 in swags	WG5 L2 (1)

Lackford: 8 pots

1 × A5 with J1 in swags	Corpus No. 2839

1 × A5? with J2 in swags	Corpus No. 937
1 × A1b with J2 in swags	Urn No. 50.161A/B
1 × A4 with J1 in swags	Corpus No. 2760
1 × A4 with J1? in swags	Corpus No. 2059
1 × D2 var. 1 with J2 in swags	Urn No. 50.146B
1 × D2 var. 3 with J2 in swags	Urn No. 50.153
1 × D3? with J1 in swags	Corpus No. 933

Westgarth Gardens: 1 pot, 1 sherd

1 × A8b? with J2 in swag	W.G.G. Grave 1
1 × J2 with J2 in swag	W.G.G. Grave 1

Scheme 3b. Total: 5 pots

West Stow: 1 pot

1 × A6 with F3 and J3 in triangles	Corpus No. 1005

Lackford: 3 pots

1 × A5 with E in triangles	Corpus No. 939
1 × A4 with J1? in triangles	Corpus No. 2058
1 × A? with J? in triangles	Corpus No. 936

Little Wilbraham: 1 pot

1 × A5 with J2 in triangles	Corpus No. 2625

Scheme 4a. Total: 15 + 1? pots

Illington: 11 + 1 pots

1 × A8a, D2 with G in swags	Corpus No. 2128
1 × A8a, D2 var. 1 with G in swags	Corpus No. 2127
1 × A8a, C var. with G in swags	Corpus No. 2136
1 × A8b?, D2 var. 1 with F5 in swags	Corpus No. 4073
1 × D2 var. 1? C with G in swags	Corpus No. 2135
1 × D1, A8b with D1 & F5 in swags	Corpus No. 2129
1 × D1 var., B2 with F2 in swags	Corpus No. 2133
1 × A2, F4 with F4 & A2 in swags	Corpus No. 2134
1 × B3, D2 var. 2 with F4 in swags	Corpus No. 2130
1 × B3, F4 with F4 in swags	Corpus No. 2132
1 × A9, B2? with J2 in swags	Corpus No. 2131

Variety

1 × B3, F4 with M in swags	Corpus No. 2138

West Stow: 1 pot

1 × D4, A8b? with J1 in swags	Hut 44(1)

Lackford: 3 pots
    1 × D3?, A1a with J1 in swags   Corpus No. 2872
    1 × A1a, D3? with J1 in swags   Corpus No. 2791
    1 × H, A with J in swags   Corpus No. 966

Scheme 3a or 4a. Swag or triangle fragments. Total 42 + 1?

Illington: 6
    1 × A11 with M in swags   Corpus No. 4071
    1 × F4 with F4 in swags   Corpus No. 4072
    1 × B2 with F2 in swags   Corpus No. 4075
    1 × G–C. var.,? swag, G   Urn No. 376
    1 × F4? with F4 in swags   Urn No. 298
    1 × G in swags   Urn No. 327(iii)

Thetford (Red Castle): 1
    1 × B2 with D1 in swags   R.C. 4B

West Stow: Total 44 + 1? pots
    4 × 2 line swags–E   Hut 49(2), Hut 49(3), WE6 L2,
                                        Hut 49(4)

    4 × 1 line swags–J1   Hut 6, Hut 35(1), Hut 19(7),
                                        ?WB6 L2 (1)

    10 + 1? × 2 line swags–J1   : A3 with J1   Ditch 54
                            : A5 with J1   Hut 45(1)
                            : A4 with J1   WC5 L2(4), WF3 L2(1)
                            : A? with J1   Hut 53(1)
                                 plus: Hut 34(1), Hut 49(5), WE3 L2(2),
                                        F104(5), Hut 53(2), WC5 L2(3),
                                        WE7 L2

    3 × A4 with swags J2   WE4 L2(1), Hut 22,over(3)
    1 × 1 line swags J2   Hut 19(8)
    4 × 2 line swags J2   WG4 L2(2), Hut 22,over(1), WD3 L2(1)
                                        U.S. L2(7)

    7 × swag J1   WE3 L2(1), Ditch 101, Hut 16,
                                      WD3 L2(2), WG5 L2(7), Hut 49(6)
                                      U.S. L2(4)

    1 × 2 line swag J?   WG4 L2(2)
    1 × 3 line swag J?   Hut 52
    1 × ? swag with A5   WC2 L2
    1 × ? swag with A3   WC6 L2(1)

5 × ? swag E   Pit 436, Hut 45(7), Hut 45(5),
                                                      Hut 45(6), Hut 49(7)

2 × ? swag J?   WC6 L2(2), Hut 34(2)

Lackford: 2
    1 × J1 in swag   Corpus No. 926
    1 × J2 in swag   (Sherd with Urn 50.92)

Scheme 4b. Total: 3 pots

Rushford: 1 pot
    1 × A?–?J–?J in triangles

West Stow: 1 pot
    1 × A8b, B2 with E & J2 in triangles   Hut 66

Lackford: 1 pot
    1 × K, A3 with J1 in triangles   Corpus No. 938

Scheme 3b or 4b. 2 pots

West Stow
    1 × ? × J2 in triangle   WE6 L2

Icklingham
    1 × ? × J1 in 2 line triangle   115/1

Scheme 3 or 4. 1

West Stow
    1 × A4,? swags with J2   U.S. L2 (8)

Scheme 2/4. Two lines stamps or one line stamps plus swag—incomplete; at West Stow those with two lines of stamps are probably from *Scheme 4* pots

Illington: 1
    1 × D2 var. 1–A2–?   Urn No. 327.ii

West Stow: 4
    1 × D?–A3–?   WG5 L2(3)
    1 × C–J?–   WH3 L2
    1 × A3–D4–   Hut 19(2)
    1 × J2–   WG5 L2(6)

Scheme 5a. Total: 3 pots

Illington: 1 pot
    1 × A8a   Urn No. 313

West Stow: 2 pots

   1 × A4   Feature 104(2)

   1 × J2   Feature 104(1)

Scheme 5b. Total: 9 pots + 1? + 1 var.

Illington: 1 pot

   1 × A10   Urn No. 324

West Stow: 6 pots + 1? + 1 var.

   3 × A4   Hut 44(2), Hut 45(2),
                                         over Hut 50(2)

   1 × A5   Hut 44(3)

   1 × A6   Corpus No. 3996

   1 × A1a   Corpus No. 4002

   1 × A6   WE4 L2

Variety

   1 × A1b + N   Over Hut 50(3)

Lackford: 3 pots

   1 × A8?   Corpus No. 930

   1 × A4   Urn No. Z19366

   1 × A1b   Corpus No. 929

Scheme 6a. Total: 7 pots

West Stow: 6 pots

   1 × A7; panels B2–C; swags E, alt. J2   Hut 49(1)

   1 × vertical boss with swags, J2   Hut 40(2)

   1 × vertical boss with swag, J2   Hut 19(6)

   1 × vertical boss with swag, J2   Hut 19(9)

   1 × vertical boss with panel; swag J2   M6.H

   1 × vertical boss with panel; A6? E;
       swag J2   M62

St John's, Cambridge: 1 pot

   1 × A1b, D4 var. H1 and N in panels,
      2 line swags, with J2   Corpus No. 286

Scheme 6. Panel and boss, probably *Scheme 6a*

West Stow: 13 sherds

   1 × A1a with D4 and H2 (panels)   Hut 19(4)

   1 × A8b with C and J? (panels)   WC5 L2(1)

   1 × A3 in panel   WF5 L2

   1 × A5 plus ? J   Hut 40(1)

1 × B2 in panel	WC6 L2(3)
2 × B2 in 2 panels, plus C	Over Hut 12; WC5 L2(5)
1 × C in panel	WG5 L2(2)
1 × J2 in panel, plus C	Hut 34(3)
1 × D4 in panel	Hut 19(1)
1 × D3 in panel	Hut 19(5)
1 × D? in panel	Hut 19(3)
1 × vertical boss plus B2	Hall 5(1)

Scheme 6b. Total: 2 pots

West Stow: 1 sherd

1 × N and A1a, swastika fragment	WB6 L2(2)

Lackford: 1 pot

1 × A1b above, with A1b, J1, H2, D3? (panels) and A1b, J1, H2 and D3? below	Corpus No. 931

Scheme Unknown (sherds)

Illington: 2 sherds

1 × ? swag, M and A11	Urn No. 365
1 × ? × A8b × 2 + ?	Urn No. 327 iv

West Stow: 60 sherds

1 × A1a	WF3 L2(2)
1 × A1b	Hall 5(2)
3 × A3	Hut 35(2); Ditch 141, WC5 L2 (6); Hut 36
12 × A4	Feature 104(3); Hut 22 (over)(2); Hut 40(3); WG8 L2; Hut 15; Unstrat.L2(9); WE4 L2(1); Hut 19(10); Hut 3(1); Hut 45(10); Hut 45(4); Ditch 67C
3 × A5	Hut 42; Hut 44(4); Unstrat.(1)
3 × A6	WG5 L2(5); WG4 L2(4); WG6 L2
1 × A6?	N6 L2
1 × A8a	Hut 50(over)(4)
8 × A?	Feature 104(4); Unstrat.(2); Hut 25(over); Hut 3(2); Hut 50(over)(5); Hut 44(5); WC5 L2(7); WE5 L2(1)
3 × B2	Hut 66(1); WH4 L2; Hut 2

1 × C	WG4 L2(1)
1 × D2 var. 1	WC5 L2(2)
2 × D3	Pit 63; WC5 L2(8)
3 × D4	WB6 L2(3); WC5 L2(9); WG5 L2(8)
1 × D4	Hut 14
5 × D?	2 × Hut 17(over) (1 and 2); WG3 L2; Unstrat.L2(3); Unstrat.L2(6)
1 × E	Hut 45(8)
4 × J1	Hut 34(4); Hut 17(over)(3); Hut 55; Unstrat.L2(5)
4 × J2	WG5 L2(4); WH5 L2; WE5 L2(2); Hut 66(2)
1 × L plus A?	Hut 45(9)

Marginals: ? Illington/Lackford workshop

Scheme 3a.

Illington:

1 × A11, swags A11	Corpus No. 2137

Lackford:

1 × P, swags P	Corpus No. 2845
1 × Q, swags Q	Corpus No. 2846

Scheme: One horizontal line of stamps

West Stow:

1 × A6	Hut 57

The Marginals:

The marginals from Illington and Lackford, listed above, are not used with other Illington/Lackford stamps, but closely follow the decorative schemes which so distinguish this workshop that they must be considered as possible products. That from West Stow, however, has an A6, as used on other Illington/Lackford pieces from West Stow, but is distinct in having only one line of stamps between lines very high on the shoulder, a style not otherwise known for this workshop.

FABRICS

The ten main fabrics with three additional varieties are listed above, p. 191; these fabrics have been defined as the result of macroscopic examination using a hand lens and, where identifiable, are given in the catalogue.

Of the 222 vessels or sherds which can be attributed to the Illington/Lackford workshop, 215 have had their fabrics classified.

Table 3: Distribution of decorative schemes, by site

Schemes	C. A.	Ill.	Rush.	Thet.	W. S.	Lkd.	Ick.	WG. G.	L. W.	St J.	Totals
I		8									8
2		4									4
I or 2		I									I
3a		6			5	8		2			21
3b					I	3			I		5
4a		11+ I var.			I	3					16
3a or 4a		6		I	45	2					54
4b			I		I	I					3
3b or 4b					I		I				2
3 or 4					I						I
2 or 4		I			4						5
5a		I			2						3
5b					7+ I var.	3					11
6a					6					I	7
6a (Probably)					13						13
6b					I		I				2
Scheme Unknown	2				60						62
Marginals		I			I		2				4
	?	42	I	I	150	23	I	2	I	I	222

Table 4: Total numbers of times fabrics occur, by site

Fabric		Ill.	Thet.	W. S.	Ick.	Lkd.	WG. G.	L. W.	St J.
Fab.	I	7		100		4			
	I?	I				2		I	
	I var.	4		I		4			
	2	5	I	I					
	2 var.	2		I					
	2?			I					
	3	5		I					
	3 var.	I							
	4	4		I					
	5	2		10					
	6	4		13	I	I			
	6?				2				
	7	4		5		I			
	7?			I	I			I	
	8	I							
	9	I		I		2			
	9?				I				
	10			12		I			
Fab.	?	2		2		6			

There is little coincidence apparent overall between the fabric types and decorative schemes, and between fabric types and stamp links. Where they occur they are almost all at Illington. This is perhaps not surprising as the majority of the complete vessels come from that site. The links noted as of possible significance are:

(a) Urns CN 2142, 2143, and 2147. All are from Illington, of decorative scheme 1. All have a zone of the D1 stamp above a zone of A8b. The first two vessels belong to fabric 2, and the third to fabric 2 variety.

(b) Urns CN 2149 and 4074. Both are from Illington and belong to scheme 1 and are of fabric 3. Both are decorated with zones of the A8b and the B2 stamps.

(c) Urns CN 2146, 2145, and 2135. All are from Illington and belong to fabric 3. The first two urns show the C and D2 stamps; Urn CN 2145 has an additional zone of the A8a stamp. Urn CN 2146 belongs to scheme 1 and CN 2145 to scheme 2. CN 2135 belongs to scheme 4a, but is linked to the other urns by the use of the C and D2 variety 1 stamps.

(d) Urns CN 2125 and CN 2126. Both belong to scheme 3a and fabric 7. Both are decorated with the A8a stamp; CN 2125 has in addition D1 and CN 2126 stamp D1 variety.

But stamp links can be in different fabrics, e.g.

(a) Illington. Urn CN 2145, fabric 3 has the A8a, C, and D2 stamps, while Urn CN 375, in fabric 7, has the A8a, C, and D2 var. 1 stamps.

Apart from the examples listed above, it is difficult to be certain if there really is little coincidence between the fabrics and the use of certain stamps and decorative styles, or if this is due to the method of determining fabrics. But fabrics 6 and 7, which are quite distinct from the others, having red inclusions, equally show no pattern nor even a particular bias towards any one site.

CONCLUSIONS

There is little doubt from a study of the vessel forms, decorative schemes and stamp links that the 222 vessels and sherds which form the basis of this survey are the products of a single workshop. Forty per cent (i.e. 90 out of 222) of the vessels and sherds belong to decorative schemes 3a and 4a, i.e. those with one or two zones of stamps and swags filled with stamps. These vessels come from Illington, Thetford, West Stow, Lackford, and Westgarth Gardens. Despite these similarities two distinct groups emerge:

1. A northern group: Illington and perhaps Thetford;

2. A southern group: West Stow, Lackford, Westgarth Gardens, Icklingham, Little Wilbraham and St John's.

The *northern group* is distinguished by:

1. Decorative schemes (fig. 2):

(a) presence of schemes 1 and 2;

(b) absence of pendent triangles (schemes 3b or 4b) and rarity of chevrons (scheme 5b);

(c) absence of elaborately decorated vessels of schemes 6a and 6b, i.e. vessels with panels and vertical bosses.

2. Stamps (see Table 1):

(a) extreme rarity of the J stamp (raised dot-in-circle)—only one vessel at Illington has this, associated with an A and a B stamp;

(b) extreme rarity of the E stamp. One vessel only from Illington has this, combined with an A7;

(c) the absence of stamps A1a and A1b, A3–A6, D2 var. 3 and D4, F3, H1–2, K and N;

(d) even in the decorative schemes 3a and 4a, which are the commonest schemes in both the southern and northern groups, the combinations of stamps used are very different.

Table 5: Distribution of stamps in schemes, by site

Illington	Thetford	West Stow	Lackford	Westgarth Gardens
Scheme 3a				
A–E = 1		A–J = 5	A–J = 5	A–J = 1
A–H = 1			D–J = 3	J = 1
A–D = 1				
D–D = 1				
Scheme 3b				
B–A–J = 1		D–A–J = 1	D–A–J = 2	
F–D–A = 2			H–A–J = 1	
F–D–B = 2				
F–B–M = 1				
G–C–A = 1				
G–D–A = 2				
G–D–C = 1				
F–A = 1				
F–B = 1				
Scheme 3a or 4a				
F–F = 1	B–D = 1	A–J = 8	J = 2	
F–B = 1		A = 2		
G–C = 1		J = 26		
F = 1		E = 9		
G = 1				

These stamps are not shown in their correct position on the pot but have been arranged in some cases to show more clearly the links. The stamps which are unique to the northern group and those that are shared by both groups can be seen most clearly in Table 2.

The southern group is distinguished by:

1. Decorative schemes:

    (a) absence of schemes 1 and 2;

    (b) use of pendent triangles and chevrons;

    (c) presence of elaborately decorated bossed and panel pots. West Stow, Lackford, St John's.

2. Stamps:

    (a) the common use of the combination of A and J and D and J stamps in schemes 3a and 3b, 4a and 4b, and 6a and 6b;

    (b) the extreme rarity of the F stamps. A single vessel from West Stow has an F3 stamp;

    (c) the absence of stamps A9, A10, B1, B3, C var., D1–D2, D2 var. 2, D5, F1, F2, F4, F5, G, H3, I;

    (d) the use of the 'N' stamp.

    The distinction by decorative scheme and stamp use into northern and southern groups is not borne out by the fabrics. The limitations of distinguishing fabrics by hand lens only are fully appreciated, but fabrics 6 and 7 at least are quite distinct in hand specimens from the others in that they contain red inclusions of perhaps pounded pot or tile. It could be argued that such distinctive fabrics would be made in a single centre by a particular potter. Vessels made from one or other of these fabrics belong to all decorative schemes except 5a (represented by only 3 vessels) and 6b (represented by only 2 vessels). They are found at Illington, West Stow, Lackford, Westgarth Gardens, Little Wilbraham, and Icklingham and are absent only from Thetford and St John's, both sites which are represented each by a single vessel. Within these two fabrics the distinctive stamp combinations of the northern and southern groups are maintained. For example, taking decorative schemes 3a and 4a, at Illington the five vessels or sherds attributed to these schemes have the stamp combinations A8a–D1; A8a–D1 var.; A8a–D2 var. 1–G; B3–D2 var. 2–F4; G–C var.; at West Stow: A4–J2; D4–A8b–J1; A5–J; at Lackford: A4–J?; at Westgarth Gardens: A2?–J2. The same division emerges from the other decorative schemes. It is also worth noting that at Illington two of the pots of decorative scheme 1 have the stamp combination, A8b and B2 and in scheme 3a, A8axD1, and A8axD1 var.

Lethbridge[20] drew attention to the elaborately decorated pots from Lackford (CN 931) and St John's (CN 286), as they stood out clearly from the other vessels. Twenty fragments of these elaborate vessels were found in the excavation of the West Stow settlement, ten of which were recovered from the primary contexts of five of the sunken-featured buildings, the remainder of the sherds scattered over the site, clearly indicating that these were not specially made for funerary purposes as suggested by Myres in Lethbridge.[21] The discovery of vessels belonging to most of the decorative schemes in the West Stow settlement suggests that there was little distinction between good quality domestic pots and good quality funerary vessels.

It is still not possible to resolve the problem of the production centre of this distinctive pottery; the changes in style between the northern and southern groups could represent an itinerant potter or potters developing styles over a period of time, or equally a shift in trading patterns, if a single centre was involved. It is still possible that this could have been at West Stow or one of the neighbouring villages. The presence of antler pot-stamps and the clay dump at West Stow strongly suggests that decorated pottery was made in village communities of this sort despite the lack of any evidence of kilns or bonfires that could be proved to be for firing the pottery.

SITES PRODUCING ILLINGTON/LACKFORD POTTERY
Literary references to sites which are noted in Meaney (1964) are not given below.

Norfolk
Castle Acre; County No. 3781; NGR TF 797 156
Unpublished: cremation cemetery discovered in 1857. Excavations in late nineteenth century and 1961 (in West Acre parish—unpublished).
Note in Norwich Castle Museum records states there is a Illlington/Lackford sherd in New Place Museum, Stratford-on-Avon in H. Houseman collection.
Meaney 1964, 172.

Illington (Wretham parish), County No. 1047; NGR TL 948 898
Unpublished: predominantly cremation cemetery excavated by Group Captain Knocker, 1950. Further surface find of sherds, 1974.
Norwich Castle Museum 220.950; 562.974.
Meaney 1974, 176, where noted as a mixed cemetery.

Rushford (Brettenham parish); County No. 6076; NGR perhaps TL 933 834
Unpublished: cremation cemetery of probably more than 200 urns found between the late seventeenth and the mid nineteenth century.

The urn identified as by the Illington/Lackford potter by Dr Myres is illustrated in the G. Burton MSS in Maidstone Museum.

Meaney 1964, 169.

Red Castle, Thetford; County No. 5746/c.1; NGR TL 860 830

Published: Knocker (1969) p. 137, fig. 8,7. Pagan Saxon sherds including one from Illington/Lackford workshop from occupation soil beneath probable eleventh century ringwork.

Norwich Castle Museum 167.957.

Suffolk

West Stow Cemetery: County No. 22; Settlement: County No. 2; NGR TL 795 714

Inhumation cemetery, with an indeterminate number of cremations found, 1849. In this report considered in conjunction with the nearby settlement excavated from 1957–72; interim in West (1969). Cemetery finds in Moyse's Hall, Bury St Edmunds; Museum of Archaeology and Ethnology, Cambridge; British Museum; Ashmolean, Oxford; Settlement finds in Moyse's Hall Museum and Suffolk Archaeological Unit, Bury St Edmunds.

Meaney 1964, 233.

Icklingham: County No. 33; NGR TL 783 719

Published: West and Plouviez 1976, 102, fig. 44, 95. Stray sherd from Romano-British site.

Lackford: County No. 1; NGR TL 774 715

Cremation cemetery excavated by Lethbridge, 1947. Finds in Museum of Archaeology and Ethnology, Cambridge and Ashmolean, Oxford.

Meaney 1964, 229.

Westgarth Gardens, Bury St Edmunds: County No. 30; NGR 845 633

Unpublished: predominantly inhumation cemetery with some cremations excavated by West (1972). Finds in Moyse's Hall Museum, Bury St Edmunds.

Cambridgeshire

Little Wilbraham: NGR TL 560 577

Published: Neville 1852. Cemetery discovered before 1847, excavated 1851.

The single Illington/Lackford urn recognized from this cemetery is in the Museum of Archaeology and Ethnology, Cambridge.

Meaney 1964, 70.

St John's College, Cambridge: TL 441 588
Unpublished: Mixed cemetery found in 1888.
The single Illington/Lackford urn recognized from this cemetery is in the
     Museum of Archaeology and Ethnology, Cambridge.
Meaney 1964, 62.

THE CATALOGUE

The catalogue is arranged by site in the order of the decorative schemes. Myres's
Corpus numbers are given under CN with urn numbers in brackets; other site
numbers or urn numbers are given for those not included in the Corpus.

The decorative schemes including both lines and stamps are described from
the upper part of the vessel to the lower, but are written horizontally to save space.

Number	Design	State	Fabric
Illington:			
SCHEME 1			
CN 2144 (147B)	$10 \times D2 \times 4 \times A8a \times 4$	Complete	Fab. 1
CN 2142 (123)	$10? + \times D1 \times 4 \times A8b \times 4$	nearly C	Fab. 2
CN 2143 (144)	$7 + \times D1 \times 4 \times A8b \times 4$	nearly C	Fab. 2
CN 2147 (173)	$7 + \times D1 \times 3 \times A8b \times 3$	nearly C	Fab. 2 var.
CN 2149 (34B)	$13 \times A8b \times 4 \times B2 \times 3$	C	Fab. 6
CN 4074 (177)	$11 + \times A8b \times 4 \times B2 \times 4$	nearly C	Fab. 6
CN 2146 (10)	$8 + \times C \times 4 \times D2 \times 4$	nearly C	Fab. 3
CN 4076 (170 in Corpus, now 384)	$1 + \times G \times 4 \times C$ var. $\times 5$	nearly C	Fab. 1
SCHEME 2			
CN 2145 (141)	$10? + \times A8a \times 3 \times C \times 3 \times D2 \times 3$	nearly C	Fab. 3
Urn No. 375	$5? + \times A8a \times D2$ var. $1 \times 4 \times C \times 4$	nearly C	Fab. 7
CN 2152 (268)	$15? + \times D5 \times 4 \times F1 \times 4 \times B1 \times 4$	nearly C	Fab. 4
CN 2141 (68)	$6 + \times H3 \times 4 \times D2 \times 4 \times D5 \times 4$	nearly C	Fab. 5
SCHEME 1 or 2			
CN 2150 (46)	$1 + \times A8b \times 4 \times I \times 3$	not C	Fab. 1
SCHEME 3a			
CN 2139 (7)	$8 \times A10 \times 3 \times 2$ line swags M, 2–1	C	Fab. 3
CN 2140 (41A)	$12 \times A7 \times 4 \times 2$ line swags E, 4–1	C	Fab. 1
CN 2125 (288)	$13 \times A8b \times 4 \times 2$ line swags D1, 6/5–1	C	Fab. 7
CN 2126 (35)	$11 \times A8b \times 4 \times 2$ line swags D1 var., 4/3–1	C	Fab. 7
CN 2124 (102)	$10 \times D2$ var. $1 \times 3 \times 3$ line swags D2 var. 1, 4–1	C	Fab. 1
Urn No. 327(i)	$12 \times A8a \times 4 \times 2$ line swags H? $\times$? stamp	not C	Fab. 1 var.

Number	Design	State	Fabric
SCHEME 4a			
CN 2128 (262B)	11 × A8a × 4 × D2 × 4 × 2 line swags G, 6–1	C	Fab. 4
CN 2127 (23)	12 × A8a × 4 × D2 var. 1 × 4 × 2 line swags G, 3–1	C	Fab. 6
CN 2136 (25)	12?+ × A8a × 4 × C var. × 4 × 2 line swags G, 3–1	not quite C	Fab. 1
CN 4073 (350)	9 × A8b? × 4 × D2 var. 1 × 3 × 2 line swags F5, 4/5–1	not C	Fab. 2
CN 2135 (287)	9?+ × D2 var. 1? × 4 × C × 3 × 2 line swags G, 3–1	not quite C	Fab. 3
CN 2129 (264)	9 × D1 × 4 × A8b × 3 × 2 line swags alt. D1 & F5, 5–1	C	Fab. 1
CN 2133 (28)	1 + × D1 var. × 4 × B2 × 3 × 2 line swags F2, 6/5–1	nearly C	Fab. 1 var.
CN 2134 (125A in Corpus, now 126)	8 × A2 × 6 × F4 × 8 × 3 line swags alt. F4 + A2 (1 mixed), 6/5–1	C	Fab.4
CN 2130 (87A)	4?+ × B3 × 3 × D2 var. 2 × 3 × 2 line swags F4, 2–1	not quite C	Fab. 7
CN 2132 (235)	7 × B3 × 3 × F4 × 3 × 3 line swags F4, 2–1	C	Fab. 4
CN 2131 (229)	12 × A9 × 4 × B2? × 3 × 2 line swags J2, 4/5–1	C	Fab. 1?
Variety			
CN 2138 (238)	7 × B3 × 4 × F4 × 4 × 3 line swags M, 2–1 × 2 × 1	C	Fab. 9
SCHEME 3a or 4a			
CN 4071 (280)	4?+ × A11 × 3 × 2 line swags M, 2–1	not quite C	Fab. 3
CN 4072 (289)	3?+ × F4 × 2 × 2 line swags F4, 3–1	not C	Fab. 8
CN 4075 (297)	? × B2 × 3 × 2 line swags F2, 5/6–1	not C	Fab. 3 var.
Urn No. 376	2?+ × G × 5 × C var. × 6 × ? swags G	not C	Fab. 6
Urn No. 298	? × F4? × 6 × 3 line swags F4, 6/5–1	not C	Fab. 2 var.
Urn No. 327(iii)	? × 4 × ? × 2 line swags G	not C	Fab. 1 var.
SCHEME 2 or 4			
Urn No. 327(ii)	? × D2 var. 1 × 5 × A2 × 4?+	not C	Fab. 1 var.
SCHEME 5a			
Urn No. 313	6? × A8a × 4 × 2 line swags × 3 lines	not C	Fab. 5
SCHEME UNKNOWN			
Urn No. 365	2 × ? × swag M alt. with A11	not C	Fab. 2
Urn No. 327 (iv)	6? × A8b × 2?+	not C	Fab. 3
MARGINAL (SCHEME 3a)			
CN 2137 (44)	15 × Grp. 1 × 4 × 3 line swags Grp. 1, 5–1	C	Fab. 2

Number	Design	State	Fabric
Rushford:			
SCHEME 4b			
	9 × A? × 4 × ? stamp × 2 × 2 line triangles ?J? 4–1	C	No fab.
Thetford (Red Castle):			
SCHEME 3a or 4a			
R.C. 41B	? × B2 × 2 × 1 line swags D1	not C	Fab. 2
West Stow:			
SCHEME 3a			
CN 2060 (Oxf.1909.435)	9 × A4 × 4 × 2 line swags J2?, 4–1	C	Fab. ?7
Hut 45(3)	9 × A8b × 3 × 2 line swags J1, 3 +–?1	nearly C	Fab. 1 var.
Pit 64	7 × A3 × 7 × 1 line swags J1, 5–1	C	Fab. 9
Above Hut 50(1)	10 × A4 × 4 × ? swag J?	not C	Fab. 1
WG5 L2(1)	9 × A? × 3 × 2 line swags J1, 4–1	C	Fab. 1
SCHEME 3b			
CN 1005 (Cemetery M.H.K10)	6 × A6 × 2 × 2 line triangles, F3 & J3 alt. random	C	Fab. 10
SCHEME 4a			
Hut 44(1)	9 × D4 × 8 × A8b × 9 × 2 line swags J1, 5–1	C	Fab. 7
SCHEME 3a or 4a			
Hut 49(2)	2 line swag E, 7? +–1	Not C	Fab. 1
Hut 49(3)	2 line swag E, 5? +–1	Not C	Fab. 1
WE6 L2	2 line swag E, 5? +–1	Not C	Fab. 1
Hut 49(4)	swag E	Not C	Fab. 1
Hut 6	1 line swag J1, 3? +–1	Not C	Fab. 1
Hut 35(1)	3 + × 1 line swag J1, 4–1	Not C	Fab. 6
Hut 19(7)	1 line swag J1	Not C	Fab. 7
WB6 L2(1)	? 1 line swag J1	Not C	Fab. 1
Ditch 54	? × A3 × 9 × 1 line swag J1, 3 +–?	Not C	Fab. 1
Hut 45(1)	? × A5 × 4 × 2 line swags J1, ?–1	Not C	Fab. 6
WF3 L2(1)	? × A4 × 4 × 2 line swags J1, 2 +–	Not C	Fab. 5
WC5 L2(4)	2 + × A4 × 5/6 × 2 line swags J1, 4 +–	Not C	Fab. 1
Hut 53(1)	? × A? × 4 × 2 line swags J1, 3 +–	Not C	Fab. 1
Hut 34(1)	2 line swag J1, 4? + – 1	Not C	Fab. 1
Hut 49(5)	2 line swag J1, – ?	Not C	Fab. 1
WE3 L2(2)	2 line swag J1, –	Not C	Fab. 5
F104(5)	2 line swag J1, –	Not C	Fab. 5
Hut 53(2)	–A? × 4 × 2 line swags J1, 3 +–?	Not C	Fab. 1

Number	Design	State	Fabric
WC5 L2(3)	2 line swags J1	Not C	Fab. 1
WE7 L2	? 2 line swags J1	Not C	Fab. 1
WE4 L2(1)	? × A4 × 4? line swags J2, 4 +−	Not C	Fab. 1
Hut 22 (over) (3)	1 + × A4 × 2? line swags J2	Not C	Fab. 5
Hut 19(8)	1? + ?line swag J2, −	Not C	Fab. 1
WG4 L2(2)	1 + × 2 line swag J2, 2 +−?	Not C	Fab.6
Hut 22 (over) (1)	2 line swag J2	Not C	Fab. 1
WD3 L2(1)	3 + × ?line swag J2	Not C	Fab. 1
US L2(7)	5 + × 2 line swag J2	Not C	Fab. 6
WE3 L2(1)	−swag J1, −	Not C	Fab. 5
D.101	3 + × ? swag J1	Not C	Fab. 7
Hut 16	3 + × ? swag J1, −	Not C	Fab. 1
WD3 L2(2)	Stamp frag. × 4 × ? swag J1, −	Not C	Fab. 1
WG5 L2(7)	3 + × swag J1, −	Not C	Fab. 1
Hut 49(6)	Swag J1, −	Not C	Fab. 6
US L2(4)	3 + × swag J1, −	Not C	Fab. 6
WG4 L2(2)	2 line swag J?	Not C	Fab. 1
Hut 52	3 line swag J?	Not C	Fab. 3
WC2 L2	? swag A5, −	Not C	Fab. 1
WC6 L2(1)	? swag A3, 5−1	Not C	Fab. 1
Pit 436	? swag E, −	Not C	Fab. 1
Hut 45(7)	? swag E	Not C	Fab. 1
Hut 45(5)	4? + × E, ? swag	Not C	Fab. 1
Hut 45(6)	4 + × ?swags E, 3? +−	Not C	Fab. 1
Hut 49(7)	? swag E, −	Not C	Fab. 1
WC6 L2(2)	2 + × ? swag J?, −	Not C	Fab. 1
Hut 34(2)	4 + × swag J?, −	Not C	Fab. 6
SCHEME 4b			
Hut 66	14? + × A8b × 4 × B2 × 4 × 2 line triangles alt. E + J2, 4 +−1	nearly C	Fab. 5
SCHEME 3b or 4 b			
WE6 L2	? × J2 in triangle	not C	Fab. 1
SCHEME 3 or 4			
US L2(8)	? × A4 × 4 × ? swags J2, 4 +−	not C	Fab. 1
SCHEME 2 or 4			
WG5 L2(4)	? × D? × 6 × A3 × ?	not C	Fab. 1
WH3 L2	? × C × 3 × J? × ?	not C	Fab. 1
Hut 19(2)	? × A3 × 3 × D4 × ?	not C	Fab. 5
WG5 L2(6)	3? + ×J2 × 3 × ?	not C	Fab. 1
SCHEME 5a			
Feature 104(2)	2 + × A4 × 4 × 2 line swags × ? 1 line	not C	Fab. 4
Feature 104 (1)	9 ×J2 × 3 × 2 line swags × 1 line	C	Fab. 10

Number	Design	State	Fabric
SCHEME 5b			
Hut 44(2)	$5 + \times$ A4 $\times$ 3 $\times$? line chevrons $\times$? line	not C	Fab. 1
Hut 45(4)	$3 + \times$ A4 $\times$ 4 $\times$ 3 line chevrons $\times$? line	nearly C	Fab. 7
Over Hut 50(2)	8? $+ \times$ A4 $\times$ 3 $\times$?2 line chevrons $\times$? line	not C	Fab. 10
Hut 44(3)	$4 \times$ A5 $\times$ 3 $\times$? line chevrons $\times$? line	not C	Fab. 1
CN 3996 (settlement)	$7 \times$ A6 $\times$ 3 $\times$ 3 line chevrons $\times$ 3	C	Fab. ?
CN 4002 (WE6 L2)	$8 \times$ A1a $\times$ 3 $\times$ 3 line chevrons $\times$ 1	C	Fab. 2 var.
CN 824 (WE4 L2)	? $\times$ A6 $\times$ 2 $\times$?2 line chevrons $\times$? line	not C	Fab. 10
Variety:			
Over Hut 50(3)	$1 + \times$ A1b $\times$ 3 $\times$ 3 line chevrons with N $\times$? line	not C	Fab. 1
SCHEME 6a			
Hut 49(1)	? $\times$ A7 $\times$ 4 Vertical bosses with panels: $2 \times$ B2 $\times$ 3 $\times$ C $\times$ 3 $\times$ 2 line swags alt. E, 8–1; J2, $4 + -$	not C	Fab. 2
Hut 40(2)	Vertical boss with 2 line swags J2, $4 + -1$	not C	Fab. 6
Hut 19(6)	Vertical boss with 2 line swag J2	not C	Fab. 1
Hut 19(9)	Vertical boss with 2 line swag J2	not C	Fab. 5
M6–H	Vertical boss with panel. 4? $+ \times$ 2 line swags J2, $3 + -$?	not C	Fab. 6
M6(2)	Vertical boss with panel $- \times$ A6? $\times$ 4 $\times$ E $\times$ 4 with $\times$?1 line swag J2, $4 + ? - $?	not C	Fab. 6
SCHEME 6a (Probably)			
Hut 19(4)	$4 \times$ collar $\times$ 3 $\times$ A1a $\times$ 2 Vertical bosses with panels $1 \times$ D4 $\times$ 3 $\times$ H2 $\times$ 1 $+$?	not C	Fab. 1
WC5 L2(1) + WE5 L2	Vertical boss with panel, with $1 \times$ A8b $\times$ 3 $\times$ C $\times$ 4 $\times$ J?	not C	Fab. 1
WF5 L2	Vertical boss + panel with A3	not C	Fab. 1
Hut 40(1)	Vertical boss + panel, ? $\times$ A5 $\times$ 3 $\times$?J	not C	Fab. 1
WC6 L2(3)	Panel with B2	not C	Fab. 1
Over Hut 12	2 panels. $1 + $? $\times$ B2 $\times$ 3 $\times$ C $\times$ 2	not C	Fab. 1
WC5 L2(5)	Panels, probably with vertical bosses. B2 $\times$ 3 $\times$ C $\times$ 3	not C	Fab. 10
Hut 34(3)	Panels with vertical bosses. 3? $+ \times$ J2 $\times$ 3 $\times$ C	not C	Fab. 1
Hut 19(1)	Panel. 2? $+ \times$ D4 $\times$ 2 $+$?	not C	Fab. 1

Number	Design	State	Fabric
Hut 19(3)	Vertical boss with panel with D?	not C	Fab. 10
Hall 5(1)	Panel with B2	not C	Fab. 1
Hut 19(5)	Panel with 1 + ×D3−	not C	Fab. 1
WG5 L2(2)	Panel; C	not C	Fab. ?

SCHEME 6b

WB6 L2(2)	Raised swastika frag. with N. A1a between arms	not C	Fab. 1
	3 line panel outline		

SCHEME UNKNOWN—ALL SHERDS

Number	Design	State	Fabric
Hut 35(2)	A3		Fab. 1
Feature 104(3)	8 × A4 × 3 +		Fab. 5
Hut 22 (over) (2)	7 × A4 × 3 +		Fab. 10
Hut 40(3)	11 + × A4 × 3? +		Fab. 1
WG8 L2	9 + × A4		Fab. 1
Hut 15	7 + × A4		Fab. 1
US L2(9)	2 + × A4 × 3		Fab. 10
WE4 L2(1)	4 + × A4 × 2 +		Fab. 1
Hut 42	9 × A5 × 3		Fab. 1
WG5 L2(4)	3? + × J2 × 3		Fab. 1
WG5 L2(5)	7 + × A6		Fab. 10
Hut 44(4)	7 × A5 × 1 +		Fab. 7
WG4 L2(4)	2 + × A6 × 2?		Fab. 1
Hut 19(10)	4? + × A4 × ?		Fab. 1
Hut 3(1)	6? × A4		Fab. 1
US (1)	−A5−		Fab. 1
Hut 45(10)	6 + × A4		Fab. 1
Hut 36	7 × A3 × 6 + ?		Fab. 5
WG6 L2	−A6−		Fab. 1
Feature 104(4)	7 × A?−		Fab. 1
US (2)	6 + × A?		Fab. 1
Hut 45(4)	2 + × A4 × 1 +		Fab. 6
Hall 5(2)	8 × A1b × 3 + ?		Fab. 1
WF3 L2(2)	2 + × A1a × 1 +		Fab. 1
Hut 25 (over)	2 + × A?		Fab. 1
Hut 3 (2)	4 + × A?		Fab. 6
Ditch 141	4 + × A3		Fab. 1
WC5 L2(6)	2 + × A3		Fab. 1
Hut 66(1)	4 + × B2 × 4 +		Fab. 1
WH4 L2	1 + × B2 × 3 +		Fab. 1
	cf. Hall 5 panel fragment		
Hut 2	6 + × B2 × 1 +		Fab. 1
WG4 L2(1)	−C × 3		Fab. 1
Pit 63	4 + × D3 × 1 +		Fab. 1
WB6 L2(3)	2 + × D4 × 2 +		Fab. 1

Number	Design	State	Fabric
WC5 L2(9)	–D4–		Fab. 1
WC5 L2(2)	1 + × D2 var. 1 × 1 +		Fab. 1
WC5 L2(8)	5 + × D3 × ?		Fab. 10
Hut 17 (over) (1)	4 + × D? –		Fab. 1
WG3 L2	–D? –		Fab. 1
Hut 17 (over) (2)	–D? × 3 +		Fab. 1
US L2(3)	1 + × D? –		Fab. 1
WG5 L2(8)	–D4–		Fab. 1
US L2(6)	1 × D? –		Fab. 1
Hut 45(8)	3 + ? × E × 2? +		Fab. 1
WH5 L2	–J2–		Fab. 1
WE5 L2(2)	–J2–		Fab. 1
Hut 34(4)	–J1–		Fab. 1
Hut 17 (over) (3)	–J1–		Fab. 6
Hut 55	–J1–		Fab. 1
US L2(5)	–J1–		Fab. 6
Hut 66(2)	–J2–		Fab. 1
Hut 45(9)	–A? × 4 × L–		Fab. 1
Hut 50 (over) (5)	–5 + × A? –		Fab. 1
Hut 44(5)	–3 + × A? –		Fab. 1
WC5 L2(7)	–2 + × A? –		Fab. 1
WE5 L2(1)	–3 + × A? –		Fab. 1
Ditch 67, C	1 + × A4 × Frag. stamp		Fab. 1
Hut 50 (over) (4)	8 × A8a × 1 +		Fab. 10
Evison N6 (1) L2	4? + × A6?		Fab. 1
Hut 14	2? + × D4? × 2 +		Fab. 2?

MARGINALS

Hut 57	2 × A6 × 1. Though the A6 stamp suggests that this pot comes from the Illington/Lackford workshop, the decorative scheme and its position is quite unlike anything else which is attributed to this workshop.	C	Fab. 10

Lackford:

SCHEME 3a

CN 2839 (50.118)	10 × A5 × 4 × 2 line swags J1, 5–1	C	Fab. 1 var.
CN 937 (48.2481) Urn No.	11 × A5? × 4 × 2 line swags J2, 4–1	C	Fab. 1?
50.161A/b	8 × A1b × 3 × 2 line swags J2, 3–1	not quite C	Fab. 1 var.
CN 2760 (48.2479 = 50.91 in Corpus)	8 × A4 × 3 × 2 line swags J1, 4–1	C	Fab. 1 var.
CN 2059 (Oxf. 1927.78)	9 × A4 × 3 × 2 line swags J1?, 5–1	C	Fab. ?6

Number	Design	State	Fabric
Urn No. 50.146b	10 × D2 var. 1 × 4 × 2 line swags J2, 3+−1	not quite C	Fab. 1
Urn No. 50.153	10?+ × D2 var. 3 × 4 × 2 line swags J2, ?6−1	not quite C	Fab. 10
CN 933 (48.2476)	7 × D3? × 5 × 1 line swags J1, 4−1	C	Fab. ?9
SCHEME 3b			
CN 939 (50.86)	10 × A5 × 4 × 2 line triangles E, 3/4−1	C	Fab. 1 ?
CN 2058 (Oxf. 1927.77)	13 × A4 × 4 × 2 line triangles J1, ?6−1	C	Fab. ? 7
CN 936 (48.2480)	?6 × A? × 3 × 2 line triangles J?, 4−1	C	Fab. ?
SCHEME 4a			
CN 2872 (50.92)	7 × D3? × 6 × A1a × 5 × 1 line swags J1, 3−1	C	Fab. 9
CN 2791 (50.233)	8 × A1a × 3 × D3? × 3 × 2 line swags J1, 5−1	C	Fab. ?
CN 966 (No No.)	?4 × H × 4 × A × 4 × 1 line swags J, 4−1	C	Fab. ?
SCHEME 3a or 4a			
CN 926 (50.126a)	5?+ × 1 line swags J1, 4−1	not C	Fab. 9
Sherd with Urn No. 50.92	2 line swags J2, 5+−1	not C	Fab. 1 var.
SCHEME 4b			
CN 938 (48.2477)	5 × K × 5 × A3 × 5 × 1 line triangles J1, 4−1	C	Fab. 6?
SCHEME 5b			
CN 930 (48.2478)	7 × A8? × 3 × 3 line chevrons × 3	C	Fab. 1
Urn No. Z19366	10 × A4 × 3 × 3 line chevrons × 3	C	Fab. 1
CN 929 (49.3)	8 × A1b × 3 × 3 line chevrons × 3	C	Fab. ?
SCHEME 6b			
CN 931 (48.2475a)	6 × collar × 3 × A1b × 4	C	Fab. 1

CN 931 (48.2475a)

Vertical bosses with panels
Swastika with N alt. with slashed
   swastika panels:
   1 A1b; A1b below N
   2 J1; J1 below
   3 H2; H2 below N
   4 J1; A1b below
   5 A1b; J1 below N
   6 J1; A1b below
   7 D3?+H2; A1b below N
   8 A1b; H2 below
   9 H2; J1 below N
   10 J1; H2 below

Number	Design	State	Fabric
MARGINALS (SCHEME 3a)			
Lackford:			
CN 2845 (50.167)	8? × P × 4 × 2 line swags spaced P, 3–3	not quite C	Fab. ?
CN 2846 (49.55)	4 × Q × 4 × 2 line swags Q, 6–?	not quite C	Fab. ?
Icklingham:			
SCHEME 3b or 4b			
115.1	1? + × 2 line triangles J1, 5–1	not C	Fab. 6
Westgarth Gardens			
SCHEME 3a			
Grave 1 (1)	6 × A8b? × 5 × 1 line swags J2, 3–1	C	Fab. 6
Grave 1 (2)	2 + × J2 × 5 × 1 line swags J2, 3–1	sherd	Fab. 7
Little Wilbraham:			
SCHEME 3b			
CN 2625 (48.1266)	12 × A5 × 4 × 2 line triangles J2, 5–1	C	Fab. 7
St John's, Cambridge:			
SCHEME 6a			
CN 286 (Z16296)	8 × collar × 4 × A1b × 4 × D4 var. Vert. bosses with panels. 4 × H1 × 4 × N × 3 × 2 line swags J2, 7/5–1	C	Fab. 1?

Bibliography

BURTON, REV. G., 'An account of Roman urns and other antiquities found in England', ?1754 or 1794. MS in Maidstone Museum.

KNOCKER, G.M., 'Excavations at Red Castle, Thetford', *Norfolk Archaeol.* XXXIV (1969), 119–86.

LETHBRIDGE, T.C., *A Cemetery at Lackford, Suffolk, Cambs. Antiq. Soc., Quarto Pub. N.S.* VI (Cambridge, 1951).

MEANEY, A.L.S., *A gazetteer of Early Anglo-Saxon Burial Sites* (London, 1964).

NEVILLE, R.C., *Saxon Obsequies* (London, 1852).

SALWAY, P., 'The Roman Fenland', in *The Fenland in Roman Times,* ed. C. W. Phillips. Royal Geographical Research Series 5 (London, 1970), 1–21.

WEST, S.E., 'The Anglo-Saxon village of West Stow: An Interim report of the excavations, 1965–8', *Medieval Archaeol.* XIII (1969), 1–20.

WEST, S.E., with JUDITH PLOUVIEZ, 'The Romano-British site at Icklingham', *East Anglian Archaeol.* 3, *Suffolk* (1976), 63–125.

Notes

1. Lackford Corpus Numbers: 2058, 2059, West Stow CN 2060, Ashmolean Museum and West Stow CN 1005, Moyse's Hall Museum. Throughout this paper Myres's 1977 (No. 147) corpus numbers are used where possible and identified by CN before the number. Vessels and sherds not included in the corpus are identified by their Museum or excavation number.

2. Myres, 1937 (No. 31), 391.

3. Lethbridge, 1951, 6.

4. Myres, 1969 (No. 122), 132.

5. Lethbridge, 1951, 6.

6. A note in Norwich Castle Museum records a sherd identified by Dr Myres in the Revd H. Houseman Collection of 1891 in the New Place Museum, Stratford-upon-Avon. A recent change of staff there (April 1979) made it impossible to check this sherd.

7. Myres, 1969 (No. 122), 135, Map 10.

8. See pp. 210–12 above for brief details and bibliographies of all the sites.

9. For convenience the finds from these two sites have been amalgamated.

10. The Lackford cemetery has sometimes been referred to as Cavenham (the next parish).

11. See Lethbridge, 1951, plan 1. For clarity, only 2 of the Dykes have been shown in Fig. 1 in this paper.

12. Myres and Green, 1973 (No. 181), 258–62 and Map 3.

13. G. Burton Mss. See entry p. 47 for references.

14. Lethbridge, 1951, 4.

15. Myres, 1977 (No. 147), 61.

16. West Stow cemetery (CN 2060), Lackford (CN 2058, 2059) in the Ashmolean Museum, Oxford; Lackford (CN 929) in the Derby Museum and Lackford (CN 936). We are deeply indebted to Mr David Brown and Mrs Freda Waters for the information about the pots at Oxford and Derby and to Miss Mary Cra'ster of the Museum of Archaeology and Ethnology, Cambridge, who most generously allowed us to study the vessels there during a period of reorganization of the Museum.

17. This work was carried out by Miss Gill Bussell at the University of East Anglia, to whom we are grateful.

18. When this paper was ready for the printer we received a manuscript from Lady

Briscoe of an article classifying stamps. The differences in the method of classification were so great that no compromise was possible without rewriting this paper.

19. We are grateful to Dr J.N.L. Myres and the Cambridge University Press for permission to reprint these.
20. Lethbridge, 1951, 6.
21. Lethbridge, 1951, 6.

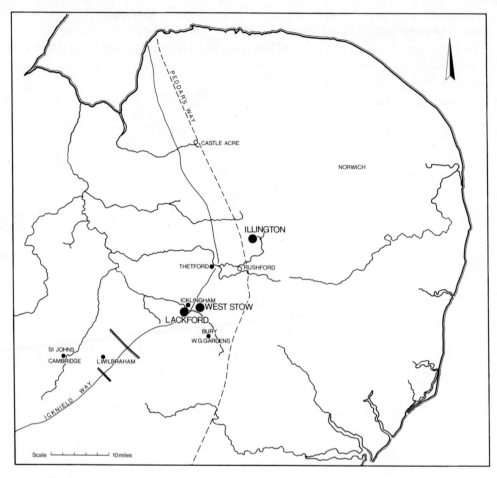

FIG. 1. The distribution of Illington/Lackford sites. The open circles represent material not seen by the authors, and the river system is based on Fenland in Roman times (Salway 1970).

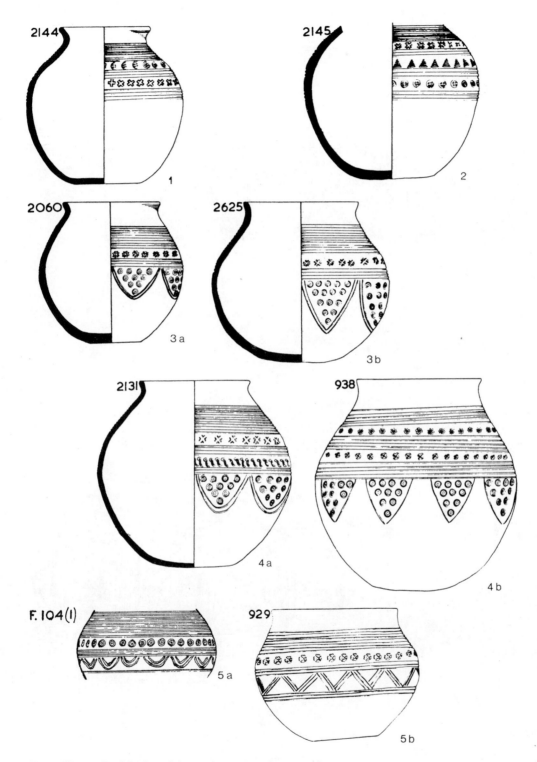

Fig. 2. Illington/Lackford workshop—decorative schemes 1–5b.

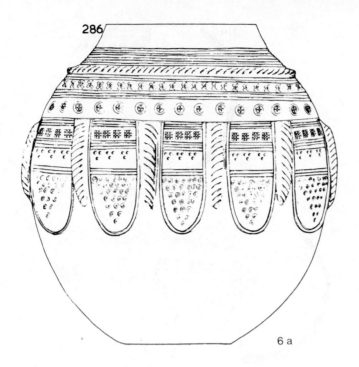

6 a

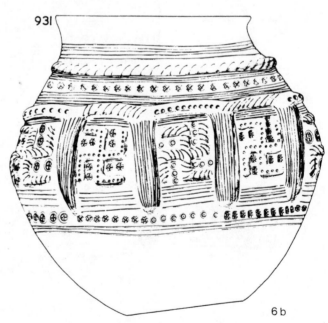

6 b

Fig. 3. Illington/Lackford workshop—decorative schemes 6a and b.

Swastika patterns

DAVID BROWN

One of the styles of decoration of Anglo-Saxon pottery to which Nowell Myres has drawn particular attention is that which combines stamps of animals, interlace and swastikas on a number of pots, most of which come from East Anglia.[1] He has attributed these pots to workshops appropriately named 'animal stamp workshops'. Both animals and interlace have inevitably been compared with the decoration of metal objects and manuscripts; my concern here is with the swastikas, and I am pleased to be able to add from this same corner of England another swastika for his consideration.

This new swastika is on an enamelled bronze disc from Great Barton, Suffolk (fig. 1). The disc is flat, 34 mm in diameter; in the centre a swastika pattern is contained within a square with a loop at each corner, and between the sides of the square and the edge of the disc are pairs of roundels joined by two lines. The disc is enamelled, mostly in red, but with yellow in the corners of the square, the loops and the roundels, and with eight pieces of millefiori embedded in the red in the more open spaces, four inside and four outside the square. The millefiori is chequer-patterned with nine squares, opaque white in the corners and centre alternating with a translucent dark (brown?) colour. In places the millefiori has been inserted on its side so that the chequer pattern is not fully visible. The surface of the bronze has been tinned; the back is also covered with tin, presumably the remains of solder.

This object was collected by Joseph Warren of Ixworth who described it in his manuscript catalogue[2] as follows:

1853   I had brought me from Great Barton a very curious enamelled ornament. It may have been the front of a fibula. It is of bronze & have been silvered, some of which is remaining as well as some of the enamel, the colours are Red, Yellow, White and Black, of a very complicated pattern, the Bronze in one part very near decayed by Age. I think it is of the Saxon period.

Warren's collection was bought by Sir John Evans. Sir John considered this disc to be medieval, and it was therefore not included among his Anglo-Saxon objects which were given to the Ashmolean Museum in 1908, but among his medieval objects given in 1927. It was registered as number 1927.6390 and described as a 'mug or dish stamp'; it was put away with other medieval things . . . and probably never even seen by E.T. Leeds!

The association of red and yellow enamel and millefiori in a swastika pattern immediately brings to mind that group of enamels which Françoise Henry has discussed in relation to Irish finds of the eighth century,[3] for these are some of the distinctive features of that group. But the Great Barton disc lacks other important features of the group; for example, its pattern is not so well laid out, nor is its enamel placed in deep cells divided by thin bronze walls. In its over-all shape, in its tinned surface and in its solder-scarred back, the Great Barton disc has far more the appearance of a hanging bowl escutcheon of which numerous examples are known from seventh-century finds in England.

Forgetting the design for a moment, the basically red enamel with small spots of yellow and millefiori is the same as on the 'Northumberland' escutcheons[4] in the British Museum, and similar to those where millefiori alone is embedded in red (Sutton Hoo bowls 1 and 3, Barlaston and Scunthorpe).[5] These pieces, and others enamelled in plain red, show considerable variety in the skill with which they have been engraved and enamelled, and the Great Barton disc, though not of the highest quality in this respect, is certainly within the known range. If it shows any difference, it is the advance in technique in placing the yellow in separate compartments in the bronze rather than floating in the red as on the 'Northumberland' pieces.

The design of the Great Barton disc is perhaps less easily accepted. Normally with escutcheons the surrounding frame dictates the arrangement within; but here there is a square within a circular frame, and the intervening spaces are occupied by fillers derived, perhaps, from a running scroll. There is a similar square within a circle on one of the Scunthorpe prints, but there the spaces seem to be filled with enamel rather than further designs, as within the square on the square-framed escutcheon on Sutton Hoo bowl 1. As for the swastika, I do not see any influence from the so-called zoomorphic swastikas from Faversham and on Sutton Hoo bowl 2, for these are merely balanced arrangements of four elements within a circle.[6] Neither has the rectangular layout, nor the surrounding square of the Great Barton swastika. In its strangeness and unsuitability in this position, this element of the design seems to me to be one which has been taken straight from another object in another medium.

There are several sources from which a square-framed, self-contained, compact swastika arrangement of this type might have been copied; probably they are all interrelated. The first is late Roman metalwork. The decoration on large chip-carved military buckles of the late fourth century is based predominantly on spirals, but also includes rectangular arrangements, and some surviving buckles have compact swastikas formed of interlocking T-shapes;[7] a notable example is the buckle from Herbergen, Oldenburg, Germany[8] (fig. 2,1). Perfect compact swastikas derived from this sort of model are a feature of the famous quoit brooch style buckle and plates from Mucking[9] (fig. 2,2). Pieces such as this could have carried the design forward to the end of the fifth century, but barely beyond, so that while they are a possible source for the motif, they are probably too distant in time to be considered seriously.

The compact swastika was also picked up by the cloisonné jewellers who used it as an element of four T-shaped stones, garnets, and glass, in a number of objects of the late fifth and early sixth centuries[10] (fig. 2,3–5). When used in this way the design remains always a complete self-contained square, and the swastika is not developed to cover the surface of the object. As a design element it proved unattractive or unadaptable and did not survive long. This second, and chronologically more likely, source for the motif can probably also be discounted, for no examples of it on cloisonné jewellery have yet been found in England.

The third source for compact swastikas is the stamps on pottery (fig. 3). Swastika stamps occur along with animals and interlace on the products of Myres's animal stamp workshops, and in combination with other less distinctive stamps on a variety of pots which are generally dated to the sixth century; Myres suggests that the animal stamp workshops may have been in operation as late as the end of the sixth and the beginning of the seventh centuries. Myres's *Corpus* makes it possible now to compile a distribution map of pots with swastika stamps (fig. 4), and to see that they were in use not only in East Anglia, but also in Lindsey and across the Humber at Sancton. The freestyle swastikas, scratched on pots as opposed to being stamped, indicate exactly the same area. As a source for the design on the Great Barton disc, stamps on pots have the advantage not only of a greater and later chronological spread than the decorative objects described above, but also of widespread use in England; and it seems that, of the three possibilities, they are much the most likely. However if they were the source of the design, then we must expect that the Great Barton disc was made within the area of their distribution. Is that possible?

The traditional view of hanging bowls, whether they be thought of as British or Irish, or simply Celtic, or Pictish, presumes that they were made outside, or at least on the periphery of, the Anglo-Saxon parts of the country, and were traded to, or looted by, the Anglo-Saxons. But why should this remain so? As long ago as 1940, Kendrick proposed a Midlands or East Anglian workshop on the basis of the distribution of a number of finds of which Scunthorpe and Sutton Hoo were the chief;[11] and it would be possible to use the same argument to associate the Great Barton disc with such a workshop, were it not that a better foundation can be given to the claim.

Vera Evison has recently drawn attention again to that group of Anglo-Saxon objects which are embellished with spots of enamel.[12] These were first noticed and listed in 1924 by Cyril Fox who commented on their localized distribution.[13] Adding to his list, I now know of nineteen of these objects, square-headed brooches, cruciform brooches, saucer brooches, wrist clasps and even a swastika brooch, centred on central East Anglia with outliers in the Nene valley and in Kent (fig. 5). Careful examination and analysis of a selection of these objects has shown that the enamel, whatever its present appearance, was originally red, and the same high lead red cuprite glass as the enamel on hanging bowls.[14]

Here then is certain evidence that there were in East Anglia in the sixth century metalworkers who knew and could make use of enamelling techniques. Inevitably the only objects that we are able to recognize as being made by these metalworkers are the 'Anglo-Saxon' ones, but there seems no reason to suppose that they would not also have acquired the knowledge to produce objects in the hanging bowl tradition. The Great Barton disc fits into place beautifully if it is explained in this way—an enamelled disc, perhaps for a hanging bowl, with a design taken from the stamps on local pottery. No doubt it would appear a bit of a mess to the masters of the Durrow spiral escutcheons; but it would be perfectly acceptable to the East Anglian metalworkers whose links with the traditional patterns were tenuous, or even non-existent.

There is another aspect of the Great Barton disc that fits in well with this explanation. This is the yellow enamel. The study of enamel colours is bedevilled by the fact that the familiar red enamel changes, on deterioration, to a pale yellow colour which is usually distinguishable from the original yellow enamel only by its different consistency; the deteriorated version is chalky or powdery rather than glassy. For example there is a Durrow spiral escutcheon from Barrington, Cambs., in the Ashmolean Museum. It is yellow to look at; it has always been described as yellow enamel, and it is illustrated as yellow by E.T. Leeds in the colour plate in *Celtic Ornament*.[15] However the yellow material is very soft and powdery, and removal of a small part of it has revealed the original hard red enamel beneath. Originally this escutcheon was bright red. So it was with many pieces. One cannot trust other people's descriptions; nor, I discover to my embarrassment, can one even believe one's own eyes, unless the enamel can be examined under magnification and tested with a needle, and ultimately by analysis.[16] This last process has so far identified, amongst circular hanging bowl escutcheons, only three with original yellow enamel: the 'Northumberland' pieces, the Benty Grange animal discs[17] and the Great Barton disc. Also analysed at the same time, to test a hunch about the origin of the yellow enamel, were three opaque yellow glass beads from graves at Stanlake, Oxon., Faversham, Kent, and Haslingfield, Cambs. The compositions of the Faversham and Haslingfield beads and of the three yellow enamels were distinctive, and sufficiently close to suggest that they had a common origin. It seems then that the metalworkers in East Anglia were not only innovators in design, but also in technique, adding yellow from beads to their enamelled objects in a way which would probably have been unthinkable to traditional enamel workers.

Summing up, we can say that the Great Barton disc is like the enamelled discs from hanging bowls of which most of the dated examples are seventh century; that it owes its design to the swastika stamps current on the pottery of East Anglia and Lindsey during the sixth century; that it uses yellow glass beads such as were in use in the sixth and earlier part of the seventh century to make a contrasting yellow enamel; and finally, that it is the sort of technical and artistic break with traditional methods that would not be unexpected in a workshop such as we know must have existed in East Anglia in the later sixth century.

Although the Great Barton disc is an isolated piece, and a rather second-rate-looking piece at that, there is no reason why other similarly inspired pieces should not have existed, and there are in fact good reasons for believing that they did; for the swastika motif appears, if infrequently, on later objects showing that it became a small, but established, part of the artistic repertoire of the seventh and eighth centuries.

The swastika motif appears on one of the millefiori panels found by Rosemary Cramp at Monkwearmouth[18] (fig. 5,1–3). The panel is made up of nine squares, eight of which have the same basic design, assembled from square rods each made out of four interlocking T-shapes, two in a dark colour and two in a light colour. These interlocking T-shapes which give the swastika effect, are created by a simple adaptation of the common chequer pattern, but they are not found in millefiori on pieces earlier than this which itself cannot be earlier than the late seventh century.

Swastikas appear in manuscripts. In the Durrow Gospels,[19] on the cross carpet page fronting St Matthew's gospel, f. 1ᵛ, the square panels at the centres of the arms of the cross are filled either with swastikas of four interlocking T-shapes (fig. 6,4), or with a chequered imitation of millefiori. In view of the Monkwearmouth find it is of particular interest to find these two designs in the same relative positions. More ambitious, on Durrow f. 125^v, the carpet page preceding St Luke's gospel, swastika squares fill two of the rectangular panels which provide the framework for the page; (fig. 6,5) larger in size, these squares are filled with four interlocking stepped shapes rather than simple T's. In the Lindisfarne Gospels[20] swastikas appear only on the carpet page before St John's gospel, f. 210^v, where there are four isolated square panels set in a background of interlace; (fig. 6,6) the swastikas filling the squares are drawn in black outline, two clockwise, two anticlockwise. And, in the early eighth-century *Collectio Canonum*,[21] a Northumbrian manuscript preserved in Cologne, swastikas are used as filling for the corner squares of the border which frames the decorative initial D on the first page (fig. 6,7). There are five of these swastika squares and all contain blocks of four; three of the five have interlocking L-shapes, two interlocking T-shapes. In these three manuscripts, the swastika is used in a discrete way, filling corners and small panels, always in self-contained squares, never expanding into a more complex design.

Finally, the swastika is prominent on the anthropomorphic escutcheons of the bowl from Løland[22] and the bucket from Oseberg[23] (fig. 6,8–9), both in Norway. The Løland escutcheon has a square panel enamelled with four red T-shapes set against a yellow background; the Oseberg escutcheon has a central millefiori-filled cross dividing the panel into four small squares each enamelled with four yellow T-shapes set against a red background. These two pieces fit happily into place as a natural development of the pattern which first appeared in its rather untidy form on the Great Barton disc. But both are also included by Françoise Henry in her group of eighth-century Irish enamels.[24] A major characteristic of the Irish group is the use of rectilinear L, T, and Z shaped cells for the enamel. It is not difficult to see the derivation of these cell shapes from the swastika-inspired designs we have been considering. In their rectilinear shape, in their use or imitation of enamel, and particularly in their use of yellow as well as red enamel, these swastika patterns from East Anglia and Northumbria provide a better 'origin' for the Irish group than do the cloisonné patterns of Anglo-Saxon garnet jewellery.

Much, it seems, can be traced back to that East Anglian metalworker who chose to take his designs from pot-stamps.

Bibliography

ALEXANDER, J.J.G., *Insular Manuscripts, 6th to the 9th century* (London, 1978).

BRUCE-MITFORD, R.L.S., *Aspects of Anglo-Saxon Archaeology* (London, 1974).

BRUCE-MITFORD, R.L.S., *The Sutton Hoo Ship-Burial*, Vol. 1 (London, 1975).

BRUCE-MITFORD, R.L.S., *The Sutton Hoo Ship Burial, A Handbook*, 3rd edn. (London, 1979).

BRØGGER, A.W. and SCHETELIG, H., *Osebergfundet*, Bd. II (Oslo, 1928).

BULLINGER, H., *Spätantike Gurtelbeschläge* (Brugge, 1969).

BUSCHAUSEN, H., *Die spätrömischen Metallscrinia und frühchristliche Reliquiare (Wiener Byzantinische Studien IX)* (Wien, 1971).

CRAMP, R., 'Decorated window-glass and millefiori from Monkwearmouth', *Antiq. J.* 50 (1970), 327–35.

EVISON, V.I., *The Fifth-century Invasions south of the Thames* (London, 1965).

EVISON, V.I., 'Quoit Brooch Style Buckles', *Antiq. J.* 48 (1968), 231–49.

EVISON, V.I., 'An enamelled disc from Great Saxham', *Proc. Suffolk Inst. Archaeol. and Hist.* 34 (Part 1, 1977), 1–13.

FOX, C., *The Archaeology of the Cambridge Region* (Cambridge, 1923).

HENRY, F., 'Hanging Bowls', *Journ. Roy. Soc. Antiqs. Ireland* 66 (1936), 209–46.

HENRY, F., 'Irish Enamels of the Dark Ages and their Relation to the Cloisonné Techniques', in Harden, D.B., ed., *Dark-Age Britain, Studies presented to E.T. Leeds* (London, 1956), 71–88.

HENRY, F., *Irish Art, I, the early Christian period* (London, 1965).

KENDRICK, T.D., British Hanging Bowls, *Antiquity* 6 (1932), 161–84.

KENDRICK, T.D., 'The Large Hanging-Bowl', in 'The Sutton Hoo Ship Burial', *Antiquity* (1940), 30–4.

KENDRICK, T.D., 'The Scunthorpe Bowl', *Antiq. J.* 21 (1941), 236–8.

LEEDS, E.T., *Celtic Ornament* (Oxford. 1933).

MENÉNDEZ PIDAL, R., *Historia de España, III, España Visigoda* (Madrid, 1940).

MYRES, J.N.L., *A Corpus of Anglo-Saxon Pottery of the Pagan Period* (Cambridge, 1977).

MYRES, J.N.L. and GREEN, B., *The Anglo-Saxon Cemeteries of Caistor-by-Norwich and Markshall, Norfolk* (London, 1973).

PETERSEN, J., *British Antiquities of the Viking Period found in Norway* (Schetelig, H., ed., *Viking Antiquities in Great Britain and Ireland,* part V) (Oslo, 1940).

RUPP, H., *Die Herkunft der Zelleneinlage* (Bonn, 1937).

SALIN, B., *Die altgermanische Thierornamentik* (Stockholm, 1904).

SMITH, R.A., *British Museum Guide to Anglo-Saxon Antiquities* (London, 1923).

WERNER, J., *Katalog der Sammlung Diergardt*, Bd. I, *Die Fibeln* (Berlin, 1961).

Notes

1. Myres, 1977 (No. 209), 62–3; Myres and Green, 1973 (No. 181), 59–61.
2. Now in the Dept. of Antiquities, Ashmolean Museum.
3. Henry, 1956, 83–8.
4. Smith, 1923, 50; Kendrick, 1932, fig. 4.
5. Bruce-Mitford, 1975, nos 109 and 111; illustrated in Bruce-Mitford, 1979, 19, 43, 62; Kendrick, 1932, fig. 4 and pl. V; Kendrick, 1941, pl. LIII.
6. Kendrick, 1932, fig. 7; Bruce-Mitford, 1979, 62.
7. Bullinger, 1969 *passim*.
8. Evison, 1965, pl. 9.
9. Evison, 1968, 53.
10. Examples are a gold reliquary from Varna, Bulgaria (Buschhausen, 1971, C 1, 263, Taf. 3), a Frankish radiate-headed brooch in the Fitzwilliam Museum, Cambridge (Rupp, 1937, Taf. XIX, 4), two Frankish quatrefoil brooches (Werner, 1961, 37, Taf. 37); and a semicircular Visigothic buckle plate in the Sammlung Diergardt, Cologne, a sword scabbard from Joches, Marne (Salin, 1904, 107), a buckle from Castiltierra, Segovia (Menéndez Pidal, 1940, 456), and a rectangular buckle plate in the RGZM Mainz.
11. Kendrick, 1940, 30–1; Kendrick, 1941, 237–8.
12. Evison, 1977, 3.
13. Fox, 1923, 283, 294.
14. This analysis, by Dr M. Hughes at the British Museum Research Laboratory, will be published in a future volume of *Anglo-Saxon Studies*.
15. Leeds, 1933, 150–1, colour plate; Henry, 1936, 231, pl. 33, 5.
16. As note 14.
17. Bruce-Mitford, 1974, 225, pl. 76.
18. Cramp, 1970.
19. Trinity College, Dublin Ms A. 4. 5 (57); Alexander, 1978, no. 6.
20. British Library, Cotton Ms Nero D. IV; Alexander, 1978, no. 9.
21. Dombibliothek, Cologne, Cod. 213; Alexander, 1978, no. 13.
22. Petersen, 1940, 91.
23. Brøgger and Schetelig, 1928, 72–4.
24. Henry, 1956, 83–8.

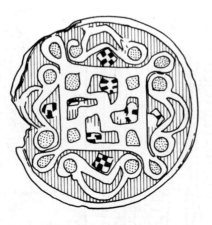

FIG. 1. Bronze disc with red and yellow
enamel and millefiori, from Great
Barton, Suffolk.   Scale 3/2.

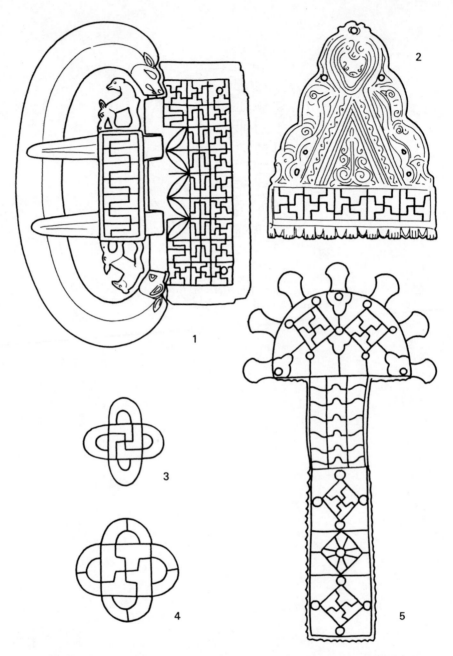

Fig. 2. Outline drawing of objects with swastika decoration: 1. Late Roman chip-carved buckle from Herbergen, Oldenburg, Germany; 2. Fifth-century belt plate from Mucking, Essex; Frankish garnet cloisonné brooches; 3. From Concevreux, Aisne; 4 and 5. Unprovenanced. (All about actual size.)

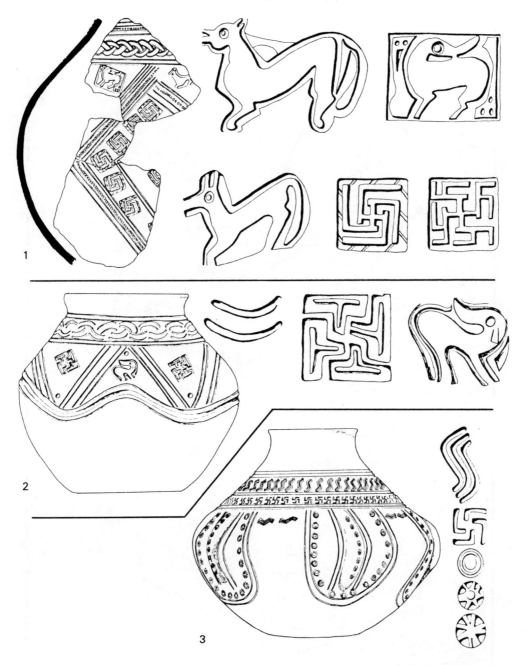

Fig. 3. Swastika-stamped pottery: 1. Caistor-by-Norwich, Norfolk; 2. Lackford, Suffolk; 3. Newark, Notts. Scales, pots 1 : 4, stamps 1 : 1. (After Myres; *Corpus* nos 1884, 997, 3543.)

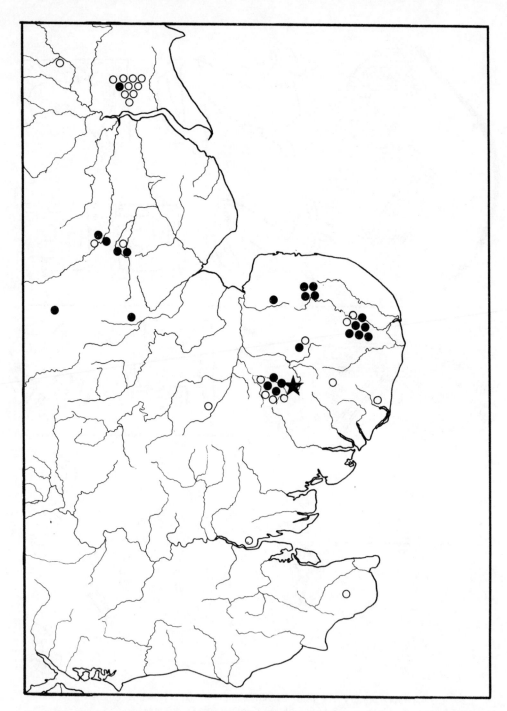

Fig. 4. Distribution map of pottery with stamped swastikas (spots) and freestyle swastikas (circles), compiled from Myres's *Corpus*. Sites plotted are: York, Sancton, Newark, Loveden Hill, Thurmaston, Melton Mowbray, Spong Hill, Castle Acre, Caistor-by-Norwich, Illington, Shropham, Lackford, Cambridge, Redgrave, Snape, Mucking, and Bifrons. The star marks Great Barton.

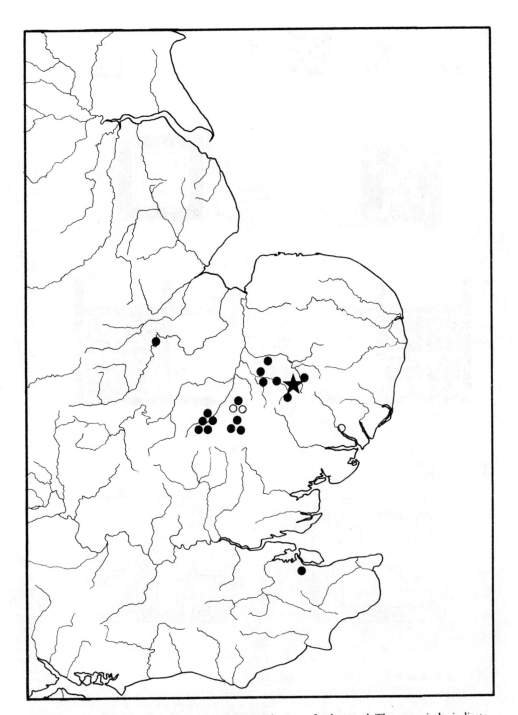

Fɪɢ. 5. Distribution map of Anglo–Saxon objects with spots of red enamel. The open circles indicate less certain occurrences. Sites plotted are Nassington (1), Barrington (5), Mildenhall (2), Ixworth (1), West Stow (1), Bury St Edmunds (1), Linton Heath (3), Little Wilbraham (1 + 2?), Lakenheath (1), Ipswich (1?), Faversham (1). The star marks Great Barton.

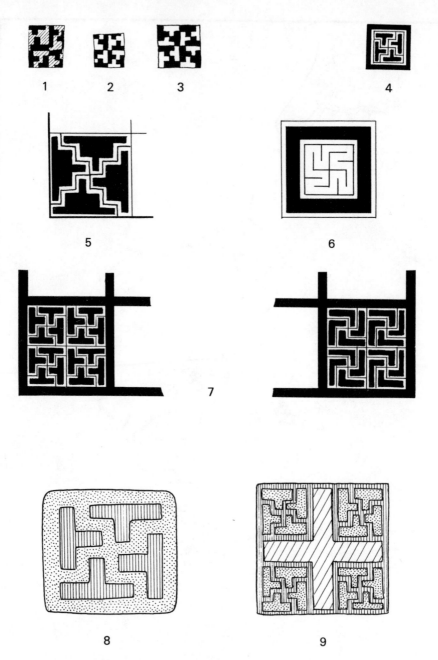

F𝗂𝗀. 6. Schematic drawings of swastika patterns: 1–3, millefiori from
Monkwearmouth; 1. Translucent blue and opaque pale green; 2. Translucent blue and
opaque white; 3. Intended pattern of millefiori free of distortion; 4. Durrow Gospels f.
1$^\text{v}$; 5. Durrow Gospels f. 125$^\text{v}$; 6. Lindisfarne Gospels f. 210$^\text{v}$; 7. *Collectio Canonum* f. 1;
8. Løland escutcheon, red and yellow enamel; 9. Oseberg escutcheon, yellow and red
enamel around a central millefiori cross. Scales 1–7 about twice actual size; 8–9, about 4 : 3.

I I

Wharram: Roman to Medieval

J.G. HURST

Introduction

Wharram is situated in the County of North Yorkshire (until 1974 East Riding) about half-way between York and Scarborough, some 7 miles (10 km) south-east of Malton, near the north-western corner of the Wolds. The area comprises a chalk plateau, about 500 ft (150 m) above sea level, dissected by a network of steep-sided winding dry valleys. The research project, which was started thirty years ago by the Medieval Village Research Group on the earthworks of the deserted village of Wharram Percy with the excavation of two sample peasant house sites,[1] has since expanded with the help of the Department of the Environment to investigate the church,[2] parsonages, and water mill in an attempt to study as many aspects of the medieval village as possible.[3]

During the last ten years a series of sections has been cut through the various boundaries defining the medieval tofts and crofts, showing that many of these are on the same lines as Romano-British features, while Romano-British and Anglo-Saxon settlements have been found underlying the medieval remains. In the last five years the project has been further expanded by C. Hayfield, to study the whole landscape of the two parishes of Wharram Percy and Wharram le Street comprising some 11,000 acres (4,500 hectares). A combination of aerial photography by A. Pacitto, fieldwalking, and geophysical survey by the Ancient Monuments Laboratory, has revealed an extensive Romano-British landscape of settlements at approximately half-mile intervals, linked by trackways lined by rectangular enclosures (figs. 1 and 2 and pl. XIV).

This scattered pattern seems to have subsisted through the Anglo-Saxon period, with nucleation, into at least six villages in Wharram Percy parish and one in Wharram le Street, taking place in late Saxon times; two of the Wharram Percy settlements were finally amalgamated into a single village, Wharram Percy, in the middle of the thirteenth century: this was deserted in the early sixteenth century, and three of the other four known villages in its parish are also deserted. In the two parishes, only Wharram le Street and Thixendale now survive. There is at present no firm evidence suggestive of continuity from Romano-British to Anglo-Saxon times in the greater part of the two parishes, since no excavation has yet been undertaken outside the deserted village of Wharram Percy itself. There are however a number of indications. The main emphasis of this paper will therefore be on the features actually in the deserted village of Wharram Percy, where extensive excavation has taken place.

There are three main aspects of the village site which have produced evidence for continuity or discontinuity: first, the general layout of the medieval earthworks on the western plateau seems to reflect very strongly the pattern of Romano-British lynchets, enclosure boundaries and roads; second, the Areas 9 and 10 enclosure and the North Manor, also on the western plateau, contain indications of Romano-British settlement with manorial sites on top; third, the valley terrace west of the stream contains extensive traces of Iron Age and Romano-British settlement, but with an apparent gap until the eighth century and the subsequent building of a sequence of churches. This evidence will now be given in more detail; this will be followed by a consideration of the nature of continuity, both in the village itself and in its parish setting, and, finally, by a critical discussion of the character of the evidence for continuity.

1. *The Western Plateau*

The most prominent feature on the western plateau at Wharram Percy village is a linear earthwork; this is a lynchet running from the south-western tributary valley known as Drue Dale northwards for 500 yards (450 m) to an east–west road (fig. 3 and pl. XII). It is pre-medieval as it is cut through by medieval roads, and, when it was utilized as the boundary between the medieval tofts and crofts, it was either left as a slope or cut back and faced with a wall by the various peasants. Parts of it were levelled in the open area between Areas 8 and 9. The size of the lynchet suggests that it was formed by ploughing over a long period, which ought to extend back into the Iron Age if the Romano-British settlement, which it is thought was situated to the west of the Area 10 Manor house site, was built in its lee. The east–west road seems to have provided the main access from the valley to the first-century fortified farm to the north-west of the site; it then continued westwards, out beyond the enclosures.

Sections through the western boundary of the medieval crofts and the boundary between crofts 10 and 12 show that there were Romano-British boundary ditches running along the same lines. A section through the headland running obliquely to the west of Area 8 also showed a Romano-British ditch on the same line, suggesting that this anomalous shape is Romano-British in origin.

Further checks must be made, but it looks very much as though the basic plan of the medieval village on the western plateau is determined by the layout of Romano-British enclosures. That some of the smaller subdivisions may also be early is suggested by the network of small rectangular enclosures which have been shown by air photography to extend westwards on the line of the croft boundaries, beyond the western boundary bank of the village, where they were levelled for the medieval open fields. In addition, although sections have so far failed to show a Roman origin for the northern boundary of the north manorial enclosure, in its eastern part this forms a considerable break in slope emphasizing a periglacial hollow which may have been utilized. More important is the fact that sample areas dug in 1979 to the north of this boundary have located no occupation and only a small scatter of abraded Romano-British and medieval sherds suggesting manuring and agriculture. This therefore seems to have been the northern boundary of the settlement from Romano-British times onwards.

2. *Areas 9 and 10 and the North Manor*

The crofts of Areas 9 and 10 form a well-defined rectangular enclosure bounded on the east by the top of the lynchet. The northern boundary has been shown to be on a Romano-British alignment and it is likely that the western and southern boundaries are also; the fact that these banks are more pronounced (pl. XII), is not, however, evidence for an earlier origin, as in the twelfth century the Area 10 manor house was surrounded by a stone wall, whereas the other croft boundaries were built only of soil and rubble. The Romano-British ditch, like the later medieval one, is only 2 ft (60 cm) wide and 2 ft (60 cm) deep, so for the alignment to have survived it must have been more than a simple bank and ditch; the most significant feature of the boundary is likely to have been a hedge. The twelfth-century stone wall is built on a bank which could be a Roman survival but which is more likely to be the Anglo-Saxon boundary to this enclosure.

The earliest building so far located in Area 10 was the camera block of a twelfth-century manor house thought to belong to the Chamberlains, and which was abandoned in 1254 when the Percies amalgamated the two manors into one. After this the area was quarried and later filled in for the building of fourteenth- and fifteenth-century peasant houses.

When 8,825 sq ft of Area 10 toft were excavated in the 1950s only a scatter of 23 Romano-British and 10 Anglo-Saxon sherds were found, though it was noted that these were fairly fresh and not abraded for manuring. When a 750 sq ft extension was dug in 1977/8 to the west, to look for more evidence for twelfth-century manorial buildings, many more sherds of Romano-British and 106 sherds of Anglo-Saxon pottery were found. These increased considerably in number as the dig progressed westwards, suggesting that Romano-British and Anglo-Saxon buildings were fairly close. The most obvious place for these is in the western half of toft 10, in the lee of the lynchet. It is hoped that in 1980 a major programme of excavation of this area will be started by G. Milne to determine the nature of any settlement there and to try to establish whether there really is continuity in this enclosure. At the same time more sections will be cut through the boundaries to test their date and nature.

The trapezoidal enclosure in the north of the village (pl. XIII) contains a complex series of earthworks of buildings round a series of courtyards, which have been interpreted as a twelfth- and thirteenth-century manor—presumably that of the Percies. The question must be asked as to whether this north manorial enclosure was subdivided to serve the various purposes of the manor or whether these were fitted into an already existing pattern. The latter seems possible, but must be checked by further excavation. There is clear evidence for a complex Romano-British settlement within the enclosure, though the boundaries have not yet been demonstrated to be early. The first evidence came from a trial trench across the south wall of the suggested hall (K) in 1961, when a series of ditches, gullies, and post-holes and a burial, associated with pottery of the second to fourth centuries, were found.

The excavation of a 40 ft (12 m) square in the south courtyard, between 1977 and 1979, has also located a complex of Romano-British features, so a nucleus of the Romano-British settlement is not only in the same area as the medieval manor house but is concentrated under and near the main manorial buildings. No Anglo-Saxon structures have so far been located but there is sufficient Anglo-Saxon pottery to suggest continuity. In addition, the large size of the Romano-British sherds, and the lack of evidence for any ploughing, suggests that there was no major post-Roman disturbance in this area. In 1980 P. Rahtz hopes to extend the area already opened to explore the extent and nature of the Romano-British occupation, and to try to determine the nature of any occupation in the Anglo-Saxon period.

3. *The Valley Terrace*

On the valley terrace, as might be expected from the presence of eight sets of springs along the junction of the chalk and the underlying Upper Jurassic clay, there is occupation of uncertain nature from Neolithic times, with the first features dating to the Pre-Roman Iron Age, ranging over an extensive area. They have been found over 100 ft (30 m) south of the church, under the church, north of the church, and at the south end of the garden south of the cottages; a total distance of over 100 yds (90 m). In addition an isolated crouched burial with a C14 date of 80 bc was found north-west of the church. This occupation continued throughout the Roman period with pottery from the first to fourth centuries, but there then seems to be a gap in occupation until the eighth century. Continuous settlement would have been expected on this sheltered terrace close to water rather than on the exposed western plateau 50 ft (15 m) above. The finds of early Anglo-Saxon pottery from nearly twenty years' excavation amount to only nine sherds from the church and eight from the Glebe area to the north.

The exact nature of the eighth century and later occupation is uncertain, as it is now unlikely that the first church can be dated earlier than the post-Scandinavian period in the tenth century. Nevertheless, there was earlier activity, as is shown by the finding of more than six sceattas dating between AD 750 and 839 together with a fragment of a late eighth-century cross. At the moment it looks as though there was only minimal activity in the early Anglo-Saxon period on the valley terrace, unless it took place well to the north under the cottages. Charlotte Harding and P. Chitwood have started excavating large new areas north of the graveyard and south of the cottages to establish the sequence there. After the experience of Area 10 it would be rash to say yet that there was no Anglo-Saxon domestic occupation on the terrace.

Discussion: A. The Parish

The concept of continuity has two aspects: firstly, continuity of exploitation of the resources of the land which may take place from varying centres, and secondly, settlement in the same place with tenurial or proprietorial continuity. The problem of continuity is not confined to the period between AD 350 and 700 and it is just as crucial in studying the total landscape history of Wharram to consider the changes from the Mesolithic to the Neolithic, the clearance of primary woodland, the impact of the later Bronze age land division as evidenced by linear earthworks (the so-called ranch boundaries), what happened in the Iron Age, and above all whether the major new landscape of roads and enclosures, apparently laid out in the Romano-British period, was created *de novo* or was influenced by earlier layouts, as seems to have been the case between the Roman and medieval periods.[4] On the medieval village site at Wharram Percy the south-north lynchet does seem to be pre-Roman and to have influenced the later layout, while elsewhere in the parish many of the linear earthworks survived: some were made into roads, while others still continue as parish boundaries. But a great deal more must be done to the parish survey before these points can be resolved and this paper is concerned with the problem of what happened in the area between Roman and medieval times.

In the parish, while there may have been continuous exploitation of the land, there was no need for it always to be organized from the same centres. Whatever happened in the early Saxon period, there was a major change in late Saxon times with the concentration of the scattered Anglo-Saxon settlements into nucleated villages, as a result either of the churches being built, or—and more likely as there was not a church at every village—consequent upon the reorganization of agricultural activities, more specifically the formalization of the open field system. Other such changes in the exploitation of the area can be more clearly seen in later, better documented times, when the medieval nucleated villages with their arable open fields were replaced in the late fifteenth and early sixteenth century by large sheep walks requiring only a single farm, and when the eighteenth-century improvers returned the Wolds to arable, run not from villages but from isolated farms such as Wharram Percy and Bella.

At Wharram le Street one of the two Roman villas is situated just east of the medieval village site with its Saxon church, but the exact relationship of the villa to other early settlement still has to be investigated (fig. 1). At Burdale in Wharram Percy (fig. 2), which was also deserted, an area of the site was recently ploughed, producing sherds of Romano-British, Anglo-Saxon, and medieval pottery.

In view of the difficulty of locating Anglo-Saxon sherds when fieldwalking a Romano-British settlement, it is hard to tell how many of these sites continued into, or were reused in, the early and Middle Saxon periods. Of the fifteen scattered Romano-British settlements so far located and fieldwalked in the Wharram parishes, fourteen have a preponderance of fourth-century pottery including the late Crambeck and Huntcliffe wares. It is not possible to say how early they were established, as ploughing may not have disturbed the lower layers. Five of these sites have produced Anglo-Saxon pottery in limited quantities, and as most of it is middle Saxon the evidence for continuity is at present uncertain. In addition three other scattered sites have been found producing only Anglo-Saxon pottery. The only Anglo-Saxon burials so far found were secondaries in Bronze Age Barrows along the ridgeway south boundary of Wharram Percy Township excavated by Mortimer.[5] The impression therefore is of scattered middle Saxon settlements fewer in number than the Romano-British sites. As late Saxon pottery has only been found at the medieval nucleated village sites, this strongly suggests that the nucleation into larger settlements took place in the classic period of eighth- or ninth-century shuffle.

The complex network of Romano-British trackways and enclosure boundaries is strongly reflected in the present road and boundary alignments. This is to be expected along the valley from Thixendale to Burdale and Fimber (fig. 2) as there is no other way a route could go; the medieval villages were about one mile apart with every alternate Romano-British settlement abandoned. In the area around Wharram Percy the present roads are generally along Romano-British alignments with gentle curves changed into sharp corners to accommodate the blocks of ridge and furrow. It is therefore tempting to suggest that the Romano-British road system survived through till middle Saxon times, with the present roads established at the same time as the open fields were laid out in late Saxon times. It is also reasonable to postulate a continued use of the area for arable or for grazing, organized from scattered settlements which might change their positions in the Anglo-Saxon period. The lack of firm evidence for the sub-Roman and early Saxon periods, however, does raise difficulties for suggesting complete continuity. But if there was a break, it has to be explained why many of the tracks survived and why at least some of the middle Saxon settlements were on the same sites as the Romano-British ones.

B. The Medieval Village Area

The nature and extent of continuity seems to have been different in the Wharram parishes as a whole from the situation in the village of Wharram Percy, where there seems to have been much more continuity of settlement. This is only natural as the half-mile stretch of the valley, with its numerous springs, is a preferred site for settlement, and people are likely to have returned again and again to the same site after any break. There are today one or two springs at Wharram le Street, Thixendale, Raisthorpe, and Burdale, but nowhere else in the parishes is there such an abundance.

In the area of the medieval village of Wharram Percy there is more definite evidence than from the parish as a result of excavation. There does seem to be strong evidence, not only for continuity of exploitation of the land from Roman to Saxon times, but also for continuity on two of the three Romano-British settlements under the later village. As the two sites, Area 10 and the northern manorial enclosure, are not situated in obvious positions close to water or other topographical features, it is unlikely that the two medieval manors would have been built exactly over the two Romano-British farms if there had been any considerable break in settlement in the early Saxon period. It is possible to argue that the physical survival of silted ditches and degraded banks could have affected later decisions on layout, but, as the Romano-British farms were built of timber, they would not have left any earthworks or other physical traces so that the earlier building sites would not have been obvious. The two medieval manor houses were either over or adjacent to, and certainly in the same enclosures as, the two Romano-British farms; this can hardly have happened without some proprietorial or tenurial continuity. A possible alternative is that there were not just two Romano-British farms on the western plateau, but a farm in each of the enclosures. If this was so it could be just chance that the later manor houses were built over two of them. In view of the pattern of scattered Romano-British settlement in the rest of the Wolds this seems to be unlikely, but it is a point to be considered.

The situation on the valley terrace is complicated by the present lack of evidence for early Saxon occupation, but this may be found in further excavation north of the church and burial ground. If there was no continuity of settlement it would be most remarkable if two exposed sites on the western plateau, quite a long way from water, survived, while the preferred site on the valley terrace was abandoned. There must have been some strong tenurial or other reason for this. In late Saxon times it could be argued that the terrace was given to the church and that it was the glebe, but this does not explain an early Saxon gap.

Conclusion

The research project at Wharram therefore suggests that there was a continuity of exploitation of the land, though possibly from shifting centres, over most of the parishes between AD 350 and 700, but that at the medieval village site of Wharram Percy, because of its situation as a preferred site close to abundant water, there was continuity of settlement with some proprietorial or tenurial continuity. The nature and reliability of the archaeological dating evidence for this continuity must now be considered.

Roman coins and pottery continued at least till the end of the fourth century. From the large quantities of late fourth-century pottery found and the presence also in large quantities compared with other Saxon sites in Yorkshire, of middle Saxon pottery, associated with sceattas from AD 750 onwards, the gap to be filled from the dating point of view is the sub-Roman fifth century and the early Saxon sixth and seventh centuries. In the absence of any features excavated so far containing only clearly identifiable early Saxon pottery, the evidence for continuity of occupation in Areas 10 and the north manorial enclosure must depend on pottery which might be datable to this period. The sub-Roman period is the most difficult as, after the end of the minting of Roman coins and the increasing possibilities after several hundred years of occupation of residual Roman pottery every time the soil is turned over, it is almost impossible to be sure which is sub-Roman pottery. When Saxon structures or features are found, as surely they will be in the next few years, the main hope will be to discover features stratified over or cutting into late fourth-century deposits and containing no Anglo-Saxon pottery, or sherds which may be definitely assigned to the fifth century by their decoration or form associated in seriated groups. There is some body of opinion that late fourth-century Roman pottery was produced into the fifth century, and that with continued use after production stopped it could last another generation or so. At the same time the coarse handmade local wares, which seem to continue largely unchanged through the Roman period from their Iron age beginnings, could also be made to the end of the fifth century. Until definite pottery types datable to the British period in Elmet and its surroundings can be identified it will be very difficult to fill in the sub-Roman period.

In the early Saxon period it is possible to identify three main groups of pottery which fill the gap of the sixth and seventh centuries. First the decorated wares, of which there are two sherds from Area 10 and 16 from the *Grubenhaus* to the north-east of the north manorial enclosure. Secondly the grass-tempered sherds, which despite the lack of dating in the north are, from evidence in the south and Midlands almost certainly early Saxon in date, though not necessarily very early. There are no examples from the north manorial enclosure but over 20 from Area 10, amounting to 50 per cent of the Saxon sherds. This is a surprising number in view of the supposed lack of grass-tempered pottery in the north of England.[6] Thirdly there are the handmade Anglo-Saxon sherds which can be firmly separated from the coarse Romano-British and Iron Age sherds. They are mainly likely to be early Saxon in date, although they continue parallel with the wheel-made middle Saxon Whitby-type sherds, as is shown from Whitby Abbey itself.[7] There are over twenty from Area 10 as well as a further forty-seven sherds which may be either Roman or Saxon. There are only so far twenty-seven sherds identified from the north manorial enclosure, but more of the pottery still has to be processed.

These numbers, plus five more sherds from the south boundary of the north manorial enclosure, tend to support the possibility of continuous occupation in the north manorial enclosure and Area 10 in the early Saxon period. There is at present better evidence from Area 10 but only a sample from the north manorial enclosure has been processed. It must also be borne in mind that any comparisons which can be made at present, between the nature of continuity at Wharram

Percy village on the one hand, and in the remainder of the parishes on the other hand, are largely based on different kinds of archaeological evidence. The possibilities of fieldwalking and crop-marks which have revealed so much elsewhere in the parishes are almost non-existent in the permanent pasture of the village: the south-west corner of the first-century Roman farm, for example, was invisible before the field beyond the Department of the Environment guardianship fence was cropped with barley in 1973. For the same reason, the collection of sherds over the sites elsewhere in the parishes has been far more extensive, albeit superficial, than in the village, where large tracts have not been sampled at all. Elsewhere, there has been no excavation; in the village itself, the full story has only been obtained by excavation in 4 per cent of the area under guardianship: what discoveries yet undreamt of may lie beneath the remainder, must indeed give us pause. It is a very sobering thought for any interpretation of the line of tofts 5 to 17 as an example of medieval planning that the ladder form of these is identical to similar features which are typical of the Romano-British landscape between the scattered settlements and alongside the trackways elsewhere in the parish (fig. 1 and pl. XIV). But excavations in Areas 10 and 6 tofts did not locate any east–west Romano-British boundaries along the lines of the rungs of a possible ladder.

To try to get some more definite evidence of the nature and full extent of the Romano-British and Anglo-Saxon settlements, and to discover their relationship to the two medieval manor houses, it is hoped to start in 1980 a ten-year programme of investigation of the north manorial enclosure and Area 10 each offering a control for the other. At the same time, it is hoped to strip as much as possible of the valley terrace to try and see if there was pre-AD 750 occupation in that area. The larger the area that is opened, the better the chance there will be of getting more dating evidence for those difficult centuries which are the concern of this book. It is most alarming for any policy of extensive sample excavation that no evidence of Romano-British or Anglo-Saxon occupation was found in the 1950s in Area 10 apparently within a few feet of the *foci* of these settlements.

So far, however, one sees a picture of long-continued exploitation of this part of the Wolds, but exploitation which varied in intensity and which was perhaps controlled from frequently changing centres, a pattern which was continued with the desertion of the nucleated villages in the sixteenth century and the return to single scattered farmsteads. The nucleated village was but an interlude in a sequence of continuing change.

Bibliography

ANDREWS, D.D., and MILNE, G. (eds.), *Domestic Settlement I: Areas 10 and 6, vol. I* of J.G. Hurst (ed.), *Wharram: A Study of settlement on the Yorkshire Wolds, Society for Medieval Archaeology Monograph Series* VIII (London, 1979).

BROWN, P.D.C., 'Some notes on grass-tempered pottery', in M. Farley, 'Saxon and Medieval Walton, Aylesbury: Excavations 1973–4', *Records of Bucks.* XX (1976), 191–3.

HURST, J.G., 'The Pottery', in D.M. Wilson (ed.), *The Archaeology of Anglo-Saxon England* (London, 1976^a), 283–348.

HURST, J.G., 'Wharram Percy: St. Martin's Church', in P.V. Addyman and R. Morris (eds.), *The Archaeological Study of Churches, Council of British Archaeology Research Report* XIII (London, 1976^b), 36–9.

HURST, J.G., 'The Wharram Research Project', in N.J. Higham (ed.), *The Changing Past* (Manchester, 1979), 67–74.

RAHTZ, P.A., 'The concept of continuity in settlement studies', *Medieval Research Group Annual Report* XXIV (1978), 35–6.

MORTIMER, J.R., *Forty Years' Researches in British and Saxon Burial Mounds of East Yorkshire* (London, 1905).

Notes

1. Andrews and Milne, 1979.
2. Hurst, 1976[b].
3. Hurst, 1979.
4. Rahtz, 1978.
5. Mortimer, 1905.
6. Brown, 1976.
7. Hurst, 1976[a], 304–6 and 309.

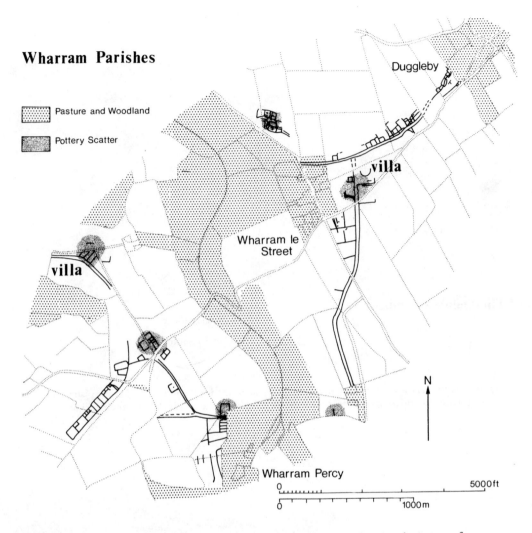

Wharram Parishes

Pasture and Woodland

Pottery Scatter

Duggleby

villa

Wharram le Street

villa

N

Wharram Percy

0   5000 ft

0   1000 m

Fig. 1. Plan of the central area of Wharram Percy and Wharram le Street showing the pattern of Romano-British tracks and settlements.

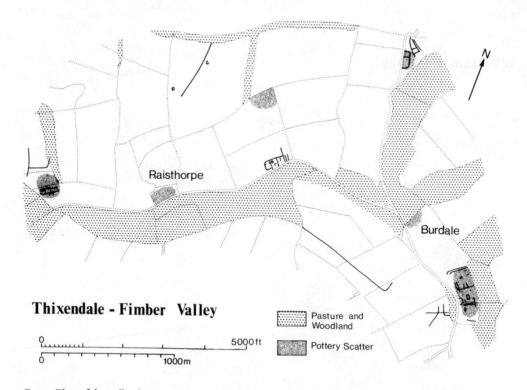

Thixendale - Fimber Valley

Raisthorpe

Burdale

Pasture and Woodland

Pottery Scatter

0 —————————— 5000 ft
0 —————————— 1000 m

FIG. 2. Plan of the valley between Thixendale (off the plan to the west) and Fimber (off the plan to the south-east) with spaced Romano-British settlements, the alternate ones surviving through till medieval times.

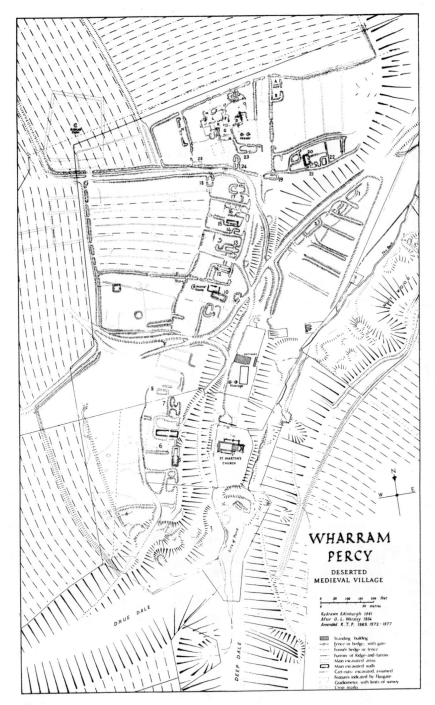

Fɪɢ. 3. Plan of Wharram Percy showing the earthworks of the medieval village set in a pattern of Romano-British earthworks.

PLATES

I. Carved head of J.N.L. Myres on the doorway of the Bodleian Library *(Thomas Photos Oxford)*

II. Hørløk, grave 3, from the north, with (empty) oak coffin (p. 3)

III. Hørløk, grave 40, from the north, with pots above and beside the coffin (p. 3)

IV. Højvang 1952, grave 2, from the west (p. 3)

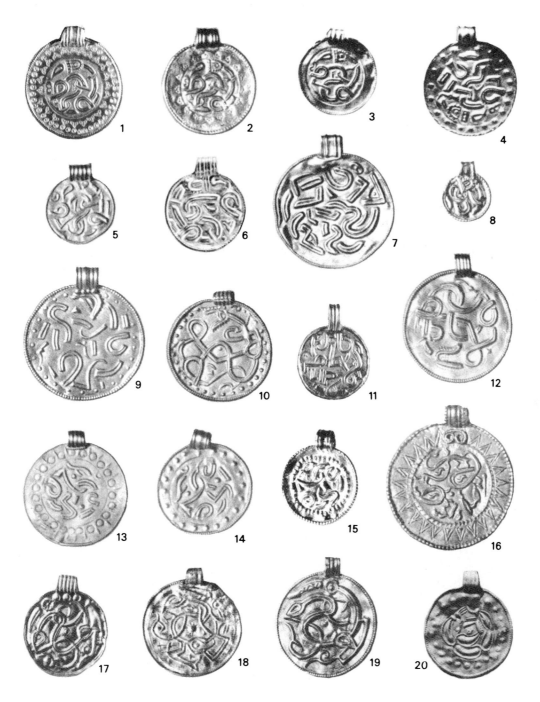

V. 1–19 Jutish type D bracteates, 1–8 variety 1, 9–12 variety 2, 13–15, 17–19 variety 3, 16 indeterminate. 20 B bracteate, 1 Hérouvillette 39, 2 Sarre 90, 3–4 Finglesham D3, 5 and 13 Bifrons 29, 6 Buckland Dover 20, 7, 9, 10, 16 Sarre 4, 8 Bad Kreuznach, 11 Hérouvillette 11, 12 Bifrons 63, 14 Bifrons 64, 15 Lyminge 16, 17 Wörrstadt, 18 Schretzheim 33, 19 Obermöllern 20, 20 Freilaubersheim 68. (p. 14)   Scale 1/1

VI. Ornaments associated with gold bracteates in grave finds, 1–2 Bifrons 29. 3–4 Lyminge 16.
5–6 Wörrstadt. 7 Schretzheim 33. 8 Bad Kreuznach. 9–11 Obermöllern 20. 12–14 Freilaubersheim 68.
(p. 21f)   Scale 1/1

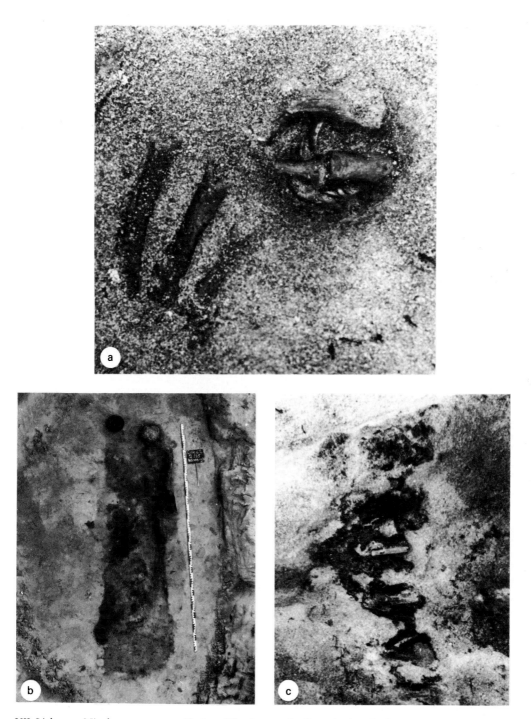

VII. Liebenau, Nienburg, grave 119 (A 1)   a. The rings on the finger *in situ*   b. Grave 119 (A 1)   c. The belt mounts *in situ*, with remains of bronze and leather (p. 61f)

a

b

c

VIII. a–c. Dörverden, Verden: silver-inlaid iron strap
mounts (p. 75f)   Scale 4/3

a

b

IX. a. Bremen-Mahndorf: iron plate inlaid with brass   b. Bremen-
Mahndorf: strap end with remains of silver inlay (p. 77)   Scale 3/2

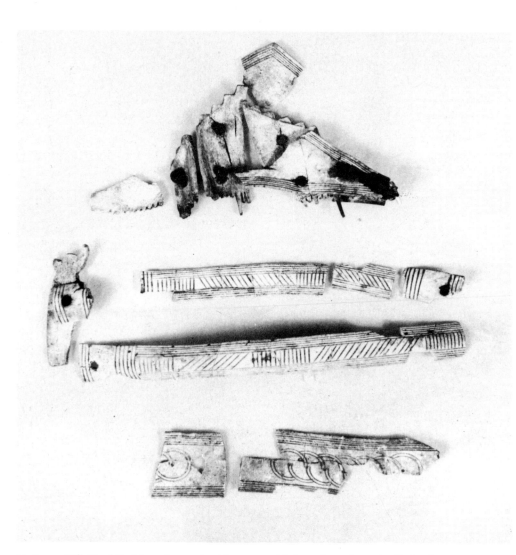

X. Spong Hill, Norfolk, triangular comb with zoomorphic barred case (p. 109)   Scale 1/1

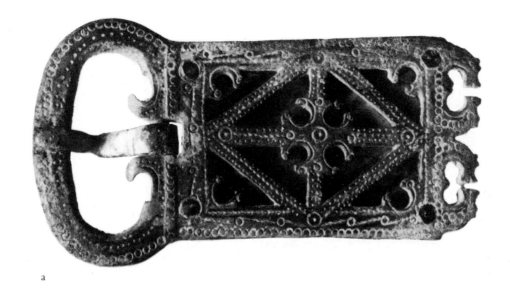

a

b

XI. a. Amiens, France, bronze buckle, Ashmolean Museum   b. Mitcham, London, bronze buckle (p. 134)
Scale 2/1

XII. Oblique air photograph of Wharram Percy, from the south, showing the earthworks of the village with the lynchet running across the site. Taken 4th June 1970. (p. 243)

XIII. Wharram Percy from the north under snow showing the north manorial enclosure, the Areas 9 and 10 enclosure and their relationship to the other village earthworks. Taken 1st January 1971. (p. 244)

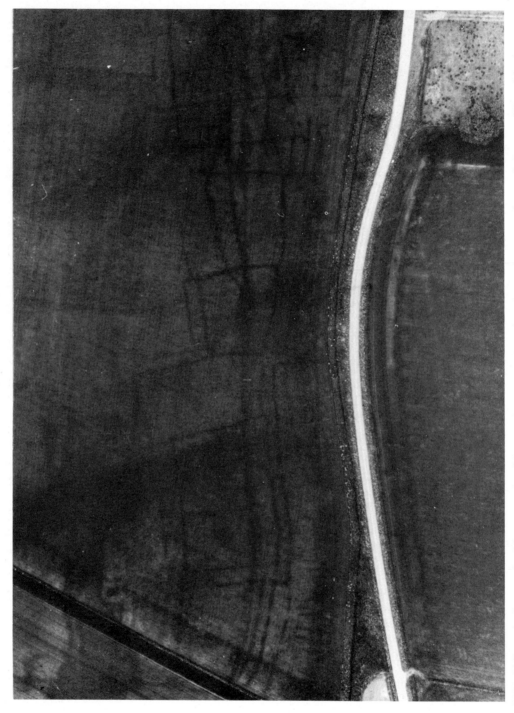

XIV. Oblique air photograph of the cropmarks of the complex Romano–British settlement between Wharram le Street and Duggleby (see Fig. 1). (p. 250)   (*A.L. Pacitto*)

DA155
.A6